The Impact
of
Reapportionment

The Impact
of
Reapportionment

Timothy G. O'Rourke

Transaction Books
New Brunswick, New Jersey

Copyright © 1980 by Transaction, Inc.
New Brunswick, New Jersey 08903

Library of Congress Catalog Number: 78-62883
ISBN: 0-87855-290-1 (cloth)
Printed in the United States of America

Library of Congress Cataloging in Publication Data

O'Rourke, Timothy
 The impact of reapportionment.

 Bibliography: p. 197
 Includes index.
 1. Apportionment (Election law)—United States—
States.   2. Legislative bodies—United States—States.
I. Title.
JK2493.076   328.73′07′3452   78-62883
ISBN 0-87855-290-1

Table of Contents

List of Tables ix

Preface xiii

Chapter   *Page*

One   The Impact of Reapportionment: An
               Introduction   1
               Reapportionment: Some Theoretical Issues
               The Impact of Reapportionment: Focus
               and Methodology
               Reapportionment in Six States:
               Organization and General Overview

Two   Reapportionment and Representation:
               Turnover, Legislator-Constituency Relations,
               and Legislator Characteristics   27
               Reapportionment and Legislative Turnover
               Reapportionment's Impact on
               Legislator-Constituency Relations:
               Elections and Representation

Reapportionment's Effects on
Legislator Characteristics
Concluding Comments

Three   The Impact of Reapportionment on
Republican and Democratic State
Legislative Fortunes   47
The Partisan Impact ·of Reapportionment
The Partisan Impact of Reapportionment:
The Special Case of Multimember Districts
Reapportionment's Effects on
Intraparty Representation
Reapportionment and Internal Party
Organization: Subdistricting and
County Chairmen's Power
Concluding Comments

Four   The Effects of Reapportionment on
Legislative Leadership and Procedure   73
Legislative Leadership and Procedure:
A Preliminary View of the Impact of
Reapportionment
The Impact of Reapportionment on
Committee Leadership
The Impact of Reapportionment on
Chamber Leadership
The Effects of Reapportionment on
Procedure: An Exploratory Analysis
Legislators' Perceptions of the
Effects of Reapportionment on
Legislative Leadership and Procedure
Legislators' Perceptions of Reapportion-
ment's Impact on Internal Party Power
Concluding Comments

Five   The Impact of Reapportionment on
Legislative Conflict   95
Possible Effects of Reapportionment
on Legislative Conflict
Reapportionment and Changing Patterns
of Conflict
Legislators' Perceptions of Reappor-

tionment's Impact
Reapportionment and Roll Call Voting
Conclusions

Six   The Effects of Reapportionment on
             State Policies   119
             Reapportionment and Policy: An
             Overview
             The Impact of Reapportionment on the
             Distribution of State Expenditures
             in the Six Sample States
             Legislators' Perceptions of Policy Changes
             Induced by Reapportionment
             The Impact of Reapportionment: A
             Look at Previous Research and
             Some Conclusions

Seven   The Impact of Reapportionment:
             Summary and Conclusions   147
             The Levels of Reapportionment Effects:
             Conclusions
             Reapportionment in the Six Sample
             States: Conclusions
             Reapportionment: Final Considerations

Appendix A The 1973 Questionnaire Survey of
             State Legislators   163

Appendix B Sources for Data on the Six Sample
             State Legislatures   169

Appendix C Supplementary Data on the Impact of
             Reapportionment on the Six Sample
             State Legislatures   175

A Selected Bibliography 197

List of Tables

Table		Page
1-1	State Legislative Apportionment, Party Competition, and Party Cohesion Prior to Mid-1960s Reapportionment	10
1-2	Selected Characteristics of the Six Sample States	14
1-3	Population and Legislative Representation of Metropolitan Counties in the Six Sample States, 1959-74	18
2-1	Legislative Turnover in the Six Sample States by Chamber, 1959-74	30
2-2	Percentage of Legislators with Four or More Years Experience Before (1959-63) and After (1969-73) Reapportionment, by Chamber	39
3-1	Republican Percentage of Central City, Suburban, and Nonmetropolitan Seats in the Six Sample Legislatures by Chamber, 1959-74	49
3-2	Partisan Division of Seats in Largest Suburban and Established Central City Counties in New Jersey by Chamber, 1960-74	61

4-1 Population Index and Legislative Index for
Committee Chairmanships Held by Legislators
from Central City and Suburban Counties, 1959-74   76

4-2 Top Internally-Elected Officials for Upper
and Lower Houses by Constituency Type and
Party in the Six Sample States, 1959-74   82

4-3 Number of Standing Committees by Chamber
in the Six Sample Legislatures, 1959-74   85

4-4 Legislators' Elaborations of the Impact of
Reapportionment on Chamber Organization and
Procedure in the Six Sample Legislatures
(Senate and House Responses Combined)   89

4-5 Legislators' Elaborations of the Impact of
Reapportionment on the Distribution of
Power within Their Respective Political
Parties in the Six Sample Legislatures
(Senate and House Combined)   91

5-1 Legislators' Perceptions of Major Sources
of Conflict in New Jersey and Tennessee by
Chamber, 1957 and 1973   98

5-2 Legislators' Perceptions of Major Sources of
Legislative Conflict in Four Sample States
by Chamber, 1973   99

5-3 Legislators' Perceptions of Most Important
Sources of Legislative Conflict Other Than
Partisan for the Six Sample States, 1963
and 1973   100

5-4 Legislators' Perceptions of Sources of Conflict on
Major Issues in the Six Sample States in 1963   101

5-5 First Most Important Source of Conflict Perceived
by Kansas Legislators, 1965 and 1973   103

6-1 Proportion of Total State Aid to Local Governments Distributed to Metropolitan Counties
in the Six Sample States, 1962 and 1971-72   124

6-2 Relationship between Legislative Representation
and Population and Share of State Aid and
Population for Metropolitan Counties, 1961-62
and 1971-72   126

6-3 Proportion of Total State Aid to Municipalities
Distributed to Cities of the Largest Population
Category in the Six Sample States, 1962 and
1971-72   128

6-4   Elaborations of Legislators Who Believed
Reapportionment Had Affected Legislation
Introduced or Adopted in the Six Sample
Legislatures (Senate and House Combined)   132

6-5   Legislators' Perceptions of Issues Affected by
Reapportionment in the Six Sample Legislatures   134

6-6   Legislators' Perceptions of Interest Groups
Increasing or Decreasing Lobbying Pressure as
a Consequence of Reapportionment   137

A-1   Response Rates to Mail Questionnaire on
Reapportionment   165

C-1   Reapportionment Activity in the Six Sample
States, 1960-73   177

C-2   Percentage of Legislators in the Six Sample States
Citing the Effects of Reapportionment with
Regard to Single-Member Districts and Size
of Legislative Districts   179

C-3   Percentage of Legislators with Four or More
Years Experience in the Six Sample States by
Chamber, 1959-74   180

C-4   Characteristics of Legislators in the Six Sample
States by Chamber, 1959-74   181

C-5   Percentage Distribution of Central City, Suburban,
and Nonmetropolitan Seats within Republican
and Democratic Parties in the Six Sample States
by Chamber, 1959-74   185

C-6   Percentage Distribution of Committee Chairmanships according to Party and Constituency in the
Six Sample Legislatures by Chamber, 1959-74   188

C-7   Distribution of Legislators' Responses to Question
of Whether Reapportionment Had Induced
Changes in Chamber Organization and
Procedure in the Six Sample Legislatures   190

C-8   Percentage Distribution of Legislators' Responses
to Question of Whether Reapportionment Had
Induced Changes within Their Respective
Parties in the Six Sample Legislatures   191

C-9   Legislators' Perceptions of Reapportionment's
Impact on the Most Important Sources of
Legislative Conflict in the Six Sample States
by Chamber, 1973   192

C-10   Legislators' Responses to Question of Whether

Reapportionment Had Affected Legislation
Introduced in the Six Sample Legislatures   193
C-11   Legislators' Responses to Question of Whether
Reapportionment Had Affected Legislation
Adopted in the Six Sample Legislatures   194
C-12   Proportion of State Highway Expenditures on
State-Administered Roads Expended in
Metropolitan Counties in the Six Sample
States, 1965 and 1972   195

Preface

The character and quality of representation give form and substance to democratic government. The achievement, or better, the pursuit of fair representation must always remain a central concern in a democratic society. The Supreme Court's "one man, one vote" decisions as applied to state legislatures have provided the opportunity to reexamine the meaning of fair representation and to assess how changing the basis of representation may alter the operation and policies of government.

The completion of this study on the impact of reapportionment on six state legislatures has left me indebted to many individuals. My greatest debt is to my wife Karen, who supplied a judicious mix of encouragement and sympathy throughout the project and assisted in the data collection and the preparation of the manuscript. Richard H. Leach of Duke University provided extensive guidance and advice at all stages of the research and writing.

In addition to Professor Leach, a number of other scholars have read and commented on earlier versions of the manuscript; their suggestions have certainly improved my work. Allan Kornberg, Thomas Spragens, and Sheridan Johns of Duke University and Elmer L. Puryear of Campbell College also made helpful criticisms. Donald G. Balmer of Lewis and Clark College, Alan L. Clem of the University of South Dakota, Paul C. Dolan of the University of Delaware, Lee S. Greene of the University of Tennessee, and Alan Rosenthal of Rutgers University read the manuscript and provided special insights into the politics of their respective states. Victor Hobday of the University of Tennessee supplied valuable information on the Tennessee legislature.

I owe a particular debt of gratitude to the state legislators who responded to my mail questionnaire and to State Senators Donn J. Everett of Kansas and Raymond H. Bateman of New Jersey who consented to lengthy telephone interviews.

Campbell College provided a grant which greatly aided revision of the manuscript for publication. The editorial board of Transaction Books made valuable suggestions on revision and expedited the publication process. Emmy Lou Hamshar and Patrice Thompson rendered exemplary secretarial assistance. Robert V. Ramsey checked the accuracy of the tables and corrected a number of errors.

This book is dedicated to my daughter Shannon, born just as the manuscript was completed; may this project be as well conceived. It is also dedicated to my parents; may it be as full of wisdom.

TIMOTHY G. O'ROURKE
Buies Creek, North Carolina

The Impact
of
Reapportionment

Chapter One

The Impact of Reapportionment: An Introduction

Reapportionment: Some Theoretical Issues

Since 1962 state legislatures have undergone extensive redistricting in order to comply with a series of federal court decisions setting out the "one man, one vote" principle. State legislative redistricting occurred throughout the period of 1962-74. First, legislatures submitted to reapportionment in the face of the Supreme Court's rulings in *Baker v. Carr* (1962), *Reynolds v. Sims* (1964), and subsequent decisions which struck down population-based malapportionment. Then in the early 1970s, states modified legislative districts to take into account population movements revealed in the 1970 census.[1]

It bears reiterating that the central element in the long string of federal court rulings on state legislative apportionment is that, as nearly as practicable, representative districts within each house of the legislature must be of equal population.[2] The assertion of this doctrine produced significant alterations in patterns of state legislative districting. But it should be recognized that the federal

1

courts in general and the U.S. Supreme Court in particular have, in the process of defining this doctrine, failed to deal directly with a number of issues closely related to the "one man, one vote" theorem. The judicial interpretation of "one man, one vote" is, therefore, somewhat incomplete and ambiguous in its application to the state legislatures. At this point, there is no clear-cut Supreme Court ruling on the use of multimember districts nor on the question of gerrymandering (which has not been foreclosed by the equal-population standard). Multimember districting, in some instances, has been held to violate the equal representation standards established by the Supreme Court, especially in cases in which it can be shown that its use dilutes the voting strength of racial minorities. However, multimember districts per se do not violate the "one man, one vote" doctrine even though a strong case can be made, on purely mathematical grounds, that they do.[3] Similarly, the Supreme Court has not ruled on the issue of partisan gerrymandering, although some state courts have taken on the issue.[4]

Significantly, legislative reapportionment, undertaken to bring about compliance with the equal-vote principle, is not a uniform phenomenon in all states. In large measure, this is due to the unresolved judicial issues noted above. Some state legislatures employ single-member districts exclusively, while others use a combination of multimember and single-member districts. This is a circumstance with some import on the evaluation of the comparative impact of court-ordered reapportionment. Furthermore, legislative schemes in the fifty states may embody varying degrees of partisan gerrymandering. The extent and effectiveness of this practice will help determine who wins and loses in a partisan sense, due to reapportionment activity within a state. The crucial point in this discussion is that the equal-population standard is not invariable in application. This standard, in its application, does not necessitate nor has it in fact produced identical districting patterns in state legislatures. To study reapportionment in the aftermath of *Baker* and *Reynolds* is to examine more than the simple application of a single standard. In terms of the present analysis, reapportionment will encompass all districting changes adopted in the states during the period, 1962-74, which takes into account redistricting activity of both the mid-1960s (in response to the major court decisions) and the early 1970s (in response to the 1970 census and consistent with the equal-population standard). The present analysis of the impact of reapportionment focuses on an extended range of activity charged by *Baker* and *Reynolds* but not entirely accounted for by the judicial holdings.

Apart from the simple consequence of a fairer distribution of legislative seats according to population, the possible effects of reapportionment are not immediately apparent. The question of whether reapportionment could affect partisan balance in legislatures or legislative policy making, or what sequence of events set off by reapportionment could lead to changes in party fortunes or policy outcomes is a question too frequently overlooked in studies of the impact of reapportionment.

A useful approach to the analysis of that impact might be to classify potential effects into four categories based upon the conditions under which reapportionment may alter elements in the legislative process.[5] The first category, which might be called first-level effects, embraces the representational changes produced directly, though not necessarily, by any modification of legislative districts in a state. Remedying malapportionment, to whatever extent, requires reducing the size of the population of some legislators' districts and enlarging the size of others' districts. Presumably these alterations could affect legislator-constituency relations which may be sensitive to absolute district size. Even minor changes in legislative districts (adding or subtracting a given number of voters) can affect legislator-constituency relations. For example, a new group of voters added to a district could introduce considerable uncertainty into a previously stable electoral situation.[6] To the extent that legislative redistricting requires consolidation of less populated districts and subdivision of heavily populated districts, higher than normal turnover in the legislature is a probable and even necessary outcome as some incumbents will be displaced. As the examples imply, first-level effects result from the mechanics of redistricting, that is, the alteration in district populations inherent in the redistricting process. First-level effects do not depend on the actual makeup or group composition of the populations involved, and thus we can expect them to occur in virtually every state legislature which undergoes redistricting. The extent of first-level effects, of course, would not be uniform, but would derive from the degree of malapportionment prior to reapportionment.

Second-level effects, which embrace the impact of reapportionment on group and partisan balance in the legislature, derive from the distribution of social, economic, and political characteristics in the state's population. Unlike first-level effects, which are inherent in the very practice of redistricting, second-level effects depend upon the political landscape. A simple illustration points out the distinction between the two. Consider the impact of redistricting on two-party balance in a state legislature. If all voters supported one party or if supporters of both parties were randomly distributed throughout a state, then any apportionment scheme, whether or not based on the equal-population standard, would produce virtually the same results in terms of partisan balance in the legislature.[7] Of course, in reality, Democrats and Republicans are not randomly distributed, and Democratic and Republican support among voters is often highly concentrated in given population areas. The impact of any apportionment scheme in distorting partisan representation in the legislature versus that in the population rests upon the uneven distribution of Republicans and Democrats across districts. Reapportionment's impact on partisan balance will depend to a large degree on the relative concentration of Republicans and Democrats in previously malapportioned areas and upon the extent of gerrymandering tied to the new reapportionment plan.

More obviously perhaps, this same analysis also extends to urban-rural conflict. Independent of the degree of malapportionment existing prior to reapportionment, reapportionment's impact on urban-rural representation depends on the specific urban-rural and suburban distribution of the population.

Third-level effects include the impact of reapportionment upon legislative procedure, committee organization, patterns of legislative conflict such as urban-rural and partisan divisions, and party leadership and organization. Practices and procedures within the legislature follow constitutional and statutory strictures, formalized rules, long-standing habits and traditions, and the short-term pressures produced by varying issues and shifting majorities. Moreover, partisan, regional, or urban-rural legislative conflict often assumes regularized patterns over a number of sessions. How reapportionment would directly affect the "institutional" legislature is by no means clear. If reapportionment leads to changes in legislative operation, it seems probable that it would do so by producing significant changes in partisan or group balance in the legislature which would in turn force changes in legislative organization and procedures.

If the link between reapportionment and changes in legislative procedure appears somewhat strained, the possible connection between reapportionment and policy outcomes, which may be classified as fourth-level effects, is even more improbable. In order for reapportionment to bring about measurable policy change, a series of developments rather than the single event of redistricting must transpire. First, reapportionment must lead to abnormally high turnover or, at the very least, enough district modification to alter legislative representation in a detectable fashion. To the degree that policy reflects group demands, redistricting must produce sufficient modification of group representation in the legislature (for example, the distribution of urban-rural or partisan interests) to make policy change likely or possible. If these first two conditions are met, measurable policy change would still require surmounting a variety of institutional barriers. Within the legislature, for example, stability in committee chairmanships and party leadership positions might mitigate major policy innovation despite substantially altered membership. In addition, legislative decision making must function within the context of previous decisions or laws and budgetary restraints which can limit policy innovation. It should be readily apparent that fourth-level effects, being several steps removed from the immediate impact of reapportionment, are likely to result only if reapportionment has produced sweeping changes in patterns of representation.

This classification of the effects of reapportionment is not exhaustive, but suggestive. It is important to recognize that some effects do not fit clearly into a single category. If reapportionment led, for example, to the election of younger legislators, it is not clear whether this condition would derive from the electoral openings created by the mere fact of redistricting (a first-level effect) or by the distribution of voter interests favoring younger legislators (a second-level effect). The classification scheme is lexical inasmuch as fourth-level effects presuppose significant changes induced by reapportionment at the first, second, and third levels. Therefore, the categories impose an order upon the analysis of reapportionment's effects.

The analysis of the four levels of effects leads to the theory that the impact of reapportionment leading to significant changes at levels three and four would be most pervasive in those states in which (1) malapportionment had been severe and operated to misrepresent in a fundamental way urban and rural interests in the legislature; [8] (2) interparty competition was weak and, therefore, allowed population-based interests such as urban and rural interests a more direct impact on legislative conflict; (3) party organization in the legislature was weak as indicated by low party cohesion and, as a result, population-based interests were more likely to serve as the basis for legislative conflict and to determine both legislative organization and policy.[9] Each of these three conditions merits fuller attention.

Since the extent of districting changes involved in reapportionment would depend upon the extent of previous malapportionment, the assertion that the political impact of reapportionment would vary according to the severity of malapportionment is obvious. The problem of measuring malapportionment in light of this assertion, however, requires some consideration.

Malapportionment can be viewed in abstract arithmetical terms, that is, as the numerical or percentage deviation from the standard of equally populated districts. In addition, malapportionment can be seen in the context of political interests as the overrepresentation or underrepresentation of definable group interests (for example, urban or rural, Republican or Democratic) competing in the electoral arena. The latter concept of malapportionment, which takes into consideration substantive electoral interests seeking legislative representation, is undoubtedly more salient in the examination of the political consequences of malapportionment than are the simple arithmetical concepts. The interest-based concept of malapportionment is, however, extremely difficult to quantify.[10]

In contrast, the purely arithmetical view of malapportionment is readily quantifiable, and there are several valuable indices in this regard. One of the most useful is the Dauer-Kelsay Index of Representativeness which shows the minimum percentage of a state's population needed to elect a legislative majority.[11] In 1962 prior to major reapportionment activity, both houses of state legislatures scored over 40 percent in only six states. The range extended from 8 percent in the Nevada Senate to 48 percent for the Oregon House and Senate. By 1968 both houses in every state legislature placed within six points of the 50 percent ideal.[12]

While the Dauer-Kelsay scale indicates the sheer magnitude of deviation from equal-population apportionment, it fails to show the distortion in interest representation that may accrue to such disparity. John P. White and Norman C. Thomas, employing a malapportionment measure developed by David and Eisenberg,[13] produced a highly significant classification scheme which relates malapportionment to urban and rural representation in state legislatures. While it is not an index, the analysis of White and Thomas does translate malapportionment into interest misrepresentation. White and Thomas classified states into four categories, according to the effect of malapportionment on urban-rural representation in the state legislatures in 1960. The four categories are: (1) states in which an existing rural majority in the population was strengthened in the legislature by malapportionment (eleven states); (2) states in which an artificial rural majority was created in both houses of the legislature by malapportionment (thirteen states); (3) states in which an artificial rural majority was created in one house only (four states); and (4) states in which an urban majority was retained in both houses (twenty states).[14]

The schema of White and Thomas hints that reapportionment would produce the most substantial changes in states classified in the second category; it is here that reapportionment would convert a pattern of rural dominance into one of urban dominance. Then in terms of urban-rural conflict, reapportionment looms as pivotal only for states in the second category and, to a lesser extent, in the third category. States in the first and fourth categories would undergo only slight, if any, change in terms of urban-rural balance as a result of reapportionment.

The study of White and Thomas provides an explanatory foundation for the earlier assertion that reapportionment would produce the most substantial changes in states in which malapportionment produces a fundamental misrepresentation of interests. To that assertion, however, were added the conditions that party competition was weak and party cohesion in the legislature was low. It was hypothesized that the absence of party competition and organization in the legislature allows population-based conflict to emerge more virulently in the absence of the moderating effects of party.

Although this hypothesis requires testing, there is good reason to believe that party competition itself led to fairer apportionment prior to *Baker* v. *Carr* and that two-party states were less likely than one-party states to be severely malapportioned in the first place. John G. Grumm projected a positive relationship between high urbanization and fair apportionment prior to *Baker* v. *Carr*; the well-established correlation between high urbanization and two-party competition supports the contention that two-partyism and fair apportionment are related.[15] In addition, Wayne Francis found a fairly clear pattern of high partisan conflict in the legislature measured by responses to a questionnaire coupled with good apportionment; conversely, he found that low partisan conflict was tied to poor apportionment.[16] Thus, two-party states, which were less likely to be severely malapportioned prior to 1962-64, were generally less likely to experience significant changes resulting from reapportionment.

The reasoning developed thus far now requires summation. Table 1-1 combines data from the Dauer-Kelsay Index for 1962, the White-Thomas classification scheme, and data on party competition and cohesion in state legislatures. The table makes it possible to isolate those states in which reapportionment would produce the most substantial impact. Well-apportioned states (that is, scoring forty or better on the Dauer-Kelsay scale for both houses in 1962) clearly would not undergo major changes as a result of reapportionment, nor would malapportioned states in which, according to White and Thomas, malapportionment merely enhanced in the legislature a rural majority in the population. The greatest changes would occur in states in which an artificial rural majority existed in one or both houses of a legislature because of malapportionment. Consistent with earlier arguments, reapportionment would be expected to exhibit more profound effects on one-party states in these two categories than on two-party states.

For those states which retained urban legislative majorities despite malapportionment, reapportionment should exert little influence on legislative operations, except in those two-party states in which one or both of the houses may have been very severely malapportioned to the extreme detriment of one major party. (An example of this is seen in the lower house of Connecticut, rated twelve on the Dauer-Kelsay Index; prior to reapportionment it was solidly Republican despite state-wide voting trends highly favorable to the Democrats.)[17]

Existing studies on the impact of reapportionment support the expectations already outlined. Brett W. Hawkins' study of the one-party legislature in Georgia before and after reapportionment found that reapportionment increased representation of Atlanta three-fold, produced exceptionally high turnover, led to a sharp rise in the number of black legislators, helped to shift committee control from rural to metropolitan legislators, increased urban-rural bloc voting, and stimulated the passage of more city-oriented legislation. Similarly, research has shown that reapportionment in modified one-party Florida led to very high turnover initially, transformed the legislature from one controlled by rural elements to one with an urban majority, helped bring about a dramatic rise (four-fold in the lower house, ten-fold in the upper) in Republican representation, created urban control of key committees, and stimulated party organization and party voting. Glen T. Broach's examination of roll call voting in one-party Alabama and modified one-party Tennessee before and after reapportionment found that urban-rural conflict in Alabama and party voting in Tennessee increased significantly after reapportionment. David W. Brady and Richard Murray found in an analysis of the policy effects of reapportionment in fifty states that the most significant changes in state expenditure patterns occurred in one-party and modified one-party states, predominantly in the South.[18] It is in these kinds of states, in view of the previous discussion, that reapportionment might be expected to produce third-level and fourth-level effects (refer again to Table 1-1).

In contrast, studies of two-party states such as Colorado, Illinois, New York, Pennsylvania, and Washington detected few changes attributable to reapportionment apart from initial increases in turnover and minor changes in legislator characteristics (for example, in New York) and partisan balance (for example, in New York and Washington).[19] The preceding analysis coincides with these findings. Slight exceptions to the theory promoted herein arise from Robeck's finding that party cohesion rose dramatically in the California Senate after reapportionment (the 1962 Dauer-Kelsay score was eleven) and from Davis' report that reapportionment in Connecticut helped the Democratic party to gain control of the lower house in 1966 for only the second time in this century.[20]

In general, case studies presently completed lend firm support to the propositions put forth. While some effects, such as increased turnover, appear endemic to reapportionment, major changes in legislative conflict and policy (third-level and fourth-level effects) seem more limited to a select category of states. States falling in this category include, specifically, marginally urban, severely malapportioned, and one-party (or modified one-party) states.

Although the preceding discussion indicates that a substantial body of literature on reapportionment already exists, there remains a gap between the detailed case studies of reapportionment in individual states and the qualititative and comparative analyses of the impact of apportionment on partisan balance and policies in all fifty states. Case studies can undertake a systematic examination of the impact of reapportionment at all stages of the legislative process (that is, the four levels of the effects of reapportionment). However, separate case studies may not lead to meaningful generalizations about the comparative impact of reap-

TABLE 1-1

State Legislative Apportionment, Party Competition, and Party Cohesion Prior to Mid-1960s Reapportionment [a]

Party Competition and Legislative Party Cohesion, 1963[e]

Nature of Apportionment 1960-1962[b,c,d]	One-Party States		Modified One-Party States		Two-Party States	
	Strong party cohesion in legislature	Moderate or weak party cohesion in legislature	Strong party cohesion in legislature	Moderate or weak party cohesion in legislature	Strong party cohesion in legislature	Moderate or weak party cohesion in legislature
Malapportioned						
Rural majority enhanced in both houses		AR,MS SC		KY,NC ND,VT SD		AK,ID
Artificial rural majority created in one house				MD,MO MN		AZ,MN WY
Artificial rural majority created in both houses		AL,GA	IO,KS	FL,OK TN,VA	DE	MT,NV NB
Urban majority retained in both houses		LA,TX			CO,CT IN,MI NJ,NY PA,RI	CA,IL HI,OH UT,WA
Well apportioned						
Rural majority retained in both houses			NH,WV	(ME)		OR
Urban majority retained in both houses					MA WI	

Sources: Dauer-Kelsay scores are reported in The Book of the States, 1968-69 (Lexington, Ky.: Council of State Govern-
ments, 1968), pp. 66-67. The description of the effect of apportionment on urban-rural balance is taken from
John P. White and Norman C. Thomas, "Urban and Rural Representation and State Legislative Apportionment,"
Western Political Quarterly 17 (December 1964): 728-730. The classification of party competition and legis-
lative party cohesion appears in Austin Ranney, "Parties in State Politics," Politics in the American States:
A Comparative Analysis, ed. Herbert Jacob and Kenneth N. Vines (Boston: Little, Brown & Co., 1965), pp. 65, 88.

[a]U. S. Postal Service abbreviations are used to designate states.

[b]Well apportioned states have Dauer-Kelsay scores of 40 or better for both legislative houses in 1962.

[c]White-Thomas categories are based on 1960 apportionment.

[d]Maine, though well apportioned by the above definition, had an artificial rural majority in both houses, according to
White and Thomas.

[e]While Ranney's classification of party competition is current to 1963, the classification of legislative party cohesion
is based on research conducted in the early 1950s (see n. 7 in Chapter Five).

portionment because of methodological differences; furthermore, in-depth case studies exist for only a minority of states. Quantitative studies, which will be more fully discussed in chapters three and six, typically focus on a single level of effects such as the policy impact of reapportionment. While providing the basis for broad comparative conclusions, the quantitative studies provide little insight into the process by which districting changes translate into modifications in partisan balance in legislatures or policy outcomes. The research presented here attempts to combine the depth of the case study approach with the comparative elements of the quantitative analysis.

The Impact of Reapportionment: Focus and Methodology

The present study examines the impact of reapportionment on six state legislatures including those of Delaware, Kansas, New Jersey, Oregon, South Dakota, and Tennessee. Analysis of reapportionment in the sample states should serve to confirm or disconfirm the propositions outlined. South Dakota is a predominantly rural state in which malapportionment enhanced the rural majority in the legislature; until recently the state has been solidly Republican. Oregon, an urban two-party state, was well-apportioned prior to *Baker* and *Reynolds*. Reapportionment would, it is argued, produce very little change in these two states. Delaware, Kansas, and Tennessee are states in which malapportionment created artificial rural majorities in both legislative chambers. Two-party Delaware should provide some indication of the mediating influence of party competition and organization on reapportionment's impact when compared to the modified one-party states of Kansas and Tennessee. New Jersey, a two-party state, despite malapportionment retained urban majorities in both houses. It stands as an intriguing final case, especially in view of the sharp divergence in apportionment of the House (forty-seven on the Dauer-Kelsay Index) and Senate (nineteen on the Dauer-Kelsey Index) prior to reapportionment.[21]

The sample states also differ in another way relevant to the study of the impact of reapportionment. Not only do the sample states vary in terms of level of urbanization (percentage of state population living in areas with population of 2,500 or more), they vary widely in the percentage of population living in Standard Metropolitan Statistical Areas (SMSAs). An SMSA, according to the U.S. Census Bureau, encompasses a central city having a population of 50,000 or more and the suburbs surrounding the central city. This conception more nearly captures the common-sense view of urban as big city than does the Census Bureau's definition of an urban place. The level of metropolitanization may indicate the dimensions of urban-rural conflict (that is, metropolitan-nonmetropolitan conflict) as well as urban-suburban conflict more accurately within a state than does the level of unbanization. In short, SMSA may prove to be a more valid indicator of "urban" for purposes of gauging the extent of urban-rural antagonism and the impact of reapportionment. Even though all of the sample states except South Dakota had in 1960 an urban majority by census definition, New Jersey and Delaware were substantially metropolitan and suburban in contrast to nonmetropolitan Kansas and Tennessee and marginally metropolitan Oregon.[22] Table 1-2 produces data on urbanization, metropolitanization, and suburbanization for the six sample states as well as summary data for malapportionment, party competition, and legislative party cohesion.

The present study of the six sample states already described attempts to determine the effects of reapportionment, over the period 1962-74, on a number of elements in the legislative process. These elements include legislative turnover, legislator characteristics, legislator-constituency relations, party competition for legislative seats, urban-rural and partisan conflict in the legislature, legislative procedure and organization, and legislative policy making. The undertaking makes use of existing studies on the sample states and especially of legislative roll call analyses. The new data introduced by this study include a limited collection of data on policy outcomes in the sample states, extensive materials on legislator characteristics and turnover and legislative leadership over the period 1959-74, and the results of a questionnaire sent to all state legislators in the sample states in 1973. (The questionnaire is described and reprinted in Appendix A.)

Reapportionment in Six States: Organization and General Overview

The analysis of the impact of reapportionment on the six sample states roughly proceeds along the theoretical lines laid out earlier. That is, the examination begins with a consideration of first-level effects of reapportionment (turnover and legislator-constituency relations). and progresses through investigation of sec-

TABLE 1-2

Selected Characteristics of the Six Sample States

Population Characteristics: 1960 and 1970

	% Urban		% in SMSAs		% of SMSA Suburban	
	1960	1970	1960	1970	1960	1970
Delaware	65.6	72.2	68.9	70.4	68.8	79.2
Kansas	61.0	66.1	37.4	42.3	54.0[a]	57.7[a]
New Jersey	88.6	88.9	78.9	76.9	76.3	78.8
Oregon	62.2	67.1	50.4	61.2	68.8	79.2
South Dakota	39.3	44.6	12.7	14.3	24.4	23.9
Tennessee	52.3	58.8	45.8	48.9	44.3	29.4

Dauer-Kelsay Index of Representativeness
by Legislative Chamber, 1962 and 1968

	Senate		House	
	1962	1968	1962	1968
Delaware	22	53	19	49
Kansas	27	49	19	49
New Jersey	19	50	47	50
Oregon	48	47	48	48
South Dakota	38	47	39	47
Tennessee	27	49	29	47

White-Thomas Classification of Malapportionment Effects, 1960

Rural majority retained in both houses of legislature: South Dakota
Artificial rural majority created in both houses: Delaware
Kansas
Tennessee

Urban majority retained in both houses: Oregon
New Jersey

Party Competition and Legislative Party Cohesion, 1963

	Party Competition	Legislative Party Cohesion
Delaware	Two-Party	Strong
Kansas	Modified One-Party (Rep.)	Strong
New Jersey	Two-Party	Strong
Oregon	Two-Party	Weak
South Dakota	Modified One-Party (Rep.)	Moderate
Tennessee	Modified One-Party (Dem.)	Weak

Sources: Population characteristics are taken from U.S., Department of Commerce, Bureau of the Census, United States Census of Population: 1970, vol. I, Characteristics of the Population, pt. A, sec. 1, pp. 9-5, 18-5; sec. 2, pp. 32-5, 39-5, 43-5, 44-5. Dauer-Kelsay scores are taken from The Book of the States, 1968-69 (Lexington, Ky.: Council of State Governments, 1968), pp. 66-67. The White-Thomas data come from John White and Norman C. Thomas, "Urban and Rural Representation and State Legislative Apportionment," Western Political Quarterly 17 (December 1964): 728-730. Party competition and legislative party cohesion come from Austin Ranney, "Parties in State Politics," in Politics in the American States: A Comparative Analysis, ed. Herbert Jacob and Kenneth N. Vines (Boston: Little, Brown & Co., 1965), pp. 65, 88. See also Table 1-1.

[a] Treating Kansas City (Wyandotte County) as a central city would reduce the 1960 figure to 39.0% and the 1970 figure to 40.0%. See the discussion related to Table 1-3 for an explanation of the relevance of these data.

ond-level (legislator characteristics and urban-rural and partisan balance in the legislature), third-level (legislative procedure, organization, and conflict), and fourth-level effects (public policies). Again, the reader should bear in mind that the levels of reapportionment effects are theoretical conveniences and not precise categories. While chapter organization generally follows the progression of levels, individual chapters may consider effects at two levels.

Appreciation and understanding of the analysis which follows requires a brief overview of the implementation of reapportionment in the six states under study. While the fifty states varied considerably in terms of the extent of malapportionment prior to the decisions of the Supreme Court in *Baker* and *Reynolds* (1962-64), every state legislature, including the six in this sample, underwent reapportionment activity between 1962 and 1968 in order to achieve compliance with the Court's equal-population standard. Typically, the process of fulfilling the "one man, one vote" principle involved a series of reapportionment plans rather than a single one until districting schemes met with final federal or state court approval. The high level of activity associated with initial compliance in the mid-1960s emerged again in the early 1970s with redistricting to accommodate population changes revealed in the 1970 census.

Among the sample states, the sheer number of separate reapportionment plans under which elections were held is startling. For example, the Tennessee legislature since 1960 has experienced six reapportionments (in 1962, 1963, 1965, 1966, 1972, and 1973). This means that in six elections out of seven from 1962 and 1974, legislative candidates in one or both chambers confronted district patterns which differed from those of the previous election. In New Jersey, the General Assembly (the lower house) underwent reapportionment in 1961, the Senate, in 1965; both the lower and upper houses were redistricted in 1966, 1969, 1971, and 1973. During the same time period, Kansas experienced similarly frequent redistricting. Oregon and South Dakota were redistricted in 1961 prior to *Baker* v. *Carr.* These two states, however, were redistricted only two more times, once in the mid-1960s and once after the 1970 census. Delaware, which was redistricted in 1964 under court order, was also redistricted only two more times in the next ten years.[23]

The cumulative impact of the redistricting activity following the *Baker* and *Reynolds* cases involved some significant modification of the representative strength of various population groupings within the state legislatures. The question of the impact of reapportionment on urban-rural conflict receives fuller treatment later but it is useful at this point to establish a tentative picture of that impact on population-based representation in the legislature.

In order to do this, I have used the concept of Standard Metropolitan Statistical Area to classify legislative districts in the six states during the period of 1959-74. The boundaries of SMSAs generally follow county lines, though some SMSAs embrace two or more counties. In the present analysis, SMSAs are divided into two components: (1) the central city county which contains the core city of 50,000 or more for which the SMSA is designated, and (2) the suburban county (ies) adjacent to the central city county. All districts composed of areas totally or predominantly within central city counties received the designation of central city, and constituencies composed of predominantly suburban counties were classified as suburban. Districts outside metropolitan areas were termed nonmetropolitan. One weakness of this scheme is its tendency to overstate the number of central city legislators since only a portion of the central city county's population actually lives in the central city. At the same time, of course, the central city category tends to understate the number of suburban representatives. The suburban category may at times slightly overstate the representation of suburban counties because legislative districts containing both suburban and nonmetropolitan counties are still classified as suburban. (The sources employed to classify legislative districts are listed in Appendix B.)

The classification of legislative districts in the six sample states makes two exceptions to the above formula. In Delaware, where metropolitan New Castle County holds about 70 percent of the state's population, the central city designation is limited to Wilmington City, while the suburban category refers to that portion of New Castle County outside of Wilmington. For Kansas, Wyandotte County, which contains the state's second largest city (Kansas City), is treated by the Census Bureau as a suburb of Kansas City, Missouri; in this analysis, Wyandotte is designated a central city county.

Though the definition of categories varies only for these two cases, another set of qualifications on the classification scheme must be made to take into account the facts that boundaries of existing SMSAs may be redefined over time (usually to include additional suburban counties) and that new SMSAs may be identified. To control for definitional changes, the classification of legislative districts during the period of 1959-70 recognizes as metropolitan counties those counties so designated in 1960 or at any time during 1961 through 1965. The classification of districts for the period 1971 to 1974 recognizes all metropolitan counties designated in 1970 and any counties redefined as metropolitan through early 1972. The only major shift in the data covering the period 1959-70 and the figures for 1971-74 occurs in New Jersey, where three nonmetropolitan counties (comprising about 16 percent of the state's population in 1970) were redefined as central city counties between 1970 and 1972. Representation figures for these counties, labeled *new* central city counties, are presented separately from the figures on the *established* central city counties, that is, those central city counties recognized prior to 1970. The central city and suburban categories for the other five states, however, are stable across the period of analysis. (The reader is advised, however, that additional metropolitan counties in Kansas, New Jersey, and Tennessee have been identified in Census Bureau publications since 1972.)[24]

Table 1-3 chronicles the process of compliance with the equal-population standard during the 1960s and early 1970s. The table produces data on the proportion of a state's population contained in central city counties and suburban counties for both 1960 and 1970 and the percentage of seats held by these counties in the upper and lower houses of the legislature during 1959-74. The table also indicates those legislative sessions affected by new redistricting plans. A review of the data for the sample states prior to 1963 at the time when the court decisions began to influence redistricting practices reveals considerable diversity in the extent of malapportionment. Oregon, as noted earlier, was well apportioned before the *Baker* and *Reynolds* cases, and before 1963 there was only slight underrepresentation of metropolitan areas. The South Dakota legislature tended to underrepresent its one central city county in the upper house but not in the lower; in any case, the central city county comprised less than one-seventh of the total population. Kansas and Tennessee reflect an obvious pattern in both legislatures of underrepresentation of central city counties prior to 1963. In Kansas, central city counties held only about one-fourth of their entitled representation in either house and in Tennessee, less than 60 percent in either house. In neither state do the suburban counties weigh prominently in the analysis. Malapportionment in Delaware, however, significantly underrepresented suburban areas which made up about half of the state's popula-

TABLE 1-3

Population and Legislative Representation of Metropolitan Counties in the Six Sample States, 1959-74

		Legislative Representation by Percentage of Seats[a] (Asterisk indicates new apportionment)					
State and Type of Counties	1960 Percentage of State Population	1959 (1960)		1961 (1962)		1963 (1964)	
		Senate	House	Senate	House	Senate	House
Delaware[b]							
Central City	21.5	11.8	14.3	11.8	14.3	11.8	14.3
Suburban	47.4	29.4	28.6	29.4	28.6	29.4	28.6
Kansas[c]					*		*
Central City	30.8	7.5	7.2	7.5	9.6	7.5	9.6
Suburban	8.4	5.0	3.2	5.0	4.0	5.0	4.0
New Jersey[d,h]					*		
Established							
Central City	39.0	23.8	50.0	23.8	40.0	23.8	40.0
New Central City	(14.4)	(14.3)	(13.3)	(14.3)	(13.3)	(14.3)	(13.3)
Suburban	39.9	38.1	31.6	38.1	38.3	38.1	38.3
Oregon[e]						*	*
Central City	45.6	36.7	41.6	36.7	41.6	43.3	45.0
Suburban	13.1	13.3	11.7	13.3	11.7	16.7	13.3
South Dakota[f]						*	*
Central City	12.7	5.7	10.7	5.7	10.7	5.7	12.0
Tennessee[g]						*	*
Central City	42.5	24.2	22.2	24.2	22.2	33.3	32.3
Suburban	5.1	9.1	5.1	9.1	5.1	9.1	6.1

Sources: Population figures are derived from data in U.S., Department of Commerce, Bureau of the Census, United States Census of Population: 1970, vol. 1, Characteristics of the Population, pt. A, sec. 1, pp. 9-6,7,12, 13; 18-6,7,17,18; sec. 2, pp. 32-6,7,19; 39-6,7,15; 43-6,7,15; 44-6,7, 15. Classification of counties is based on U.S., Department of Commerce, Bureau of the Census, County and City Data Book: 1967, pp. 618-621, 630, 639, 653, 660, 664-665, and U.S., Department of Commerce, Bureau of the Census, County and City Data Book: 1972, pp. 952-956, 977, 986, 1000, 1007, 1011-1012. For sources on legislative representation, see Appendix B.

[a]The years designated mark the first legislative sessions following elections. Odd-numbered years apply to every state except New Jersey, where sessions begin in even-numbered years.

[b]The central city is Wilmington City; suburban refers to that part of New Castle County outside of Wilmington.

[c]Central city counties are Sedgwick (Wichita), Shawnee (Topeka), and Wyandotte (Kansas City); suburban counties are Butler and Johnson.

TABLE 1-3 (continued)

Legislative Representation by Percentage of Seats[a] (Asterisk indicates new apportionment) covers 1965 (1966), 1967 (1968), 1969 (1970). Legislative Representation by Percentage of Seats[a] (Asterisk indicates new apportionment) covers 1971 (1972), 1973 (1974).

1965 (1966) Senate	House	1967 (1968) Senate	House	1969 (1970) Senate	House	1970 Percentage of State Population	1971 (1972) Senate	House	1973 (1974) Senate	House
*	*			*	*				*	*
22.2	22.9	22.2	22.9	15.8	15.4	14.7	15.8	15.4	14.3	14.6
44.4	45.7	44.4	45.7	52.6	53.8	55.7	52.6	53.8	57.1	56.1
*	*			*			*		*	*
22.5	14.4	22.5	29.6	30.0	29.6	30.8	30.0	29.6	32.5	29.6
10.0	4.8	10.0	9.6	12.5	9.6	11.4	12.5	9.6	12.5	12.0
*		*	*	*	*		*	*	*	*
41.4	40.0	40.0	38.8	40.0	38.8	34.6	35.0	35.0	35.0	35.0
(17.2)	(13.3)	(15.0)	(15.0)	(15.0)	(15.0)	16.2	17.5	17.5	17.5	17.5
41.4	38.3	42.5	43.8	42.5	43.8	40.6	42.5	42.5	42.5	42.5
						*			*	*
43.3	45.0	43.3	45.0	43.3	45.0	44.1	43.3	45.0	43.3	43.3
16.7	13.3	16.7	13.3	16.7	13.3	17.2	16.7	13.3	23.3	23.3
		*	*						*	*
5.7	12.0	11.4	12.0	11.4	12.0	14.3	11.4	12.0	14.3	14.3
*	*	*	*	*					*	*
36.4	32.3	42.4	42.4	42.4	42.4	43.4	42.4	42.4	42.4	44.4
9.1	6.1	9.1	6.1	9.1	6.1	5.5	9.1	6.1	9.1	6.1

[d]Established central city counties are Atlantic (Atlantic City), Essex (Newark), Hudson (Jersey City), Mercer (Trenton), Passaic (Paterson, Clifton, Passaic); new central city counties, after 1970 only, are Cumberland (Vineland, Millville, Bridgeton), Middlesex (New Brunswick, Perth Amboy, Sayreville), and Monmouth (Long Branch, Asbury Park); suburban counties are Bergen, Burlington, Camden, Gloucester, Morris, Salem, Union, and Warren.

[e]Central city counties are Lane (Eugene), Marion (Salem), and Multnomah (Portland); suburban counties are Clackamas, Polk, and Washington.

[f]The central city county is Minnehaha (Sioux Falls).

[g]Central city counties are Davidson (Nashville), Hamilton (Chattanooga), Knox (Knoxville), and Shelby (Memphis); suburban counties are Anderson, Blount, Sumner, and Wilson.

[h]Data on new central city counties, recognized after 1970, are given in parentheses for years prior to 1972.

tion, although the central city was also underrepresented. Examination of the data for New Jersey reveals a pattern of greater complexity in which the upper house underrepresented and the lower house overrepresented central city counties in 1960. Suburban counties, which were fairly represented in the upper house, suffered underrepresentation in the lower house in 1960. However, redistricting of the lower house in 1961 (prior to *Baker*) largely corrected the overrepresentation of central city counties and the underrepresentation of suburban areas.

The use of the metropolitan-nonmetropolitan division to establish the data in Table 1-3 leads to a departure from the White-Thomas account of the impact of malapportionment in legislative representation. This is not surprising in light of the differences between the definitions of urban and metropolitan, although metropolitan areas held more than three-fourths of the nation's urban population in 1960 and 1970. In the White-Thomas analysis, for example, three of the sample states (Delaware, Kansas, and Tennessee) possessed artificial rural majorities in their legislatures prior to reapportionment. Only Delaware has an artificial nonmetropolitan majority, although Tennessee was a borderline case. As noted earlier, the dichotomy of metropolitan and nonmetropolitan is probably the more appropriate indicator of real political divisions.

Table 1-3 shows the general underrepresentation of metropolitan areas prior to reapportionment. In addition the data clearly demonstrate the transition from varying degrees of malapportionment in the states to fair apportionment based on equal population through the mid-1960s. Representation figures and population figures thus gradually come into alignment. It is important to recognize that the representative balance of central city counties and suburban counties after the activity of the mid-1960s stabilizes in the states of Oregon, South Dakota, Kansas, and Tennessee. That is to say, the relative strength of central city and suburban areas in these states remains fairly constant even during the redistricting activity of the 1970s. In Delaware, however, the post-1970 activity brought a reduction in central city representation at the expense of suburban areas which hold a majority in the legislature. While established central city counties and suburban counties in New Jersey together accounted for about 80 percent of the seats in the legislature after 1966, new reapportionments in the late 1960s and early 1970s brought a gradual shift to suburban dominance, with suburban areas accounting for nearly 43 percent of legislative seats in both chambers by 1974. In contrast to 1960, when established central city counties held half of the seats in the lower houses, these counties accounted for only about a third of the seats in the Senate and Assembly in 1974. However, new central city counties after 1970 held more than a sixth of the legislative seats and perhaps the balance of power between the established central city counties and the suburban counties.

A summary of the data in Table 1-3 must emphasize several points. Reapportionment in neither Oregon nor South Dakota produced more than slight modification in existing patterns of representation. Central city counties and to a considerably smaller degree, suburban counties in Kansas and Tennessee achieved dramatic gains in representation as a result of reapportionment. Figures suggest, however, a more substantial effect in Tennessee where central city counties held about 43 percent of the seats in the legislature by 1973. In Kansas, for the same year, central city counties held just over 31 percent of the legislative seats. Reapportionment in Delaware roughly doubled suburban representation in legislature and by 1973 solidly implanted a suburban majority in both legislative chambers. In New Jersey, reapportionment enhanced the already existent metropolitan majority in both houses. Several districting plans, however, eventually established the clear dominance of suburban and new central city representation (about 60 percent in 1974) over established central city representation (about 35 percent in 1974).

Now that the dimensions of reapportionment in the six states during the period of 1963-74 have been brought into focus, it is possible to consider the specific ramifications of reapportionment on legislative activity in each state. The remaining chapters generally follow the sequence of the four levels of effects as described earlier. Chapter two focuses on first-level effects including legislative turnover and legislator-constituency relations. Chapter three examines the impact of reapportionment on interparty competition (second-level effects). Chapters four and five deal with third-level changes in legislative organization, procedure, and conflict. Chapter six analyzes the impact of reapportionment on policies (fourth-level effects) in the six states. Chapter seven summarizes the findings of the research in light of the theoretical framework laid out in this chapter.

Notes

1. *Baker* v. *Carr*, 369 U.S. 186 (1962); *Reynolds* v. *Sims*, 377 U.S. 533 (1964). The *Baker* decision simply recognized that legislative apportionment was a justiciable question, while *Reynolds* laid down the "one man, one vote" doctrine which applied to both upper and lower chambers of state legislatures. Subsequent decisions, elaborating the basic principles set out by the *Reynolds* case, are cited in n. 2 below.

2. Having established the equal-population principle in *Reynolds* and, with respect to the U.S. House of Representatives, in *Wesberry* v. *Sanders*, 376 U.S. 1 (1964), the Supreme Court still had to wrestle with the matter of defining the limits of population variation in state legislative and congressional districting plans. In subsequent cases, the Court gradually narrowed the range of population variation allowable. See *Swann* v. *Adams*, 385 U.S. 440 (1967), *Wells* v. *Rockefeller*, 394 U.S. 542 (1969), and *Kirkpatrick* v. *Pressler*, 394 U.S. 526 (1969). The present view of the Court appears to be that any deviation from precise population equality must be justified by officials responsible for districting. However, *Mahan* v. *Howell*, 410 U.S. 315 (1973), indicated that the Court would be more tolerant of deviations in state legislative districting plans than in congressional plans. In *Mahan*, the Court accepted an apportionment plan for Virginia with a total variation of 16.4 percent (the percentage representing the combined deviation of the largest and smallest districts from the average population for all districts). The operative limit for state legislative apportionment plans, however, appears to be "under 10 percent" total variation. See *Connor* v. *Finch*, 431 U.S. 407 (1977). A concise and current summary of the development of the standards for implementing "one man, one vote" is provided in William J. Keefe and Morris S. Ogul, *The American Legislative Process: Congress and the States,* 4th ed. (Englewood Cliffs, N.J.: Prentice-Hall, 1977), pp. 68-85. Gordon E. Baker supplies an illuminating analysis of *Mahan* and related cases in "One Man, One Vote, and 'Political Fairness'—or How the Burger Court Found Political Happiness by Rediscovering *Reynolds* v. *Sims*," *Emory Law Journal* 23 (1974): 701-23. For more detailed, though less current treatments of the evolution of "one man, one vote," see these two works by Robert G. Dixon, Jr.: "The Court, the People, and 'One Man, One Vote,' " in *Reapportionment in the 1970s,* ed. Nelson W. Polsby (Berkeley: University of California Press, 1971), pp. 7-46; and the seminal study, *Democratic Representation: Apportionment in Law and Politics* (New York: Oxford University Press, 1968). Also refer to Ward E. Y. Elliott, *The Rise of Guardian Democracy: The Supreme Court's Role in Voting Rights Disputes, 1845-1969* (Cambridge, Mass.: Harvard University Press, 1974).

3. In *White* v. *Regester*, 412 U.S. 755 (1973), for example, the Supreme Court required the use of single-member districts in place of multi-member districts shown, with apparent discriminatory intent, to dilute the voting strength of blacks in one county and Mexican-Americans in another county and to reduce the possibility of the election of minority representatives to the state legislature. In *Whit-*

comb v. Chavis, 403 U.S. 124 (1971), the Court upheld the use of multimember districts per se (although in this case racial discrimination was alleged). John F. Banzhaf, III has argued that multimember districts, apart from questions of discrimination, violate the mathematical presuppositions of the "one man, one vote" principle. See his "Multi-Member Electoral Districts—Do They Violate the One Man, One Vote Principle?" Yale Law Journal 75 (1965): 1309-38. The Court in Whitcomb (pp. 145-46) recognized Banzhaf's view as having theoretical but not practical significance.

4. However, see the Supreme Court's decision in Gaffney v. Cummings, 412 U.S. 735 (1973) and the discussion of this case in Baker, "One Man, One Vote, and 'Political Fairness.' " The Court in Gaffney upheld a Connecticut plan designed to guarantee Democratic and Republican representation in the legislature roughly proportional to the statewide voting strength of the parties. Also see Gordon E. Baker, "Gerrymandering: Privileged Sanctuary or Next Judicial Target?" in Reapportionment in the 1970s, pp. 121-42. For recent state judicial activity on the issue of partisan gerrymandering, refer to Council of State Governments, Reapportionment in the Seventies (Lexington, Ky.: Council of State Governments, 1973), pp. 21-22. The reader interested in pursuing the constitutional status of gerrymandering should also examine the U.S. Supreme Court's recent holding in United Jewish Organizations of Williamsburgh, Inc. v. Carey 430 U.S. 144 (1977); the Court sustained gerrymandering designed to enhance black representation in the New York legislature and commented on the tolerable range of both racial and partisan gerrymandering.

5. The classification of effects benefits from the insightful analysis of William E. Bicker, "The Effects of Malapportionment in the States: A Mistrial," in Reapportionment in the 1970s, pp. 151-201.

6. David Braybrooke has suggested that "Persons in constituencies with reduced populations would find access to their representatives easier . . ." Douglas W. Rae, however, regards this assertion as implausible in light of the fact that, in a hypothetical case, a representative would hardly find it easier to divide his time among 10,000 constituents rather than 20,000. See David Braybrooke, "Commentary," in Reapportionment in the 1970s, p. 114, and Douglas W. Rae, "Rejoinder," in Reapportionment in the 1970s, p. 119.

7. See Robert G. Dixon, Jr., "Representation Values and Reapportionment Practice: The Eschatology of 'One Man, One Vote,' " Representation, Nomos X, ed. J. Roland Pennock and John W. Chapman (New York: Atherton Press, 1968), pp. 167-75. As Dixon notes, any districting system will affect partisan interests, precisely because the strength of interests is not uniformly distributed throughout the electorate. See pp. 174-75.

8. See especially John P. White and Norman C. Thomas, "Urban and Rural Representation and State Legislative Apportionment," Western Political Quarterly 17 (1964): 724-41. This article is given detailed consideration later in this chapter.

9. The notion that malapportionment would have its greatest impact on one-party states is treated by Bicker, p. 160.

10. The problems of measuring malapportionment are considered in de-

tail in Bicker, pp. 161-71, and in Timothy G. O'Rourke, "The Impact of Reapportionment on State Legislatures: An Interpretative Analysis" (Masters thesis, Duke University, 1973), pp. 9-33.

11. The index adds the populations of the most overrepresented (that is, the least populated) districts until a majority of legislative representation is accounted for; the sum is then divided by the total state population to produce the measure of representativeness. See Manning J. Dauer and Robert G. Kelsay, "Unrepresentative States," *National Municipal Review,* 44 (1955): 571-75, 587.

12. Dauer-Kelsay scores for all state legislatures in 1962 and 1968 are reported in *The Book of the States, 1968-69* (Lexington, Ky.: Council of State Governments, 1968), pp. 66-67.

13. Paul T. David and Ralph Eisenberg, *Devaluation of the Urban and Suburban Vote: A Statistical Investigation of Long-Term Trends in State Legislative Representation,* 2 vols. (Charlottesville, Va.: Bureau of Public Administration, University of Virginia, 1961-62), vol 1: pp.7-16. David and Eisenberg calculated for each county in the United States the ratio of its proportion of state legislative representation to its proportion of the state's population in 1960, as well as in selected previous years. The ratio, termed the relative value of the right to vote, could also be employed to measure the quality of representation for categories of counties.

14. White and Thomas, pp. 728-30.

15. John G. Grumm, "The Effects of Legislative Structure on Legislative Performance," in *State and Urban Politics: Readings in Comparative Public Policy,* ed. Richard I. Hofferbert and Ira Sharkansky (Boston: Little, Brown & Co., 1971), pp. 304-5.

16. Wayne Francis, *Legislative Issues in the Fifty States: A Comparative Analysis* (Chicago: Rand McNally, 1967), pp. 63-70.

17. *The Book of the States, 1968-69,* pp. 66-67, and I. Ridgeway Davis, *The Effects of Reapportionment on the Connecticut Legislature—Decade of the Sixties* (New York: National Municipal League, 1972), pp. 1-6.

18. Brett W. Hawkins, "Consequences of Reapportionment in Georgia," in *State and Urban Politics: Readings in Comparative Public Policy,* pp. 273-98; Douglas S. Gatlin, "The Development of a Responsible Party System in the Florida Legislature," in *State Legislative Innovation,* ed. James A. Robinson (New York: Praeger Publishers, 1973), pp. 1-45; Glen T. Broach, "A Comparative Dimensional Analysis of Partisan and Urban-Rural Voting in State Legislatures," *Journal of Politics* 34 (1972): 905-21; and David W. Brady and Richard Murray, "Reformers and Skeptics: Testing for the Effects of Apportionment Patterns on Policy Outputs," paper presented at the 1972 Annual Meeting of the Southern Political Science Association, Atlanta, Ga., 2-4 November 1972.

19. Susan W. Furness, "The Response of the Colorado General Assembly to Proposals for Metropolitan Reform," *Western Political Quarterly* 26 (1973): 747-65; Samuel K. Gove, 'Policy Implications of Legislative Reorganization in Illinois," in *State Legislative Innovation,* pp. 105-13; Richard Lehne, *Reapportionment of the New York Legislature:*

Impact and Issues (New York: National Municipal League, 1972); Robert Heath and Joseph H. Melrose, Jr., *Pennsylvania Reapportionment: A Study in Legislative Behavior* (New York: National Municipal League, 1972); and James J. Best, "The Impact of Reapportionment on the Washington House of Representatives," in *State Legislative Innovation*, pp. 136-82.

20. Bruce W. Robeck, "Legislative Partisanship, Constituency, and Malapportionment: The Case of California," *American Political Science Review* 66 (1972): 1246-55; Davis, *Effects of Reapportionment*, pp. 1-6.

21. *The Book of the States, 1968-69*, pp. 66-67.

22. The White-Thomas analysis defined "urban" according to the Census Bureau's definition of urban place. Although I have relied on the White-Thomas work in setting out the theoretical propositions to be examined, the definition employed in their article is, for the reasons noted in the text, a less adequate conception of urban than SMSA. The present study operationalizes urban primarily in terms of SMSA.

23. Reapportionment activity for all six states during the period of 1960-73 appears in summary in Table C-1 in Appendix C.

24. The classification scheme has several major assets which include: (1) its applicability to the comparative analysis of legislative districting patterns within a state over time, since most states over a period of time have utilized both at-large and subcounty districts for the central city counties; (2) its applicability to the comparative analysis of different states which employ a myriad of districting approaches involving single-member and multimember districts for metropolitan counties; and (3) the relative accuracy of this approach in identifying urban, suburban, and rural components of the population compared to alternative formulations such as the White-Thomas schema. The classification scheme is also similar to the approach used by David and Eisenberg in their 1961 examination of malapportionment in the fifty states. (See n. 13 in this chapter.) It is relatively easy in this mode of analysis to detect differences in the population strength of a county or group of counties expressed as the percentage of the state's total population and the representative strength of the same area expressed as the percentage of seats held in each chamber of the state legislature.

Chapter Two

Reapportionment and Representation: Turnover, Legislator-Constituency Relations, and Legislator Characteristics

Reapportionment and Legislative Turnover

Chapter one described first-level effects of reapportionment as those derived from the mechanics of redistricting itself, considered apart from political interests such as urban or partisan that may gain or lose depending on the distribution and strength of such interests from reapportionment. First-level effects embrace the impact of reapportionment on legislator-constituency relations or on representation in general, abstracted from the specific interest content of such representation. Perhaps the central element in first-level impact is the general disruption in legislative activity which may be produced, first, by the requirement to reapportion especially if the legislature bears the legal responsibility for redistricting; second, by the electoral uncertainty for incumbent legislators as a result of modified districting patterns; third, by changes in legislator-constituency relations spurred by changes in the size or composition of districts; and fourth, by the continuing threat to the legislature of renewed reapportionment activity as judicial challenges arise against existing arrangements.

Little attention will be given here to the distraction from general policy matters created in those states in which the legislature holds initial responsibility for reapportionment. The fact that in five of the six sample states (all but New Jersey) the legislature does have this responsibility deserves mention, especially in view of the crooked road traveled by some of the states on their way to compliance with the "one man, one vote" principle.[1]

Electoral uncertainty for incumbents is perhaps the most immediate impact of reapportionment. The problem for incumbents was enhanced in the 1960s and early 1970s by the ever-present possibility of court-imposed rather than legislated reapportionment. The fact of electoral uncertainty finds support in aggregate statistics on election outcomes and in individual experiences of incumbent legislators. Looking first at aggregate figures on legislative turnover, we find a clear relationship between reapportionment and higher turnover. Alan Rosenthal's study of turnover in all state legislatures over the period of 1963-71 found a correlation of .30 for upper houses and .19 for lower houses between *number* of reapportionments during the period and extent of legislative turnover.[2] Focusing on the sample of six states for the years 1959-74 reveals more directly the tendency of reapportionment to produce unusually high turnover.

Table 2-1 summarizes turnover data for the six sample states over the period of 1959-74.[3] One must view variations in turnover with some caution since reapportionment is only one of several operative forces which may lead to increased turnover. In a given state, short-term issues, swings in party fortunes, gubernatorial races, national issues (for example, Watergate), and presidential contests (especially unusual ones like the 1964 and 1972 races) may lead to unusually high turnover. Still, it is apparent from a review of Table 2-1 that reapportionment leads to peculiarly high turnover. In the upper and lower houses of five of the six sample legislatures, turnover is generally higher in elections under new apportionment plans than in elections using stable districts. Only in the cases of the Tennessee Senate and House is turnover for nonreapportionment years greater than it is for reapportionment years. It is not immediately clear why Tennessee should stand outside the overall pattern, although it is worth observing that turnover in both legislative chambers in Tennessee exceeds turnover rates for all other state legislative houses in non–reapportionment years.

Looking at the five states excluding Tennessee, one cannot infer from the data the precise sources of higher turnover in reapportionment years; several factors, however, deserve attention. Consolidation of lesser-populated districts through reapportionment requires some turnover. This phenomenon occurred most prominently in Kansas in 1966 when reapportionment eliminated thirty-eight incumbents in the lower house through such consolidation.[4] Subdivision of more populated districts need not eliminate incumbents, though this possibility certainly exists and will receive attention in the following section. Finally, modifications of the legislature's size in terms of the total number of seats may be a product of reapportionment. Throughout the period 1959-73, Kansas, Oregon, and Tennessee maintained stable numbers in both legislative chanbers.[5] The Delaware Senate, however, increased from seventeen seats in 1959 to twenty-one seats in 1973; the Delaware House, at the same time, grew from thirty-five to forty-one. The most dramatic changes in size occurred in New Jersey. Reapportionment activity enlarged the Senate from twenty-one to twenty-nine in 1966 and then to forty in 1968. The Assembly, in 1968, expanded from sixty to eighty. The 1968 enlargement of both the upper and lower houses helps to account for the exceptional turnover of over 70 percent in both chambers in that year. The South Dakota Senate, having thirty-five seats, remained unchanged in size throughout the period of the study, but post-1970 redistricting reduced the membership in the House from seventy-five to seventy beginning with the 1972 elections.

**Reapportionment's Impact on Legislator-Constituency Relations:
Elections and Representation**

The examination of turnover in the sample states suggests rather strongly that reapportionment produces increased electoral uncertainty for incumbent legislators. This formulation gains added support from the observations of legislators in the six states. The questionnaire sent to legislators in 1973 asked those who were incumbents running in the last election in 1972 whether reapportionment based on the 1970 census had modified their districts to the point of affecting their chances for reelection. Better than 70

TABLE 2-1

Legislative Turnover in the Six Sample States by Chamber, 1959-74
(New Members as a Percentage of Total Number of Seats Up for Election)

Legislative Session Beginning[a]	1959 (1960)	1961 (1962)	1963 (1964)	1965 (1966)	1967 (1968)	1969 (1970)	1971 (1972)	1973 (1974)	Average for Non-Reapportionment Years	Average for Reapportionment[b] ment Years
Delaware[c]										
Senate	70.0	57.1	50.0	100.0*	55.6	36.8*	0.0	47.6	46.5	61.5
House	54.3	51.4	40.0	65.7*	57.1	53.8*	46.2	48.8*	49.8	56.1
Kansas[d]										
Senate	(0.0)	45.0	(15.0)	55.0*	(2.5)	45.0*	(7.5)	40.0*	45.0	46.7
House	31.2	51.2*	26.4*	36.8*	47.2*	28.0	24.0	36.8*	27.6	39.7
New Jersey[e]										
Senate	25.0	20.0	45.5	51.7*	75.0*	(0.0)	52.5*	57.5*	30.2	59.2
Assembly	31.7	41.7*	33.3	48.3	72.5*	25.0*	58.8*	62.5*	37.8	52.1
Oregon[f]										
Senate	40.0	33.3	62.5*	26.7	40.0	33.3	60.0	53.3*	38.9	57.9
House	38.3	28.3	38.3*	33.3	28.3	31.7*	38.3	45.0*	33.3	38.3
South Dakota[g]										
Senate	22.9	34.3	31.4*	60.0	51.4*	37.1	42.9	42.9*	39.4	41.9
House	33.3	42.7	36.0*	30.7	57.3*	36.0	41.3	34.3*	36.8	42.5
Tennessee[h]										
Senate	60.6	66.7	54.5*	45.5*	57.6*	42.4*	35.3	25.0*	54.2	45.0
House	57.6	56.6	50.5*	50.5*	55.6*	52.5	46.5	40.5*	53.3	49.3

Sources: See the description of sources in Appendix B.

[a]Years in parentheses are for New Jersey, the only state of the six which holds elections in odd-numbered years.

[b]Years in which new apportionment plans were implemented are designated by asterisks.

[c]Senate terms in Delaware are four years, with about half of the seats up for election every two years, except that all seats were up for election in 1968.

[d]All Kansas senators stand for election every four years. Figures in parentheses indicate turnover in non-election years and are not averaged into the cumulative percentages in columns nine and ten.

[e]Roughly half of the New Jersey Senate stood for election in 1959, 1961, and 1963, when four-year terms were used. All Senate seats were up for election in 1965 with two-year terms only. All seats were up for election in 1967 when four-year terms again applied. There were no elections for Senate seats in 1969. In 1971, all seats were up for election for two-year terms; in 1973, all seats were up for election, with four-year terms at stake.

[f]The Oregon Senate uses staggered four-year terms. As a rule, half of the total seats are up for election in a given year.

[g]All Senate seats in South Dakota are up for election every two years.

[h]Tennessee used two-year Senate terms until 1968, when four-year terms were initiated. Terms are staggered so that roughly half of the seats were up for election in 1970 and 1972. All seats were up for election in 1968 and prior years.

percent of the incumbents in Oregon thought that redistricting activity had modified their chances for success, while slightly more than half of the incumbent respondents in Delaware and South Dakota felt that reapportionment affected their electoral fortunes either positively or negatively. Roughly 40 percent of the respondents in New Jersey and Tennessee gave similar responses, though New Jersey legislators tended to base their replies on anticipated results of the reapportionment plan to be applied to the upcoming election in 1973. Only in Kansas, where 25 percent of the incumbents indicated that reapportionment hurt or helped their election opportunities, did an overwhelming number of legislators see no major impact of reapportionment on their districts.[6]

The effects of reapportionment on election chances have several sources. In some instances, redistricting involves the consolidation of two or more districts and thereby mandates the elimination of one or more incumbents. A Kansas legislator pointed up this case when he observed "as the result of redistricting my representative district was dissolved and I was forced into a Senate race in [the] 1972 election." Looking ahead to elections to be held in 1974, an Oregon legislator observed, "I don't plan to run for the Senate again but reapportionment put me and two other incumbent senators in the same district. I supported this. They were opposed." [7]

Reapportionment may also add or subtract significant numbers of people from existing districts. Apart from the interests identified with the people added or subtracted, reapportionment may add constituents who are unfamiliar with the incumbent and thus less inclined to support him on grounds of recognition alone. Reapportionment may also remove constituents who have a record of supporting the incumbent. These are clearly first-level effects since they do not depend on the interests attached to the constituents. It is, however, fairly difficult to separate these first-level effects from the interplay of urban-rural and partisan considerations which are second-level effects. Most incumbent legislators, in fact, view district modifications in terms of interests. For example, a South Dakota state senator noted the effect of post-1970 reapportionment when he said, "I am urban and gained a rural county in my district making an almost even urban-rural split. [It] makes [it] difficult to fairly [sic] represent both." A South Dakota Democrat commented, "Many suburban and rural voters were taken out of my district. As they were mostly Republican, this increased my chances." From a Kansas legislator came this detailed analysis:

[Reapportionment] fixed my district so that I was almost a shoo-in by enlarging my party vote and setting up voting blocks that cancel out each other on many issues. This allows me to vote more as I personally see the problem. For the first time I was unopposed, previously having very hard campaigns.

In a rather special case of district modification, reapportionment may affect election outcomes by subdividing larger districts. In many states, this phenomenon was common in more populous urban and suburban districts which gained added representation during the reapportionment wave of the 1960s. However, apportionment plans replacing multimember districts with single member districts also require district subdivision even in the absence of malapportionment. Oregon, well apportioned throughout the 1960s, converted in 1971 from a combination of multimember and single-member districts to a plan relying exclusively on single-member districts. The transition, which had its strongest impact on the major metropolitan centers, apparently accounts for the exceptionally large number of incumbents who claimed reapportionment affected their reelection chances. Responding to an open-ended question on reapportionment,[8] about 46 percent of all Oregon respondents mentioned the apparent effects of the switch to single-member districts. In New Jersey, which in 1973 converted to single-member Senate districts and uniform two-man Assembly districts, about 18 percent volunteered comments on single-member districts. Respondents from Tennessee, which switched to predominately single-member districting during the 1960s (the House in 1966, the Senate in 1968), hardly mentioned this aspect of the change. We can speculate, however, that subdistricting during the mid-1960s would have produced a level of reaction in that state similar to that in Oregon. Delaware used single-member districts throughout the period under study, as did Kansas during most of the period.[9] South Dakota continues to use both single-member and multimember districts. These three states did not generate much comment on the issue.

Subdistricting may either enhance an incumbent's chances for reelection by placing him in a constituency of concentrated strength or may hurt him by diluting support previously enjoyed in a multimember district. An Oregon senator anticipated a "rough election in 1974" as a result of post-1970 subdistricting. "I was elected by Lane County at-large, but was reapportioned into rural sections of [the] county."

The consolidation, modification, and subdivision of districts through reapportionment poses hazards to some incumbent legislators and benefits to others. Apart from affecting election outcomes, reapportionment might alter legislator constituency relations in terms of legislator contact with his constituents by enlarging district populations and land area or by reducing populations and land area. In most states, the initial wave of reapportionment in the mid-1960s created geographically larger and more populous districts in rural areas. At the same time, it produced smaller districts both geographically and population-wise in urban and suburban areas. The effect of these changes, evidenced on a smaller scale in post-1970 redistricting, is open to speculation. The responses of legislators to the 1973 questionnaire, however, provide support for David Braybrooke's contention that citizen access to legislators would be enhanced in districts with populations reduced by reapportionment.[10] The corollary to this contention, that citizens in districts with increased populations might find access more difficult, also is supported by the legislators' comments.[11] About one legislator in ten in Kansas and Tennessee volunteered that reapportionment activity during both the 1960s and 1970s had resulted in districts which were either smaller and closer to the people or geographically larger and more difficult to represent effectively. Metropolitan legislators tended to view redistricting in the former and more positive way, for obvious reasons. Rural legislators, on the other hand, saw reapportionment resulting in larger and more populous districts which were more difficult to represent. While this question generated relatively few responses (7 percent) in compact and urban New Jersey, the following comments of one New Jersey assemblyman are instructive:

An example, one district in my county consists of three medium-size and one small cities [sic]. The representative has a relatively small area to cover, and since cities tend to house large families, as well as many residents who are non-citizens, his constituency are [sic] fewer in number under the "one man, one vote" concept.... A short drive from that district we find a representative must cover three entire counties to serve the same number of people.... It would seem that some consideration should be given to a formula that would consider both voter population and area.

Legislators in tiny Delaware, composed of only three counties, hardly noted this question. In contrast, nearly 6 percent of the legislators in rural South Dakota cited the difficulty in representing sprawling, sparsely-populated constituencies. About one legislator in seven in Oregon, however, commented on the impact of reapportionment in creating smaller and more manageable constituencies. The observations came predominantly from metropolitan legislators and grew out of Oregon's transition to single-member districts in 1971. Malcolm Jewell's comparative study of metropolitan legislators in seven states addressed the problem of representation in at-large multimember districts versus representation in single-member districts. From a campaigning standpoint, Jewell found legislators agreed that at-large districts were difficult to contest both in terms of cost and time.[12] However, Donald G. Balmer, who has studied state legislative races in Oregon, has suggested that conversion from at-large, multimember districts may have varying effects on campaign style and expenses. On the one hand, the use of single-member districts may raise expenditures per voter by forcing candidates competing in neighborhood races to bear the costs of metropolitan-wide advertising in newspapers, radio, and television even though the advertising is aimed at only a small segment of voters in the metropolitan area. Balmer found this to be the case in several state legislative campaigns. On the other hand, single-member districts may enhance the opportunities for a low-cost, door-to-door campaign for those candidates who have the time and friends to pursue this strategy.[13] Responses from Oregon legislators emphasized this latter possibility, reflected in the following comments by one Oregon representative: "With smaller districts, candidates with limited campaign funding have been able to run aggressive, door-to-door campaigns, which were difficult to run in larger districts. A very high number of incumbents were defeated by young newcomers in the last election."

It appears that reapportionment has led to both positive and negative changes in legislator-constituency relations. In some instances, it has produced overly large districts geographically, while in other instances it has enhanced legislator-constituency contact through the creation of smaller districts both geographically and in terms of population. Discussion of legislator-constituency relations requires, however, a final word about the impact of successive reapportionment plans on constituents' recognition of their legislators. Frequent redistricting in many states throughout the 1960s and early 1970s probably created confusion among voters about both their districts and representatives. How much confusion is not certain, though several legislators responding to the questionnaire noted this problem.

Reapportionment's Effects on Legislator Characteristics

If reapportionment exerts some influence on legislator-constituency relations, reapportionment will probably also affect the characteristics of legislators themselves. Apart from the partisan attachments of the legislators (analyzed in the following chapter), personal characteristics including legislative experience, age, sex, race, and occupation may undergo modification as a result of reapportionment. Previous studies of reapportionment, including Lehne's work on New York and Melrose and Heath's monograph on Pennsylvania, have examined the impact of reapportionment on legislator characteristics, though none have given detailed consideration to the issue of why and how reapportionment might affect such characteristics.[14]

In view of the previous discussion of turnover in the six sample states, reapportionment should lead to a decline in legislative experience overall as freshmen legislators replace veterans. The way in which the age distribution of a legislature or the number of women members might change following reapportionment is not immediately clear; two hypotheses, however, do arise. Combination, modification, and subdivision of existing districts can reduce the reelection chances of incumbent legislators and in turn create fresh opportunities for potential candidates. An increased number of these potential candidates, in contrast to prereapportionment elections, may be younger candidates or women. To the extent that wealth correlates with age (that is, income rises with age), smaller districts and reduced campaign costs may attract those young candidates who were previously financially unable to run. An Oregon legislator specifically mentioned that post-1970 redistricting created districts "small enough for a person of my means and age [to] have a chance." As urban and suburban areas are the major beneficiaries of reapportionment, they may be more willing to elect younger legislators than are rural areas.

The number of blacks elected to the legislature may also increase as a result of reapportionment, if blacks constitute a viable voting block in the state's population and have significant concentration in areas gaining representation as a result of reapportionment. In practice, this means that in states with a large population residing in metropolitan areas (specifically central cities) and gaining from reapportionment, black representation after redistricting may rise.

The distribution of occupations among a state's legislators may change as a result of reapportionment due to modified campaign costs and the shift in representation from rural to metropolitan areas. The distribution of occupations and of age, sex, and racial characteristics of legislators may vary according to party fortunes to the extent that such characteristics are not equally represented among each party's candidates. Thus, if reapportionment benefits Democrats over Republicans, the election of more Democrats may result in larger numbers of black legislators or legislators from blue-collar occupations (assuming that Democrats overrepresent such groups).

Based on the theoretical framework established in chapter one, changes in legislator characteristics constitute both first-level and second-level effects since some characteristics such as age, sex, and occupation may change because of new election opportunities created by redistricting itself (first-level effects). Other modifications in legislator characteristics (for example, race and occupation) may derive from the shift in representative strength of certain interests like black or blue-collar voting blocs or Democrats.

The earlier analysis of reapportionment's impact on legislative turnover might lead us to expect that reapportionment would be associated with a decline in overall legislative experience of representatives. If reapportionment produces higher than normal turnover, it should also lead to a reduction in the number of veteran legislators. This expectation is not clearly substantiated by the data on legislative experience in the six sample states over the period of 1959-74.

Legislative experience is measured here as the percentage of legislators who have served four or more years in their chamber (Delaware, Kansas, New Jersey) or in either legislative house (Oregon, South Dakota, Tennessee).[15] In only two of the six states (Kansas and New Jersey) is legislative experience lower in both legislative chambers when elected under new apportionment plans, as opposed to established apportionment plans. In one house of the Delaware, Oregon, and South Dakota legislatures, and in both houses of the Tennessee legislature, legislative experience is actually greater in reapportionment years than in non-reapportionment years. Solely for the New Jersey legislature does reapportioment appear to have caused a sharp decline in overall legislative experience (for example, four-year veterans constituted more than two-thirds of the Senate in 1960, 1962, and 1964, but about one-sixth of the Senate in 1968 and 1974). In this case, the decline in percentage of experienced members is partly attributable to the expansion of the Senate from twenty-one members in 1964 to forty in 1968 and the increase in membership in the Assembly from sixty in 1966 to eighty in 1968.

Whatever temporary impact reapportionment may have had on legislative experience, it is clear that reapportionment had virtually no long-term effect on the level of legislative experience in the six sample states with the exception of New Jersey. Table 2-2 reports the percentage of experienced legislators for the period 1959-63 prior to the major redistricting activity of the 1960s and for the period 1969-1973 after most of the significant reapportionment activity had been concluded. In every state except New Jersey, postreapportionment levels of experience are nearly equal to or greater than prereapportionment levels. Again, the decline in legislative experience in New Jersey appears to be partly the result of the expansion of the legislature. Drastic swings in partisan fortunes in New Jersey are a second source of the decline in experience (to be considered in chapter three).

Thus, the summary data generally suggest a nominal impact of reapportionment on legislative experience. A more accurate conclusion is perhaps that it is difficult to isolate reapportionment years in terms of changes in legislative experience. A variety of factors including shifting party fortunes may affect legislative experience. It may also be the case that first-term and second-term legislators are more vulnerable to defeat than more veteran legislators. If so, the percentage of veteran legislators may remain fairly stable even in high turnover years.

Like the data on legislative experience, the statistics on other legislator characteristics do not yield to easy and unambiguous interpretation of the impact of reapportionment. The present analysis considers characteristics including sex, race, age, and occupation for the six sample legislatures over the period of 1959-74. The data on legislator characteristics, gleaned from state manuals and legislative journals, are fairly comprehensive (with the exception of Delaware which did not publish such information during most of the period covered by the study). The data on legislator characteristics including age, sex, race, and occupation are analyzed in the following paragraphs and are reported in detail in Table C-4 in Appendix C.[16]

TABLE 2-2

Percentage of Legislators with Four or More Years Experience Before (1959-63) and After (1969-73) Reapportionment, by Chamber

	Upper House		Lower House	
	Average per Session 1959-1963	Average per Session 1969-1973	Average per Session 1959-1963	Average per Session 1969-1973
Delaware[a]	37.3	50.8	23.8	19.3
Kansas[a]	55.0[c]	52.5[c]	35.2	43.4
New Jersey[a]	71.4	32.5[c]	32.2	17.9
Oregon[b]	67.8	83.3	32.8	37.8
South Dakota[b]	40.0	33.3	39.1	34.7
Tennessee[b]	33.3	61.6	24.3	24.6

Source: Computed from data in Table C-3 in Appendix C.

[a]Figures are percentages of total chamber members who served four or more consecutive years in the chamber.

[b]Figures are percentages of chamber members who served four or more consecutive years in either house of the legislature.

[c]Sessions following non-election years are not averaged (see Table C-3).

The data on age of legislators provide two measures, the average age for each legislative chamber and the percentage of legislators aged thirty-five and under. In neither Tennessee nor South Dakota did the age characteristics of the legislatures undergo much change in the period under study. However, in the New Jersey Assembly (but not the Senate), the average age of legislators declined rather steadily over the period of analysis (the average age of the Assembly was 47.1 in 1960 and 44.5 in 1974), and the number of young legislators increased sharply (from about 8 percent in 1960 and 12 percent in 1964 to nearly 19 percent in 1974). Since the New Jersey Senate was more severely malapportioned than the Assembly, one hesitates to attribute the growing youthfulness of the lower house to reapportionment. Nevertheless, a jump from about 12 percent to over 16 percent in the proportion of young members occurred after the 1967 election when the Assembly expanded from sixty to eighty members and when, for the first time, assemblymen ran in subcounty rather than at-large county districts. Consistent with the proposition outlined above, the smaller districts and the greater number of districts created by reapportionment may have enhanced the opportunities for more youthful candidates. The analysis of New Jersey gains support from a review of the Oregon data. While the age characteristics of

Oregon legislators show little change throughout the 1960s (recall that Oregon was well apportioned in 1961), the average age in both the Senate and House declined by three years and the number of young legislators in both chambers increased sharply in the first election in 1972 after the adoption of exclusively single-member districting. However, it is easy to overestimate the influence of single-member districting on the increase in young legislators. In 1971 there were four central city legislators aged thirty-five or under in the House and in 1973 a total of seven. Since the overall total of legislators aged thirty-five and under was thirteen in 1971 and nineteen in 1973, only half of the gain from 1971 to 1973 is attributable to central city counties subdistricted in 1972. Other factors obviously affected the number of young legislators. Data on ages of legislators in Kansas and Delaware were not available, although several Kansas legislators responding to the questionnaire suggested that reapportionment had brought younger members to the legislature. No Delaware respondents, however, noted this effect. In the absence of firm figures, the impact of reapportionment on age distribution in Kansas and Delaware remains an open question.

In general, reapportionment appears to have had little influence on the age characteristics of state legislators except in New Jersey and Oregon where the impact of reapportionment on age seems slight. A similar conclusion emerges with regard to reapportionment's effect on the number of women in state legislatures. Study of the data fails to uncover any state in which reapportionment has led to either an increase or a decrease in the number of women. Even when the data suggest such a relationship, it is difficult to provide a satisfactory explanation which could account for a possible link between reapportionment and the number of women. In the Oregon House, where the percentage of women doubled over the previous session after the adoption of single-member districting in the 1972 election, the total of 15 percent was little greater than the 13 percent total of the 1959 sessions before reapportionment occurred in the 1960s.

In contrast to the absence of substantial reapportionment impact on age and sex of legislators, a rather clear pattern of effect arises in the data on the race of legislators. Reapportionment had a negligible impact on the number of black legislators in South Dakota and Oregon where the total number of blacks in the population is very small. However, in Kansas, New Jersey, and Tennessee reapportionment appears to have produced significant increases in the number of black legislators. The results are most evident in Tennessee where the percentage of black legislators rose from zero in 1963 to 3 percent and 7 percent in the Senate and House respectively in 1973. Though accurate prereapportionment data does not exist for Kansas and New Jersey, the number of black legislators after 1966 may indicate that reapportionment in those states led to greater black representation. (Blacks accounted for 3 percent of 1973 Kansas legislators and nearly 6 percent of 1974 New Jersey legislators.) Prereapportionment data on Delaware are also missing, though black representation apparently rose in the late 1960s. In 1973 black legislators comprised about 5 percent of the legislature and came exclusively from central city Wilmington which benefited little from reapportionment. The rise in black representation is thus better accounted for by the increasing percentage of black population in Wilmington than by reapportionment.

It is expected that reapportionment should produce an increase in the number of black representatives in the states of Kansas and Tennessee where central cities gained significantly in representation as a result of reapportionment in light of the concentration of blacks in central city areas. In Tennessee, the black representatives of which have come from central city constituencies, single-member districting seems to have played a more important role in producing black representation than the shift in total number of seats to metropolitan areas as a result of reapportionment. Subdistricting of central city counties virtually guarantees some black representation from cities with a heavy concentration of blacks. The rise of the black legislator in Tennessee corresponds with the adoption of single-member districts in the lower house. The proportion of black representatives increased from 1 percent in 1965 to nearly 6 percent in 1967. In the Senate, the adoption of single-member districts corresponded to an increase from zero to 3 percent in the proportion of blacks between 1967 and 1969. In New Jersey, subcounty districting may have aided black representation, but the data do not permit a firm conclusion on this point. The evidence provided here is consistent with Jewell's findings on the effects of reapportionment and specifically on single-member districting in producing greater black representation in Ohio, Georgia, and Tennessee.[17]

If single-member districts operate to favor minority representation, continued use of multimember districts may reduce the possibility of minority representation. The maintenance of multi-

member districts in western South Dakota has precluded the creation of districts having a population with a majority of Indians,
who make up about 5 percent of the state's population. This circumstance means that Indians are less likely to be elected to the
legislature.[18]

As with race, review of the data on occupations of state legislatures during 1959-73 reveals rather clear evidence of reapportionment's impact. In both Kansas' and Tennessee, reapportionment
appears related to an obvious decline in the number of legislators
whose occupation is tied to agriculture. This development derives
from the reduction in rural representation in both Kansas and
Tennessee as a result of reapportionment. The shift away from
agricultural occupations, which is rooted in the changing balance
of urban and rural elements in the legislature, might have been
expected in these two states in light of the discussion in chapter
one. The proportion of farmer-legislators in the Kansas House
dropped from 40 percent in 1959 to 23 percent in 1973; in the
Senate, the percentage declined from 20 percent to 15 percent over
the same period. In Tennessee, farmer-legislators comprised 15
percent of the Senate and 19 percent of the House in 1959, but
only 3 percent of the Senate and 7 percent of the House in 1973.
Nonmetropolitan legislative representation in Delaware, Kansas,
and Tennessee declined sharply as a result of reapportionment.
Partial information suggests that reapportionment may have led to
a reduction in the percentage of farmer-legislators in Delaware. In
1957 29.4 percent of senators and 31.4 percent of representatives
were engaged in agriculture. In 1973, the next year for which data
are available, only 9.5 percent of senators and 9.8 percent of representatives listed agricultural occupations.[19] Such change does
not appear in well-apportioned Oregon, stably rural South Dakota,
or highly urbanized New Jersey, the last having no farmers prior
to reapportionment.

While the data on legislators' occupations show several other
trends, none can be attributed to reapportionment. New Jersey, for
example, displays after 1966 a clear diminution in the percentage
of lawyer-legislators, with the percentage in the upper and lower
houses in 1974 being roughly half the 1962 proportions. Among
both Republicans and Democrats and metropolitan and nonmetropolitan legislators, this trend emerges. The pattern is difficult to
explain in terms of reapportionment's impact. One might hypothesize that a link exists between subcounty districting (which applies to data for 1968 and later years) and the decreasing

percentage of lawyers if subcounty districting reduces the advantages of recognition and wealth that one may obtain county-wide. This proposition assumes that lawyers possess such advantages; in the absence of evidence on this point, the hypothesis remains highly questionable.

Concluding Comments

The evidence presented suggests reapportionment resulted in obvious changes in the characteristics of legislators in Kansas and Tennessee, the two sample states most severely malapportioned prior to *Baker* and *Reynolds*. In both states reapportionment contributed to an increase in the number of black legislators made possible by greater representation for central city counties and to a decline in legislators from agricultural occupations as a result of reduced legislative strength of rural areas. In the context of the theory set out in chapter one, these are second-level effects, dependent on the distribution of population-based interests. As projected, they are most pronounced in those two states in which malapportionment had operated to misrepresent in a fundamental way the relative balance of nonmetropolitan and metropolitan interests. Data on characteristics of legislators in the other four sample states, with the exception of New Jersey, indicate that reapportionment produced relatively minor changes in characteristics. In New Jersey, expansion of the legislature and subcounty districting contributed to a more youthful and inexperienced membership.

Thus, the analysis of characteristics of legislators as second-level effects of reapportionment shows that the impact of reapportionment has been fairly pronounced in only two states. In contrast, the earlier examination of turnover and legislator-constituency relations, which involve first-level effects, suggests a more generalized impact. Independent of the particular circumstances prevailing in individual states, reapportionment led to increased turnover in all states except Tennessee (where turnover was extremely high in both reapportionment and non-reapportionment years) and an alteration in legislator-constituency relations in those districts modified by reapportionment. Reapportionment was also linked to changes in incumbents' electoral fortunes. Notably, even after fair apportionment had largely been achieved, the introduction of complete single-member districting in Oregon and subcounty districting in New Jersey in the early 1970s appar-

ently made legislative campaigns more feasible for potential con-
tenders and caused considerable apprehension among incumbent
legislators. These findings accord with the expectation that any
redistricting activity poses some consequences for legislator-constituency relations as outlined in the first chapter.

Notes

1. Initial responsibility for apportionment in New Jersey was given to a
   bipartisan commission in 1966.
2. Alan Rosenthal, "Turnover in State Legislatures," *American Journal
   of Political Science* 18 (1972): 612-13.
3. Table 2-1 reports the number of freshmen legislators as the percentage of the total number of seats up for election. This percentage need
   not be identical with the percentage turnover of incumbent legislators who leave office by virtue of electoral defeat or retirement. If
   the number of seats in the legislature increases from one election to
   the next, the percentage of freshmen will exceed the percentage of
   incumbents who leave office. For example, in the New Jersey Assembly, which expanded from sixty members in 1966 to eighty in 1968,
   63.3 percent of incumbents left office in 1968; however, 72.5 percent
   of the 1968 Assembly were freshmen. For the assessment of the impact of reapportionment, the percentage of freshmen may be a more
   revealing measure than percentage turnover of incumbents because it
   more clearly reflects legislative inexperience resulting from reapportionment and because expansion of legislative membership may be a
   device to preserve incumbents.
4. Analysis of William H. Cape, reported in National Municipal League,
   Apportionment in the Nineteen Sixties, rev. ed. (New York: National
   Municipal League, 1970), sec. on reapportionment in Kansas.
5. The Kansas Senate numbered 40 seats, the House 125. The Oregon
   Senate contained 30 seats, the House 60. The Tennessee Senate held
   33 seats, the House 99.
6. See question 12 on the questionnaire reprinted in Appendix A. The
   precise breakdown of responses according to percentage of incumbents who felt post-1970 redistricting affected their chances for reelection is: Delaware, 53.3 percent (of 15 incumbents); Kansas, 25.0
   percent (of 56 incumbents); New Jersey, 43.5 percent (of 23 incumbents); Oregon, 72.7 percent (of 22 incumbents); South Dakota, 53.7
   percent (of 41 incumbents); Tennessee, 38.5 percent (of 26 incumbents).
7. Comments of state legislators are taken from the questionnaire survey described in chapter one; later quotations are not footnoted.
8. See question 2 in the questionnaire reprinted in Appendix A. The
   responses are summarized in Table C-2 in Appendix C.
9. The Kansas Senate utilized some multimember districts from 1969 to
   1972. For the remainder of the period under study, the Senate used
   single-member districts as did the House for the entire period of
   study.

10. Braybrooke, p. 114 (see n. 6 in chapter one). Geographical size of districts and relative concentration of population figure more prominently in legislators' comments about representation than does the total population of the constituency.

11. See question 2 in Appendix A. These data are reported in Table C-2 in Appendix C.

12. Malcolm E. Jewell, *Metropolitan Representation: State Legislative Districting in Urban Counties* (New York: National Municipal League, 1969), p. 13.

13. Letter from Donald G. Balmer, Professor of Political Science, Lewis and Clark College, Portland, Oregon, 4 January 1978.

14. Richard Lehne, *Legislating Reapportionment in New York* (New York: National Municipal League, 1971), pp. 22-41; Heath and Melrose, *Pennsylvania Reapportionment*, pp. 29-42.

15. These data are reported in detail in Table C-3 in Appendix C.

16. The sources used to compile the data are given in Appendix B.

17. Jewell, *Metropolitan Representation*, pp. 15-18. See also Hawkins, pp. 278-79.

18. Letter from Alan L. Clem, Professor of Political Science, University of South Dakota, Vermillion, 10 June 1977.

19. Sources for these data are given in Appendix B.

Chapter Three

The Impact of Reapportionment on Republican and Democratic State Legislative Fortunes

The Partisan Impact of Reapportionment

Because Republicans and Democrats draw disproportionate support from different groups in the population, one would expect that major shifts in central city, suburban and nonmetropolitan representation would lead to alterations in partisan representation in state legislatures. Examination of this proposition is not easy, since one must try to isolate reapportionment's impact from other forces operating on partisan balance. Long-term trends favoring one party and culminating in the postreapportionment period in the late 1960s may give the illusion that reapportionment has influenced party fortunes. Short-term factors, such as the Goldwater candidacy in 1964, may also complicate the analysis.

Even accounting for other forces at work, a review of party fortunes in the six sample states over the period of 1959-74 suggests that reapportionment in several instances has led to signifi-

47

cant gains for one party or to sometimes offsetting gains by both parties. Table 3-1 summarizes Republican fortunes and, by implication, Democratic fortunes in the six states for central city, suburban, and nonmetropolitan constituencies. The most apparent instance of reapportionment's impact is in Tennessee. While the Republican share of seats increased for all types of constituencies in the period analyzed, the most significant gains occurred in central city counties which benefited most from reapportionment. In the lower house, for example, Republicans in 1973 held twenty-two out of forty-four central city seats versus three out of twenty-two seats in 1959. The dramatic increase in central city representation as a result of reapportionment enhanced Republican fortunes in the party's area of greatest growth in the central city counties. Reapportionment thus merits at least partial credit for the rise of Republicans by the late 1960s to nearly equal status with the Democrats.

In two-party Delaware, reapportionment appears to have conferred similar benefits upon the Republicans. Suburban representation rose from 24 percent to 57 percent in the Senate from 1959 to 1973; in the House it rose from 29 percent to 56 percent. Republican ascent to legislative control in 1967, and continuing through 1973, derived from the party's ability to dominate elections in suburban constituencies in spite of fluctuating and often weak support in central city and nonmetropolitan districts.

In Kansas, the impact of reapportionment upon party fortunes is more complicated, yet as apparent as it is in Delaware and Tennessee. The shift of seats from nonmetropolitan areas to central city areas undoubtedly cost Republicans seats in both the upper and lower houses. Even though Republican success rates in central city districts improved over the period under study, the Republican share of central city seats fell considerably below the party's share of nonmetropolitan seats. From 1959 to 1973 the percentage of central city seats in the Senate and House increased four times over, and in 1973 Democrats held half of these seats in the Senate and 59 percent in the House. At the same time, the gains of the Democrats in the central cities were partially neutralized by Republican dominance in an expanded number of suburban constituencies. In the lower house in 1973, Republicans held 87 percent of the fifteen suburban seats; in 1959 they had held only one out of four suburban seats.

Of the remaining three states in the sample, only New Jersey evidences some reapportionment-induced changes in party for-

TABLE 3-1

Republican Percentage of Central City, Suburban, and Nonmetropolitan Seats in the Six Sample Legislatures by Chamber, 1959-74 [a b c]

Delaware

	1959	1961	1963	1965	1967	1969	1971	1973
Senate								
Central City	50.0(2)	50.0(2)	50.0(2)	0.0(4)	25.0(4)	33.3(3)	33.3(3)	33.3(3)
Suburban	60.0(5)	40.0(5)	60.0(5)	50.0(8)	62.5(8)	80.0(10)	80.0(10)	80.0(10)
Nonmetro	20.0(10)	30.0(10)	30.0(10)	16.7(6)	50.0(6)	66.7(6)	66.7(6)	16.7(6)
Total	35.3(17)	35.3(17)	41.2(17)	27.8(18)	50.0(18)	68.4(19)	68.4(19)	52.4(21)
House								
Central City	20.0(5)	20.0(5)	20.0(5)	0.0(8)	50.0(8)	16.7(6)	33.3(6)	33.3(6)
Suburban	40.0(10)	50.0(10)	50.0(20)	31.3(16)	75.0(16)	76.2(21)	76.2(21)	73.9(23)
Nonmetro	25.0(20)	45.0(20)	25.0(20)	0.0(11)	63.6(11)	58.3(12)	41.7(12)	16.7(12)
Total	28.6(35)	42.9(35)	31.4(35)	14.3(35)	65.7(35)	64.1(39)	59.0(39)	51.2(41)

Kansas

	1959	1961	1963	1965	1967	1969	1971	1973
Senate								
Central City	66.7(3)	66.7(3)	66.7(3)	66.7(9)	66.7(9)	75.0(12)	75.0(12)	53.8(13)
Suburban	50.0(2)	50.0(2)	50.0(2)	50.0(4)	50.0(4)	100.0(5)	100.0(5)	80.0(5)
Nonmetro	82.9(35)	82.9(35)	82.9(35)	70.4(27)	70.4(27)	78.3(23)	78.3(23)	72.7(22)
Total	80.0(40)	80.0(40)	80.0(40)	67.5(40)	67.5(40)	80.0(40)	80.0(40)	67.5(40)
House								
Central City	22.2(9)	33.3(12)	33.3(12)	44.4(18)	43.2(37)	43.2(37)	48.6(37)	40.5(37)
Suburban	25.0(4)	60.0(5)	60.0(5)	83.3(6)	83.3(12)	91.7(12)	83.3(12)	86.7(15)
Nonmetro	58.9(112)	68.5(108)	75.9(108)	67.3(101)	67.1(76)	78.9(76)	73.7(76)	71.2(73)
Total	55.2(125)	64.8(125)	71.2(125)	64.8(125)	61.6(125)	69.6(125)	67.2(125)	64.0(125)

[a] Data is reported in percentages; figures in parentheses are number of legislators (all parties) in that category.

[b] Years indicate first legislative sessions following elections.

[c] The district classification scheme is described in Chapter One.

TABLE 3-1 (continued)

New Jersey

	1960	1962	1964	1966	1968	1970	1972	1974
Senate								
Established Central City	20.0(5)	20.0(5)	40.0(5)	16.7(12)	62.5(16)	62.5(16)	28.6(14)	21.4(14)[d]
New Central City[e]	[33.3(3)]	[33.3(3)]	[33.3(3)]	[40.0(5)]	[50.0(6)]	[50.0(6)]	57.1(7)	14.3(7)
Suburban	50.0(8)	50.0(8)	87.5(8)	41.7(12)	100.0(17)	100.0(17)	82.4(17)	29.4(17)
Nonmetro	75.0(8)	75.0(8)	75.0(8)	80.0(5)	57.1(7)	57.1(7)	100.0(2)	50.0(2)
Total	52.4(21)	52.4(21)	52.4(21)	34.5(29)	77.5(40)	77.5(40)	60.0(40)	25.0(40)[d]
	1960	1962	1964	1966	1968	1970	1972	1974
Assembly								
Established Central City	30.0(30)	12.5(24)	29.2(24)	8.3(24)	45.2(31)	51.6(31)	25.0(28)[d]	10.7(28)
New Central City[e]	[37.5(8)]	[37.5(8)]	[37.5(8)]	[37.5(8)]	[83.3(12)]	[83.3(12)]	50.0(14)	14.3(14)
Suburban	52.6(19)	47.8(23)	78.3(23)	47.8(23)	91.4(35)	88.6(35)	61.8(34)	20.6(34)
Nonmetro	63.6(11)	61.5(13)	61.5(13)	46.2(13)	85.7(14)	85.7(14)	100.0(4)	50.0(4)
Total	43.3(60)	36.7(60)	55.0(60)	31.7(60)	72.5(80)	73.8(80)	48.8(80)[d]	17.5(80)

Oregon

	1959	1961	1963	1965	1967	1969	1971	1973
Senate								
Central City	27.3(11)	27.3(11)	23.1(13)	23.1(13)	15.4(13)	15.4(13)	15.4(13)	15.4(13)
Suburban	50.0(4)	50.0(4)	80.0(5)	80.0(5)	100.0(5)	100.0(5)	80.0(5)	85.7(7)
Nonmetro	40.0(15)	33.3(15)	16.7(12)	33.3(12)	33.3(12)	58.3(12)	66.7(12)	40.0(10)
Total	36.7(30)	33.3(30)	30.0(30)	36.7(30)	36.7(30)	46.7(30)	46.7(30)	40.0(30)
	1959	1961	1963	1965	1967	1969	1971	1973
House								
Central City	56.0(25)	52.0(25)	44.4(27)	44.4(27)	51.9(27)	44.4(27)	33.3(27)	34.6(26)
Suburban	57.1(7)	57.1(7)	62.5(8)	50.0(8)	75.0(8)	87.5(8)	75.0(8)	28.6(14)
Nonmetro	32.1(28)	42.9(28)	48.0(25)	64.0(25)	72.0(25)	76.0(25)	76.0(25)	70.0(20)
Total	45.0(60)	48.3(60)	48.3(60)	53.3(60)	63.3(60)	63.3(60)	56.7(60)	45.0(60)

[d] Percentage and number take into account one independent.

[e] New central city counties are those central city counties recognized after 1970. Percentages for these areas prior to 1970 are given in brackets, but are not counted in overall tabulations.

TABLE 3-1 (continued)

South Dakota

	1959	1961	1963	1965	1967	1969	1971	1973
Senate								
Central City	100.0(2)	100.0(2)	100.0(2)	100.0(2)	100.0(4)	100.0(4)	100.0(4)	60.0(5)
Nonmetro	39.4(33)	66.7(33)	72.7(33)	48.5(33)d	80.6(31)	74.2(31)	64.5(31)	46.7(30)
Total	42.9(35)	68.6(35)	74.3(35)	51.4(35)d	82.9(35)	77.1(35)	68.6(35)	48.6(35)
House	1959	1961	1963	1965	1967	1969	1971	1973
Central City	87.5(8)	100.0(8)	100.0(9)	100.0(9)	100.0(9)	100.0(9)	66.7(9)	20.0(10)
Nonmetro	53.7(67)	73.1(66)	74.2(66)	54.5(66)	83.3(66)	75.8(66)	65.2(66)	55.0(60)
Total	57.3(75)	76.0(75)	77.3(75)	60.0(75)	85.3(75)	78.7(75)	65.3(75)	50.0(70)

Tennessee

	1959	1961	1963	1965	1967	1969	1971	1973
Senate								
Central City	0.0(8)	12.5(8)	9.1(11)	16.7(12)	14.3(14)	35.7(14)	42.9(14)	42.9(14)
Suburban	33.3(3)	33.3(3)	33.3(3)	33.3(3)	33.3(3)	33.3(3)	33.3(3)	33.3(3)
Nonmetro	18.2(22)	18.2(22)	21.1(19)	27.8(18)	31.3(16)	37.5(16)	37.5(16)d	37.5(16)d
Total	15.6(33)	18.2(33)	18.2(33)	24.2(33)	24.2(33)	36.4(33)	39.4(33)	39.4(33)d
House	1959	1961	1963	1965	1967	1969	1971	1973
Central City	13.6(22)	13.6(22)	12.5(32)	15.6(32)	40.5(42)	50.0(42)	47.6(42)	50.0(44)
Suburban	20.0(5)	20.0(5)	33.3(6)	16.7(6)	33.3(6)	66.7(6)	50.0(6)	66.7(6)
Nonmetro	18.1(72)	20.8(72)	24.6(61)	29.5(61)	43.1(51)	47.1(51)d	39.2(51)	44.9(49)
Total	17.2(99)	19.2(99)	21.2(99)	24.2(99)	41.4(99)	49.5(99)d	43.4(99)	48.5(99)

Sources: See Appendix B.

tunes. In New Jersey, reapportionment opened the possibility for Democratic control of the Senate, which was usually dominated by Republicans, even when a Democrat held the governorship and an Assembly majority during 1960-1963; Democrats won control of the Senate, and the Assembly, as well as the governorship, in the 1965 elections. Beyond 1965, however, the additional representation for suburban areas provided by reapportionment aided the Republican party as its greatest strength was in suburban constituencies. Republican success in the enlarged number of suburban districts in the late 1960s more than offset Republican losses caused by the reapportionment-induced reduction in the number of nonmetropolitan seats, which in most elections had been predominantly Republican. The established central city counties, which were largely Democratic, gained little in overall representation, as gains in the Senate were offset by losses in the Assembly as a result of reapportionments in 1961 and later years.

The 1967 legislative elections, which were held after the most extensive redistricting of the period under study, thus produced a Senate and an Assembly which were three-fourths Republican. Republicans won all suburban seats in the Senate and 90 percent of the suburban seats in the Assembly; suburban seats accounted for well over one-half of the enlarged Republican delegation in both chambers. The conclusion that reapportionment is the primary source of the Republican rise is weakened by the fact that the GOP carried a majority of central city, nonmetropolitan, and suburban seats in the elections of 1967 and 1969. The addition of newly defined central city counties complicates the analysis of post-1970 developments in New Jersey. It is not clear whether the new central city counties, which were defined as nonmetropolitan prior to 1970, are politically more similar to the predominantly Democratic central city counties or to the heavily Republican suburban counties. In the first wave of reapportionment activity in the late 1960s, these counties made slight gains in representation but became significantly more Republican, especially in the Assembly in which 83 percent of the seats went to Republicans in the 1967 and 1969 elections. The 1971 elections produced a drop in Republican strength in the new central city counties, although the party controlled 50 percent of these seats in the Assembly and 57 percent in the Senate. The 1973 elections, strongly influenced by Watergate, resulted in a landslide victory for the Democrats who won an overwhelming proportion of seats from new central city counties, established central city, and suburban areas as well. If the 1973 elections are excluded, however, the primary thrust of reapportionment in New Jersey appears to have aided Republicans by enhancing suburban representation and by producing no major change in the representation of the established central city counties where Democrats were strongest.

In neither Oregon nor South Dakota does it appear that reapportionment has produced significant modifications in partisan balance. Both states were relatively well apportioned prior to the Supreme Court's rulings in the *Baker* and *Reynolds* cases, and population distribution remained relatively stable over the period under study. Thus, reapportionment resulted in only slight alteration in the representation of central city, suburban, and nonmetropolitan areas; what changes did occur in partisan representation cannot be attributed to reapportionment.

A summary of the evidence of all six states suggests that partisan changes were most substantial in the states most malapportioned prior to reapportionment. Consistent with the theory outlined in chapter one, the most dramatic changes in partisan representation occurred in Tennessee where the emergence of a metropolitan majority in the legislature as a result of reapportionment corresponded to a sharp rise in the Republican share of legislative seats. The creation of a suburban majority in Delaware, also as a result of reapportionment, formed the basis for firm Republican control of both chambers; this finding also fits into the analysis of chapter one. Although changes in partisan representation in Kansas were clearly evident, they were less significant than those in either Delaware or Tennessee. Metropolitan seats comprise a slightly smaller proportion of the legislature of Kansas than that of Tennessee, but in terms of malapportionment and level of urbanization and metropolitanization, the states are similar. The stability of the Republican majority in Kansas over the period of analysis contrasts with the declining Democratic position in Tennessee. This situation is perhaps attributable to greater suburbanization in Kansas and to the strong national Republican trends in the late 1960s and early 1970s. The successes of Nixon in 1968 and 1972 undoubtedly enhanced growing Republicanism in Tennessee and helped forestall Democratic gains in Kansas.

The findings on the impact of reapportionment on partisan balance in the six sample states can be incorporated into a more general context by referring to other studies on the partisan effects of reapportionment. Perhaps the most systematic effort to determine the comparative impact of reapportionment on partisan balance is Robert S. Erikson's study of thirty-eight chambers in twenty-eight states which were reapportioned between 1962 and 1968.[1] Using the statewide vote for the U.S. House of Representatives as a measure of election results, Erikson examined the deviation of the Democratic percentage of seats in the thirty-eight chambers (all non-Southern) from a presumed 50 percent Democratic share of the statewide vote. Looking at prereapportionment elections, Erikson found that a 50-50 split of the statewide vote would give the Republicans a majority of seats in 68 percent of the chambers; after reapportionment, the same even split would net the Republicans a majority in only 42 percent of the chambers. With an even division of the statewide vote, the average seat division for all chambers was 48 percent Democratic in 1962; after reapportionment, 50.9 percent Democratic. Erikson thus concluded that reapportionment netted the Democrats a 2.9 percent seat increase overall for the thirty-eight chambers studied. Democratic gains were concentrated in states east of the Mississippi (7.4 percent increase in seats), while Republicans made slight gains west of the Mississippi (2.7 percent increase in seats). Erikson argued that Democratic gains were greatest in the large industrial and urban states of the Northeast. Erikson's findings generally support earlier studies of the partisan impact of malapportionment. One such study is V.O. Key's analysis of thirty-two, two-party states during 1930-50 which reported that, partly as a result of malapportionment, Democratic governors were three times as likely as Republican governors to face a legislature controlled by the opposition in one or both chambers.[2] The Erikson study also accords with Jewell's assertion that reapportionment would help the Republicans in the Southwest. Jewell also suggested Republicans would benefit in Southern states where, as in the Southwest, the party is urban-based. The South, however, was not included in Erikson's study.[3]

Erikson's analysis covered only three of the six sample states, but the three cases merit attention. Erikson found a prereapportionment bias of 10.7 percent in favor of the Democrats in the Delaware House; the postreapportionment bias was 10.6 percent in favor of the Democrats. In the Kansas House, a prereapportionment bias of 6.9 percent favoring Republicans became a 12.2 percent bias favorable to the Democrats after reapportionment. A prereapportionment bias of 9.8 percent favoring Republicans in the South Dakota House rose to 11.3 percent after reapportionment; in the Senate a prereapportionment bias of 2.4 percent favoring the Democrats was converted after reapportionment to a

0.7 percent Republican advantage.[4] Tufte's research on the New Jersey Assembly uncovered a reduction in bias favoring the Republicans as a result of reapportionment, although his study does not give a precise figure on the decrease.[5]

It is interesting to note that Republicans gained in Delaware after reapportionment despite a continuing Democratic bias, but in Kansas, they maintained their position despite the emergence of a Democratic bias after reapportionment. Republicans in New Jersey gained legislative strength after the reapportionment of the mid-1960s despite an apparent reduction in bias favorable to the Republican party. Thus, it appears that measuring changes in bias between periods before and after reapportionment is not equivalent to determining real partisan gains resulting from reapportionment. One source of disparity in the two approaches rests on the fact that Erikson's data estimates bias, given an even partisan split of the statewide vote. In a sense, the bias is hypothetical and may become less important as state-wide votes diverge from a 50-50 division. Tufte's work distinguishes "bias," which is projected on an even division of the state-wide vote, from "swing ratio," which expresses the relationship of change in a party's statewide vote to change in its share of legislative seats in terms of a ratio. Swing ratio estimates the percentage gain in seats as a percentage of all seats for each 1 percent rise in a party's vote. Generally, a 1 percent rise in the statewide vote nets a much greater than 1 percent rise in seats. According to Tufte's analysis, reapportionment may have enhanced the swing ratio in New Jersey—thus accounting for Republican gains after reapportionment—while reducing bias.[6] Although no data exist on swing ratios for Delaware and Kansas, the operation of the swing ratio concept may help to account for Republican strength in the face of Democratic bias in the election systems after reapportionment.

The existence of the swing ratio itself derives from the fact that geographical, winner-take-all districting virtually guarantees divergence between a party's overall proportion of the statewide vote and its proportion of legislative seats.[7] It is significant that Erikson reported a correlation of .40 between partisan imbalance and the prereapportionment Dauer-Kelsay scores of malapportionment for the thirty-eight chambers in his study. This relationship could explain only 16 percent of the variation in partisan imbalance. The correlation between the Dauer-Kelsay Index and change in partisan imbalance after reapportionment was .49, a figure which would still account for less than a fourth of the variation.[8]

Weber and Uslaner's examination of forty lower houses before reapportionment in 1962 and after reapportionment in 1968 determined that deviation from the proportionality in statewide vote and seats held by one party actually increased overall after reapportionment. However, for twenty houses examined, they also found a reduction in the relationship of Erikson's partisan bias scores and deviation from proportionality after reapportionment. (Before reapportionment r = .541, after r = .357.) [9] This would suggest that reapportionment reduced slightly the role of districting schemes in conveying advantage disproportionate to votes.

It is interesting that Weber and Uslaner take this last finding to indicate that reapportionment has reduced the role of gerrymandering, which they equate with partisan bias, in producing disproportionality between votes and seats.[10] It is hard to accept this conclusion without hesitation since only a portion of bias derives from apportionment patterns. Still, a key issue in the analysis of reapportionment's impact on partisan representation centers on its effects on gerrymandering.

Application of the equal-population standard need not foreclose gerrymandering since the creation of unequally populated districts constitutes only one tactic by which one party may enhance its electoral opportunities at the expense of another. Concentration of opposition votes in a few districts where the opposition wins by overly large majorities and distribution of the voting strength of the opposition across several districts so that the opposition forms a substantial but losing minority are two other approaches which can result in partisan advantage by forcing one party to receive wasted votes in landslide wins and narrow losses.[11] Neither of the latter approaches is inconsistent with the principle of "one man, one vote." Indeed, some observers have suggested that the Supreme Court's reapportionment rulings enhanced the prospects for gerrymandering by allowing redistricting agents, who are usually state legislatures, to ignore almost all other considerations (for example, integrity of political subdivisions) in pursuit of equally-populated districts.[12]

The evidence that exists suggests that the success, if not the frequency, of gerrymandering has not increased in the aftermath of *Baker* v. *Carr* and *Reynolds* v. *Sims*. Indeed, the opposite is more likely true. Consider post-1970 redistricting in the sample states. In Delaware, where Republicans controlled legislative redistricting, the party suffered losses in both chambers in the 1972 elections. Despite control of the 1971 reapportionment plan in South Dakota, Republicans in 1972 lost seats in both houses. Republicans also dominated a redistricting plan for the Kansas House (a federal court produced the plan for the Senate) but lost seats in the 1972 elections. Tennessee Democrats also lost seats in the lower house, although they controlled legislative reapportionment. In New Jersey and Oregon, the state legislatures did not create the districting plans used in post-1970 elections.[13]

Erikson's analysis of state legislative reapportionment after *Baker* and *Reynolds* found that in six out of seven chambers for which Democrats controlled redistricting, a Democratic imbalance resulted (that is, a greater percentage of seats than percentage of statewide votes, given a projected 50-50 split). In only four out of eight houses in which Republicans controlled reapportionment did a Republican imbalance result. In the other twenty-three chambers in Erikson's study, a court bipartisan commission, or divided government controlled redistricting.[14] While these figures give some support to the continuing use of gerrymandering, they hardly suggest an increase in gerrymandering. In fact, Erikson's finding of an overall reduction in bias for thirty-eight chambers would imply a reduction in gerrymandering.[15] This view gains added weight when it is considered that state or federal court review is a common prospect in state legislative redistricting.[16] While neither federal nor state courts have invalidated gerrymandering per se, they have applied standards of compactness and contiguity which circumscribe attempts at gerrymandering.[17]

Partisan Impact of Reapportionment: The Special Case of Multi-member Districts

Up until this point, this analysis has focused on the general effect of reapportionment on partisan representation. However, particular attention needs to be given to the role of multimember and single-member districts in the context of partisan representation, and, more important, to the effect of reapportionment upon the use of single-member and multimember districts. Presumably, changes in patterns of single-member and multimember districting may influence party competition.

Data on the use of single-member and multimember districts in state legislative apportionment plans reveal a clear trend following *Baker* and *Reynolds* favoring increased use of single-member districts and reduced application of multimember districts. Thirty-two state senates out of fifty used single-member districts exclusively in

1962, while the remainder used a combination of single-member and multimember districts. While the number of states using only single-member districts fell to twenty-seven in 1968, it had risen to thirty-six by 1973. Among lower houses, the number using only single-member districts increased from twelve in 1962 to sixteen in 1968 and to twenty-five in 1973.[18] Although federal and state court rulings on apportionment have not invalidated the use of multimember districts, there seems to be general sentiment in judicial holdings favoring the use of single-member districts.[19] Reapportionment since 1962 has undoubtedly contributed to the increased reliance on single-member districts.

Among the six sample states, four used systems employing both single-member and multimember districts prior to court-ordered reapportionment. Only Delaware and Kansas used single-member districting exclusively both before and after reapportionment, although the Kansas Senate used some multimember districts between 1969 and 1972. Among the remaining four states, South Dakota continued to use both single-member and multimember districting in both chambers after court-ordered reapportionment. Tennessee converted from a combination system to a predominantly single-member plan for the House in the 1966 elections, and an all single-member format for the Senate in the 1968 elections; by the 1972 elections, all House districts were single-member. Oregon abandoned a combination of single-member and multimember districts in favor of single-member districts in the 1972 elections. The picture is more complex in New Jersey, where the first wave of reapportionment forced the use of multimember districts in the Senate in the 1965 election; it previously had used only single-member districts. A later plan in 1973 reverted to the single-member districting formula. The Assembly followed multimember districting almost exclusively throughout the period of 1959-74, but with some important changes in the wake of court-ordered reapportionment. These changes are discussed below. Although the evidence appears in later discussion, it is important to note that following court-ordered reapportionment, three of the four states using some multimember districts either abandoned them entirely (Oregon and Tennessee) or significantly reduced their size (New Jersey); only South Dakota maintained fairly consistent use of multimember districts after the *Reynolds* decision.

The use of multimember districts in four of the sample states has had, in some instances, a considerable impact upon the relative success of the two major parties in contesting legislative seats. This impact is most pronounced in central city counties employing at-large, county-wide multimember districts. This practice tends to reduce the ability of the minority party, in some cases, to win any legislative seats. In contrast, division of the county into subcounty multimember districts or single-member districts will usually afford some legislative representation to the minority party in those subdivisions of the county where its votes are concentrated.[20]

The effect of multimember, at-large schemes in central city counties clearly surfaces in the case of Multnomah County (Portland) in Oregon. Until the reapportionment in 1971, state senators were elected at-large from Multnomah, while representatives were elected in five subcounty districts after 1955. From 1959 to 1972, Democrats controlled the entire Multnomah Senate delegation, numbering seven in 1959 and 1961 and eight thereafter. During the same period, Republicans were able to elect at least five and sometimes seven representatives to the Multnomah House delegation, which numbered sixteen from 1959 to 1962 and seventeen from 1963 to 1972. Multimember, at-large districting obviously favored the countywide Democratic majority in Senate contests, while subdistricting of House seats afforded virtually guaranteed seats for the Republican minority. Ironically, the switch to exclusively single-member districting for both Senate and House seats for the 1972 elections did not benefit Republicans, who won only three of sixteen House seats and (again) no Senate seats.

In Tennessee, House Reapportionment plans adopted in 1965 and thereafter utilized single-member districts for the largest counties (including the four major central city counties) for which at-large, multimember districts had been employed previously. The reapportionment plan adopted in 1966, which took effect in 1968, provided for single-member Senate districts, which, in the central city counties replaced at-large districts. Conversion to single-member districts undoubtedly aided Republicans, whose share of House seats in central city counties increased more than two and a half times in the 1966 legislative elections. That single-member districting contributed immensely to this gain is evident from a comparison of House and Senate results in the 1966 election. Republicans fared much worse in the Senate which did not convert to single-member districts until the 1968 elections. The 1966 results follow: [21]

County	House		Senate	
	Rep.	Dem.	Rep.	Dem.
Knox (Knoxville)	7	1	2.	0
Davidson (Nashville)	0	11	0	4
Hamilton (Chattanooga)	4	3	0	2
Shelby (Memphis)	6	10	0	6

With the adoption of single-member Senate districts for the 1968 election, Republican seats in central city counties increased two and a half times (see Table 3-1).

Changes in multimember districting and their link to partisan success in New Jersey are more difficult to analyze than in the cases of Oregon and Tennessee. Until 1965 the Senate assigned one seat per county, thus yielding a total of twenty-one seats. Although reapportionment, which began in 1965, added seats to central city and suburban counties, these counties elected multimember delegations at-large until 1971. In that year, a new reapportionment mandated the election of forty senators from forty single-member districts which included subcounty districts in central city and suburban counties. To some degree then, the at-large system applied in 1965 resulted in the continuation of the countywide, winner-take-all system under the one county, one senator formula. Republican control of multimember suburban delegations tended to offset Democratic dominance of central city county delegations. For example, in 1967 the Republicans won all five Bergen County seats and all three Union County seats, while Democrats won all four Hudson County (Jersey City) seats. It is intriguing that in that year, Republicans won all six Essex County (Newark) seats and all three Passaic County (Paterson, Clifton, and Passaic) seats, winning central city counties which were normally Democratic.[22] In the 1971 elections, Republicans held the suburban counties noted above, but Democrats won three out of five Essex County seats and all three Passaic County seats. In terms of overall seats, it is not clear that multimember districts conferred advantages to either party, though they certainly created the capacity for sharp swings in party fortunes (for example, in Passaic County). The switch to single-member districts for the 1973 elections in that abnormal year, nevertheless, raised the likelihood of a two-party split in the delegations of large suburban and central city counties in three out of four cases analyzed (see Table 3-2). In the preceding three Senate elections in 1965, 1967, and 1969,

TABLE 3-2

Partisan Division of Seats in Largest Suburban and Established Central City Counties in New Jersey by Chamber, 1960-74 [a]

| | Senate and Assembly At-Large | | | Senate At-Large; Assembly Subcounty | | | | |
	1960	1962	1964	1966	1968	1970 (No Senate Elections)	1972	1974[b]
Suburban Counties								
Bergen								
Senate	1R/0D	1R/0D	1R/0D	4D/0R	5R/0D	(5R/0D)	5R/0D	4D/1R
Assembly	6R/0D	7R/0D	7R/0D	6D/1R	10R/0D	10R/0D	7R/3D	8D/2R
Union								
Senate	1R/0D	1R/0D	1R/0D	1D/1R	3R/0D	(3R/0D)	3R/0D	2D/1R
Assembly	3D/1R	4D/1R	4R/1D	3D/2R	5R/2D[c]	5R/2D[c]	4R/2D	6D/0R
Central City Counties								
Essex								
Senate	1D/0R	1D/0R	1R/0D	4D/0R	6R/0D	(6R/0D)	3D/2R	4D/1R/1I
Assembly	7R/5D	8D/1R	5R/4D	9D/0R	7R/5D	8R/4D	6D/3R/1I	9D/3R
Hudson								
Senate	1D/0R	1D/0R	1D/0R	3D/0R	4D/0R	(4D/0R)	3D/0R	3D/0R
Assembly	7D/0R	6D/0R	6D/0R	6D/0R	8D/0R	8D/0R	7D/0R	6D/0R

Source: See Appendix B.

[a] R refers to Republicans, D to Democrats, I to Independents.

[b] Senate districts are single-member and subcounty; Assembly districts are uniform two-member districts and also subcounty.

[c] The number includes one assemblyman elected at-large by the entire county.

split results occurred in only one out of four counties in 1965 and 1969.

The New Jersey Assembly employed county at-large elections until 1965; larger counties were multimember. From 1965 until 1973, the Assembly subdistricted larger counties through a combination of smaller multimember districts having two or three assemblymen and single-member districts. Beginning in 1973, assemblymen ran from uniform two-member districts. Review of the data in Table 3-2 on the two largest suburban and two largest central city counties suggests that subdistricting has had little effect on the likelihood of a split in county delegations. Essex and Union divided seats between parties before and after subdistricting, Hudson remained solidly Democratic throughout the period of analysis, and Bergen divided more often after subdistricting. However, in the cases of Union, Bergen, and Essex, there was a greater tendency to division among Assembly seats than among the at-large Senate seats.

Multimember districting in New Jersey has apparently played a less significant role in affecting party fortunes than in either Oregon or Tennessee. At least one reason for this would be the more generalized strength of Republicans and Democrats in New Jersey; either party seems capable, even in at-large districts favorable to opponents, of mounting successful challenges in good years (for examples, the Republicans in Essex in the 1967 elections and the Democrats in Bergen in 1965). Republicans, from 1959 to 1973, never carried Mulnomah County in Oregon, and Republicans in Tennessee never gained more than a small minority of House or Senate seats in Knox and Shelby counties until subdistricting occurred.

South Dakota, the remaining sample state which has used multimember districts, is perhaps the least interesting case. Throughout the period of analysis, the only central city county (Minnehaha) elected both senators and representatives at-large and, in most years, elected a unified Republican delegation. Democrats won one out of eight House seats in the 1958 elections, three out of nine in 1970, and eight out of ten in 1972. Only in 1972 did the Democrats elect any senators; in that year, they won two out of the five seats. Because Minnehaha County has never been subdistricted, one cannot say conclusively that subdistricting would have afforded Democrats greater representation in past years. The figures do indicate that it could have only helped them.

Examination of multimember districting in Oregon, Tennessee,

New Jersey, and South Dakota leads to the conclusion that multi-member districting, or alternatively, subdistricting in metropolitan counties, whether central city or suburban, may influence the relative fortunes of the two parties. Because reapportionment in three out of the four states involved either subdistricting or single-member districting in formerly at-large counties, it modified the structure of interparty competition in metropolitan areas. This finding reaffirms the earlier and significant work of Jewell, who found that reapportionment-induced subdistricting of metropolitan counties enhances the ability of the minority party to win legislative seats otherwise unattainable in at-large districts.[23]

Reapportionment's Effects on Intraparty Representation

Earlier analysis has shown that reapportionment has affected, in particular cases, the relative strength of Democratic and Republican representation in state legislatures. A related question is the impact of reapportionment on the representation of interests within state legislative delegations of the two major parties. Changes in the proportions of central city, suburban, and nonmetropolitan legislators within a party may in turn lead to changes in the leadership and policy positions advanced by the party.

Review of the data on intraparty representation of central city, suburban, and nonmetropolitan interests for the six sample states suggests that reapportionment has led, in some instances, to obvious transformations in internal party make-up.[24] Perhaps the most intriguing case is in Tennessee, where both the Democratic and Republican legislative parties experienced substantial increases in the proportion of central city legislators as a result of reapportionment. By 1973 central city legislators constituted similiar proportions, about 42-46 percent, of Democratic and Republican legislators in both the Senate and House. This proportion of central city legislators stands in sharp contrast to pre-reapportionment levels in 1959 and 1961 when central city legislators comprised only about one-fourth of Democratic representation and one-sixth of Republican legislators. After 1967 Democratic and Republican legislators are fairly equally divided internally according to central city, suburban, and nonmetropolitan interests. Since Democrats and Republicans were closely matched after 1967 in total legislative seats in both upper and lower houses, the intraparty distribution of interests raises the question of whether party

or constituency would be more salient factors in aligning legislators on major issues. This question receives attention in chapter
six.

By enlarging the proportion of central city legislators in Kansas,
reapportionment yielded a shift in population-based representation similar to that which occurred in Tennessee. Kansas Republicans and Democrats, in contrast to their counterparts in
Tennessee, absorbed the increased number of central city seats in
unequal proportions. Kansas Republicans showed larger central
city and suburban wings by 1973 than in prereapportionment
years, but nonmetropolitan legislators still held a clear, if somewhat reduced, majority of Republican seats in the upper and lower
houses. Central city legislators, however, constituted nearly half of
Democratic seats in the Senate and House in 1973; this differs from
prereapportionment years when more than three-fourths of Democratic legislators came from nonmetropolitan constituencies. A
growing gulf emerges in Kansas following reapportionment between the predominantly suburban and nonmetropolitan Republican party and the central city-oriented Democratic party.
However, it is too easy to overstate this dichotomy, especially in
view of the fact that in absolute numbers the Republicans held one
more central city seat in the Senate than Democrats did in 1973
and nearly as many in the House (fifteen versus twenty-two for the
Democrats). Nevertheless, the divergence of the Republican and
Democratic characteristics in Kansas contrasts with the similarity
of internal representation between Republican and Democratic legislators in Tennessee.

The effects of reapportionment on internal party representation
in the remaining four sample states emerge less obviously than in
Kansas and Tennessee. In South Dakota, both Democrats and Republicans before and after reapportionment reflected the profoundly rural cast of the state's population. While Democrats in
both houses of the Oregon legislature became decidely more central city-oriented and House Republicans more nonmetropolitan,
neither change can be attributed to reapportionment as it modified
only slightly the representation of central city, suburban, and nonmetropolitan interests.

Reapportionment in New Jersey and Delaware apparently produced similar consequences for the Republican party. In both
states, reapportionment enhanced the position of suburban elements which were already dominant prior to major redistricting
activity. The Democratic party in New Jersey remained largely

central city-oriented throughout the period of analysis, although the year 1974 stands as an exception to this generalization as noted earlier. Democrats in Delaware, who were strong in central city and nonmetropolitan areas, suffered from the reduction in legislative strength in these areas as a result of reapportionment. Consequently, internal representation in the party evidences no clear patterns. The strength of the central city, suburban, and nonmetropolitan components of the Democratic legislative delegations in both the Senate and House was nearly equal throughout the late 1960s and early 1970s. In 1973, however, nonmetropolitan areas accounted for half of the Democratic seats in each house.

Reapportionment, in summary, has produced the most significant internal party changes in Tennessee and Kansas. Both of these states are modified one-party states which, prior to reapportionment, significantly underrepresented central cities. A real shift in the balance of interests in both Democratic and Republican parties occurred in Tennessee; in Kansas, a major transformation emerged in the Democratic party. Consistent with the propositions outlined in chapter one, changes in Kansas and Tennessee seem more substantial and involve clear shifts in the constituency foci of the parties than do changes in two-party New Jersey and Delaware, where internal representation and thus orientation remained fairly stable throughout the period of analysis. In Oregon and South Dakota, states which were reasonably well apportioned prior to reapportionment, reapportionment yielded virtually no alteration in internal party representation.

Reapportionment and Internal Party Organization: Subdistricting and County Chairmen's Power

The earlier analysis of the partisan impact of reapportionment devoted special attention to the effects on party fortunes of reapportionment-induced subdistricting of metropolitan counties. In connection with internal party organization at the electoral level, the impact of subdistricting may again be analyzed. Jewell's monograph, *Metropolitan Representation*, holds that subdistricting may lead to internal party divisions at the county level by reducing the control of county party officials over the nomination process.[25] Legislative candidates nominated and elected in subcounty districts may establish some independence from the county organization. Jewell found that reapportionment-induced subdistricting in Denver contributed to decentralization of party organization in both parties in the Colorado legislature. Though evidence from other metropolitan areas is less conclusive, Jewell summarized his analysis:

> Where party organizations are strong and unified and where voters have been accustomed to supporting party endorsees, the party may be able to maintain its influence over legislative nominations. Districting [i.e., subdistricting] may make it more difficult, however, for a county organization to control nominations when factional splits occur or when candidates run who have a strong local base of support.[26]

Reduction in the influence of county chairmen could only occur in those areas in which chairmen's powers over nomination and ultimate electoral success are present, if not strong. The county chairmen and party organization in general play the strongest role in electoral politics in New Jersey, among the three sample states which subdistricted as a result of reapportionment. While the questionnaire sent to legislators in the sample states did not address the issue directly, several Democratic and Republican legislators in New Jersey suggested that subdistricting (especially under the 1973 plan), had reduced the role of county chairmen at both the electoral and policy-making levels of the legislative process. One Democratic senator said:

> One of the greatest impacts of reapportionment has been on political organization. ... [W]hile assemblymen formerly ran at-large in counties, since reapportionment they have run from small (180,000 pop.) two-man districts. Especially in the larger counties this has weakened somewhat the control of the county party chairmen over his assemblymen—an "offensive" black assemblyman from Newark could be purged when elections were countywide, but regain his seat once district elections gave him a wholly black constituency.
> Until this year [1973] (when ... senators must run in single-member districts), reapportionment had resulted in countywide, multimember senate districts. Senators, especially from the large northeastern counties, have therefore been still very responsive to the wishes of their county chairmen and county political organizations. They would block judgeships their county leaders might oppose and have to maintain a

public profile that would not be "radical" for the organization.

In Oregon, where local party organizations are weak, there was no evidence that the switch to single-member districting in 1971 altered the power of county party leaders. The conversion to single-member districting in Tennessee dates back to the mid-1960s; legislators in 1973 may have thus been less inclined to reflect upon its effects. Still, a Tennessee Republican representative noted that:

> In Knox County prior to reapportionment (pre-1966) the seven representatives ran at-large. This meant the courthouse and party chairman could pretty well elect a slate of controlled men . . . Since we are now running from districts . . . more independent candidates are able to win nomination and election.

Jewell suggests that single-member districting in Shelby County may have reduced the influence of the Republican organization which had influenced the results of a few primary contests prior to the adoption of single-member districting.[27]

Coupled with Jewell's findings the tentative evidence from New Jersey and Tennessee suggests that reapportionment-induced subdistricting weakened the control of local party organizations over the election process in a few instances.

Concluding Comments

The evidence presented indicates that reapportionment has had a variety of effects upon interparty competition, distribution of metropolitan and nonmetropolitan legislators within parties, and local party organization. Consistent with the expectations set out in chapter one, the partisan impact of reapportionment emerged most prominently in those states in which malapportionment had been most severe and had operated to underrepresent in a fundamental way population-based interests. Reapportionment clearly resulted in Republican gains in the late 1960s in Delaware and Tennessee, states in which malapportionment had severely underrepresented areas of greatest Republican strength; reapportionment assisted the election of Republicans to majority control of both houses in Delaware and allowed Republicans to threaten seriously the long-term Democratic hegemony in the Tennessee legislature. To a lesser extent, reapportionment aided the minority Democrats in Kansas, a state in which Democratic gains in previously underrepresented central cities were partially offset by Republican gains in suburban areas. Reapportionment in New Jersey reduced the barriers to Democratic control in the Senate, but the expansion of suburban representation as a result of reapportionment contributed to Republican ascendency in the late 1960s. Little partisan change attributable to reapportionment occurred in Oregon or South Dakota. Reapportionment produced few major intraparty changes, but both parties in Tennessee and the Democratic party in Kansas became notably more central city-oriented after reapportionment.

Among the more subtle effects of reapportionment noted in the preceding analysis, several merit reiteration. First, evidence shows that the breakup of multimember districts contributed to more frequent party divisions in legislative delegations from populous counties in Tennessee and New Jersey (although not in Oregon) and also to a reduction in the control of local party organizations over legislative candidates in some counties in Tennessee and New Jersey. Secondly, there is good evidence that the application of the equal-population standard to state legislative districting did not enhance the potential for partisan gerrymandering in the sample states.

Notes

1. Robert S. Erikson, "The Partisan Impact of State Legislative Reapportionment," *Midwest Journal of Political Science* 15 (1971): 57-71. The analysis contained in the remainder of the paragraph summarizes the findings of Erikson, as reported in this article.
2. V.O. Key, Jr., *American State Politics: An Introduction* (New York: Alfred A. Knopf, 1956), pp. 57-59. Key's general analysis has special significance for New Jersey where Democratic governors, over the period of 1856-1965, were four times as likely as Republican governors to face opposition party control of one or both legislative chambers. On this point, see Alan Shank, *New Jersey Reapportionment Politics: Strategies and Tactics in the Legislative Process* (Rutherford, N.J.: Fairleigh-Dickinson University Press, 1969), p. 34. It is worth mentioning, however, that malapportionment is only one factor among many contributing to divided control (with the most important factor being separation of powers). Therefore, there is little reason to believe that the reapportionment revolution will ultimately lead to substantially fewer instances of divided control for state gov-

ernments in general, although in particular states (such as New
Jersey) this may be the case. (The other five sample states have
experienced divided control since redistricting in the mid-1960s.)

3. Malcolm E. Jewell, *The State Legislature: Politics and Practice* (New
   York: Random House, 1962), pp. 28-29. See also Brady and Murray,
   "Reformers and Skeptics: Testing for Effects of Reapportionment,"
   pp. 25-26.
4. Erikson, "Partisan Impact," pp. 62-63.
5. Edward R. Tufte, "The Relationship between Seats and Votes in
   Two-Party Systems," *American Political Science Review* 67 (1973):
   543-44.
6. Ibid., pp. 542-44.
7. See Douglas W. Rae, "Reapportionment and Political Democracy," in
   Reapportionment in the 1970s, pp. 91-112.
8. Erikson, "Partisan Impact," p. 67.
9. Eric M. Uslaner and Ronald E. Weber, "The Electoral Impact of
   Reapportionment," paper presented at the 1973 Annual Meeting of
   the Southern Political Science Association, Atlanta, Ga., 1-3 November 1973, p. 20.
10. Ibid., p. 21.
11. See the description of gerrymandering strategies in Andrew Hacker,
    Congressional Districting (Washington, D.C.: Brookings Institution,
    1963), pp. 46-63.
12. On this point, see Dixon, "Court, People, and 'One Man, One Vote,' "
    pp. 20-35, and Baker, "Gerrymandering: Privileged Sanctuary," pp.
    121-42. The Supreme Court's decision in *Mahan* v. *Howell* (1973)
    relaxed the requirements for equal population of districts and al-
    lowed for deviations from equality in districts following boundaries
    of political subdivisions. Recognition of the desirability of maintain-
    ing the integrity of political subdivisions (for example, wards, towns,
    counties) could limit gerrymandering.
13. An open-ended question on the impact of reapportionment included
    in the survey of legislators in the six sample states generated only
    seven mentions of gerrymandering (two in Kansas, two in New
    Jersey, two in Tennessee, and one in Delaware). See question 2 in the
    questionnaire reprinted in Appendix A. A question dealing with the
    specific effects of post-1970 redistricting (see question 11) yielded four
    responses noting the use of gerrymandering in creating districts for
    post-1970 elections. One of the four responses came from Delaware,
    the other three from Tennessee. A question dealing with the effect of
    post-1970 redistricting on individual reelection chances (see question
    12) produced several direct or implied references to gerrymandering
    which were tabulated. On each of the questions, the number of legis-
    lators mentioning gerrymandering was, therefore, quite small. The
    data, as a result, are only suggestive. However, responses from Ten-
    nessee were more numerous and more intense than those from the
    other five states. A Tennessee Republican representative, who com-
    mented on the 1973 reapportionment plan, predicted that his party
    would be ruined by the districting plan created by the Democrats. A

victim of the plan, he lamented, "It has completely taken my county away from me and all but 8,000 population ... and put me in three counties which are solidly Democratic. It will be impossible to win." It is interesting that a Democratic representative conceded that his party in 1973 "controlled [the] General Assembly and drew lines to try to reelect as many Democrats as possible and to increase the size of the majority."

14. Erikson, "Partisan Impact," pp. 69n.-70n. Divided government refers to a situation in which one party holds the governorship and the other party holds control of one or both houses of the legislature.

15. Ibid., pp. 62-65.

16. See the summary of reapportionment activity in the six sample states in Table C-1 in Appendix C.

17. In a later study of congressional redistricting which bears on the question of gerrymandering, Erikson found only scant evidence that control of redistricting after *Wesberry* worked to the advantage of the party with the opportunity to gerrymander. Erikson, in this analysis, concluded that uneven distribution of voter support ("an accident of geography") contributed more to the disproportionality of votes and seats than gerrymandering. Erikson, "Malapportionment, Gerrymandering, and Party Fortunes in Congressional Elections," *American Political Science Review* 66 (1972): 1242-44. For the contrasting view that gerrymandering continues unabated in congressional districting, see Elliott, *Rise of Guardian Democracy*, pp. 227-31. Also see Jack L. Noragon, "Redistricting, Political Outcomes, and Gerrymandering in the 1960s," *Annals of the New York Academy of Sciences* 219 (1973): 314-33. Noragon's detailed presentation includes a discussion of evidence on partisan and individual gerrymandering in congressional redistricting after *Wesberry v. Sanders* and a compelling showing that redistricting contributed to a decline in the competitiveness of congressional districts. See also John A. Ferejohn, "On the Decline of Competition in Recent Congressional Elections," *American Political Science Review* 71 (1977): 166-75.

18. "States Make Size, Electoral Changes," *National Civic Review* 57 (1968): 94-97; *The Book of the States, 1968-69*, pp. 66-67; *The Book of the States, 1974-75* (Lexington, Ky.: Council of State Governments, 1974), pp. 66-67.

19. As noted above in chapter one, n. 3, the U. S. Supreme Court in *Whitcomb v. Chavis* ruled that multimember districts do not violate the "one man, one vote" principle; but in *Connor v. Johnson*, 402 U.S. 690 (1971), the Court held that lower federal courts constructing apportionment plans should use single-member districts instead of multimember districts.

20. See Howard Hamilton, "Legislative Constituencies: Single-Member Districts, Multimember Districts, and Floterial Districts," *Western Political Quarterly* 20 (1967): 321-40; also Ruth C. Silva, "Relation of Representation and the Party System to the Number of Seats Apportioned to a Legislative District," *Western Political Quarterly* 17 (1964): 742-69.

21. The analysis and results of the 1966 elections are taken from Lee S.

Greene's perceptive commentary in Malcolm E. Jewell and Lee S. Greene, *The Kentucky and Tennessee Legislatures* (Lexington, Ky.: Department of Political Science, University of Kentucky, 1967), pp. 35-36. See also Jewell, *Metropolitan Representation*, pp. 18-19.

22. A growing majority of the population of Essex County is concentrated in the suburbs outside of Newark. Coupled with the Republican inclination of the suburbs, this factor helps to account for the Republican sweep in Essex in 1967. See "Jersey's High Court Backs Districting Proposal," *New York Times*, 3 March 1970, p. 46. Continued use of countywide multimember districts, which was abandoned in 1973, might have favored Republicans as the population advantage of suburban Essex over Newark widens.

23. Jewell, *Metropolitan Representation*, pp. 18-19. Republicans picked up seats in predominantly Democratic Cuyahoga County (Cleveland) in Ohio after the introduction of single-member districts in 1966. Republicans also gained seats in metropolitan Atlanta, Georgia, after the subdistricting of three counties during 1962-65 and expected gains from the subdistricting of Harris County (Houston), Texas. Democrats made no immediate gains, however, after single-member districting was adopted in 1966 in predominantly Republican Hamilton County (Cincinnati), Ohio.

24. The data on intraparty representation are reported in detail in Table C-5 in Appendix C.

25. Jewell, *Metropolitan Representation*, pp. 7-11, 21-26.

26. Ibid., p. 11.

27. Ibid., p. 10.

Chapter Four

The Effects of Reapportionment on Legislative Leadership and Procedure

Legislative Leadership and Procedure: A Preliminary View of the Impact of Reapportionment

The theoretical framework laid out in chapter one argues that major reapportionment-induced changes of the first and second levels of effect may not yield concomitantly significant changes at the third and fourth levels. In specific instances, a dramatic increase in central city representation (a second-level effect) may not produce a similar gain in urban representation in positions of legislative leadership, such as standing committee chairmanships (third-level effects). Third-level effects may not result if, for example, most central city legislators serve with the minority party and all chairmanships go to majority party members, or a formal chamber official such as the speaker controls selection of chairmen and chooses nonurban chairmen regardless of party. This dilution of second-level effects at the third level, which involves legislative leadership and organization, would in turn reduce the likelihood of notable changes at the fourth level, which involves policy making, since legislative procedure and power so obviously influence the shaping of policy.

The present chapter undertakes an examination of the impact of reapportionment upon legislative leadership in the six sample legislatures. It concentrates specifically on the distribution of standing committee chairmen and chamber presiding officers among legislators from different types of constituencies. The analysis also attempts to discover the effects of reapportionment upon legislative procedure. One possible effect to be examined is the relative power of standing committees in ordering and controlling legislative policy making. Finally, this discussion deals with the impact of reapportionment upon internal party power and ideology in the Republican and Democratic parties. The analysis in the first half of the chapter builds upon a base of quantitative data on leadership changes covering the period of 1959-74 for the six legislatures and upon observed changes in legislative procedure and party organization in the sample legislatures over the same period. The second half of the chapter reports the perceptions of legislators, derived from the 1973 survey, of the impact of reapportionment on legislative leadership, procedure, and internal party organization.

The Impact of Reapportionment on Committee Leadership

Standing committees play a vital role in state legislative activity, although their specific importance varies with each state legislature.[1] In legislatures in which party organization is highly cohesive and disciplined, majority party leaders or the majority caucus may control not only the selection of committee chairmen but also the consideration and reporting of legislation by the committees. To a substantial degree in both the Delaware and New Jersey legislatures, party organization dominates committee activity in the ways suggested, although in both legislatures committee autonomy is increasing.[2]

When party discipline and leadership are lacking, committees are likely to assume a far greater and more independent role in controlling the shape and passage of legislation. Such a pattern may develop in a balanced two-party environment such as that in the Oregon legislature, in which party organization is relatively weak. It may also develop in comparatively noncompetitive, one-party environments, such as those of the Kansas, South Dakota, and Tennessee legislatures, in which until recently the dominant party's majority was often large and unwieldy.[3]

Given the important yet variable role of standing committees in the state legislative process,[4] a key issue in the present analysis is the effect of reapportionment on the leadership of these committees. What has been the impact of reapportionment upon the distribution of committee chairmanships among legislators representing central city, surburban, and nonmetropolitan constituencies in the six sample states?

Table 4-1 summarizes the data on standing committee chairmen by constituency type over the period of 1959-74 which embraces both prerepportionment and postreapportionment sessions. The table examines the distribution of chairmen by constituency in relation to state population and legislative representation.[5] The population index indicates the ratio of the percentage of chairmanships held by a constituency category (for example, central city counties) to the percentage of the state's population in that category. One might hypothesize that more equitable apportionment would push ratios in any given constituency category toward unity and that malapportionment would be associated with index values greater or less than one. The legislative index computes the ratio of the percentage of chairmanships held by a constituency category to the percentage of chamber seats held by that category. The legislative index provides a clue to the independent effect of selection procedures for chairmen. If chairmen were selected randomly and without regard to constituency, the legislative index values should approach one regardless of apportionment.[6] For convenience of analysis, the data in Table 4-1 for each state are marked by a vertical line dividing sessions before major redistricting activity from postreapportionment sessions (based on the reapportionment of the mid-1960s only).

Examination of the data in Table 4-1 suggests that reapportionment did not necessarily bring about a greater share in committee chairmanships for those constituency categories benefiting from added representation even in states in which redistricting produced profound shifts in the comparative representation of different types of constituencies. The clearest instance of the contribution of reapportionment to a modified distribution of chairmanships arises in Kansas. Reapportionment increased representation of central city counties by four times and central city counties' share of chairmanship positions by an even greater margin. There is an almost steady

TABLE 4-1

Population Index and Legislative Index for Committee Chairmanships Held by Legislators from Central City and Suburban Counties, 1959-74 [a]

Legislative Session Beginning[b]	1959 (1960) Senate	House	1961 (1962) Senate	House	1963 (1964) Senate	House
Delaware[c]	D	D	D	D	D	D
Pop. Ind. - Central City	.42	.89	.42	.72	.42	.72
Leg. Ind. - Central City	.77	1.34	.77	1.08	.77	1.08
Pop. Ind. - Suburban	.48	.41	.58	.49	.38	.32
Leg. Ind. - Suburban	.77	.67	.93	.81	.62	.54
Kansas[c]	R	R	R	R	R	R
Pop. Ind. - Central City	.21	.07	.20	0	.20	.07
Leg. Ind. - Central City	.87	.32	.84	0	.84	.23
Pop. Ind. - Suburban	.38	.27	.37	0	.75	0
Leg. Ind. - Suburban	.64	.72	.62	0	1.26	0
New Jersey[c]	R	D	R	D	R	R
Pop. Ind. - Est. Central City	.21	1.71	0	1.49	.43	.43
Leg. Ind. - Est. Central City	.35	1.33	0	1.46	.70	.42
Pop. Ind. - New Central City[e]	(.58)	(.58)	(1.16)	(1.16)	(.58)	(.58)
Leg. Ind. - New Central City[e]	(.58)	(.62)	(1.17)	(1.26)	(.58)	(.62)
Pop. Ind. - Suburban	1.05	.63	.83	.63	1.05	.83
Leg. Ind. - Suburban	1.09	.79	.87	.65	1.05	.87
Oregon[c]	D	D	D	D	D	D
Pop. Ind. - Central City	.84	.77	.77	.81	.88	1.10
Leg. Ind. - Central City	1.04	.84	.95	.88	.92	1.11
Pop. Ind. - Suburban	.73	.38	1.53	1.21	.76	.76
Leg. Ind. - Suburban	.71	.43	1.50	1.35	.60	.75
South Dakota[c]	D	R	R	R	R	R
Pop. Ind. - Central City	.61	1.51	1.39	1.02	.98	2.06
Leg. Ind. - Central City	1.35	1.79	3.09	1.21	2.20	2.18
Tennessee[c]	D	D	D	D	D	D
Pop. Ind. - Central City	.29	.44	.50	.47	.74	.43
Leg. Ind. - Central City	.52	.85	.87	.90	.94	.56
Pop. Ind. - Suburban	1.23	1.23	1.04	.98	1.24	.88
Leg. Ind. - Suburban	.69	1.24	.58	.98	.69	.74

Sources: Figures are calculated from data in Tables 1-3 and C-6. The Popula-
tion Index and Legislative Index are borrowed from Brett W. Hawkins,
"Consequences of Reapportionment in Georgia," in State and Urban
Politics: Readings in Comparative Public Policy, ed. Richard I.
Hofferbert and Ira Sharkansky (Boston: Little, Brown & Co., 1971),
pp. 284-287.

[a]Key: Pop. Ind. - Population Index, which is the ratio of the percentage of
chairmanships held by legislators in a category to the percentage of
the total state population in that category of counties.
Leg. Ind. - Legislative Index, which is the ratio of the percentage
of chairmanships held by legislators in a category to the percentage of legislative seats in that category.
Est. Central City - Established central city counties (New Jersey only)
New Central City - New central city counties (post-1970, New Jersey
only)

TABLE 4-1 (continued)

1965 (1966)		1967 (1968)		1969 (1970)		1971 (1972)		1973 (1974)	
Senate	House	Senate	House	Senate	House	Senate	House	Senate	House
D	D	D	R	R	R	R	R	R	R
1.48	1.38	1.69	.55	.54	.33	.56	.85	.56	.90
1.43	1.29	1.64	.52	.75	.46	.53	.81	.58	.91
.77	.78	.86	1.24	1.36	1.51	1.20	1.46	1.50	1.32
.82	.83	.92	1.29	1.23	1.33	1.27	1.51	1.46	1.31
R	R	R	R	R	R	R	R	R	R
.71	.07	.71	.72	.54	.65	.54	.85	1.26	.93
.97	.15	.97	.75	.56	.68	.56	.88	1.20	.94
.37	0	.75	.80	1.32	.95	1.46	1.14	1.46	1.67
.31	0	.63	.70	.89	.83	1.34	1.35	1.34	1.58
D	D	R	R	R	R	R	R[d]	D	D
1.58	1.58	.64	.64	.75	.75	.58	.96	1.45	1.11
1.49	1.54	.63	.64	.74	.76	.57	.95	1.43	1.10
(.53)	(1.60)	(.87)	(1.31)	(.82)	(1.22)	1.23	.35	.62	.95
(.45)	(1.74)	(.83)	(1.25)	(.79)	(1.17)	1.14	.32	.57	.88
.77	.39	1.57	1.25	1.47	1.33	1.48	1.37	.99	1.14
.74	.40	1.47	1.14	1.38	1.21	1.41	1.31	.94	1.09
D	R	D	R	D	R	D	R	D	D
.99	.82	.73	.96	1.04	.52	.80	.62	1.66	1.22
1.04	.83	.77	.97	1.10	.52	.82	.61	1.69	1.24
.76	.48	1.09	.48	1.46	1.79	1.02	.53	.39	1.34
.60	.47	.86	.47	1.14	1.77	1.05	.68	.29	.99
R	R	R	R	R	R	R	R´	D	D
1.97	1.89	1.97	1.89	1.48	.94	.50	0	.50	.50
4.39	2.00	2.19	2.00	1.65	1.00	.62	0	.50	.50
D	D	D	D	D	R[d]	D	D	D	D
.78	.71	.82	.54	.39	.29	.38	.69	.66	.84
.91	.93	.83	.54	.39	.29	.39	.71	.67	.86
2.18	1.96	1.96	.75	3.27	0	3.04	1.82	2.60	1.65
1.22	1.64	1.10	.62	1.83	0	1.84	1.64	1.57	1.49

[b] Even-numbered years are for New Jersey only.

[c] D denotes a Democratic majority in chamber.
R denotes a Republican majority in chamber.

[d] Republicans did not constitute a majority, but organized the chamber.

[e] Index values for new central city counties recognized after 1970 are given in parentheses for years prior to 1972.

rise in central city chairmanships after the reapportionment of the mid-1960s. In 1973 central city counties held more than six times as many chairmanships by percentage in the Senate as they held in 1959 and about fifteen times as many House chairmanships as in 1959. The population index rose from .21 in the Senate and .07 in the House in 1959 to 1.26 in the Senate and .93 in the House in 1973. Suburban areas likewise made significant gains both in representation and share of chairmanships; they were, in fact, overrepresented in chairmanships relative to population after reapportionment. (See the population index for 1969-73 in Table 4-1.)

In Tennessee, where reapportionment also brought about dramatic gains in central city county representation, the increase in the share of the chairmanships in the central city counties was less significant than in Kansas. In 1969 central city counties held about the same portion of chairmanships as they held in 1959, despite the major redistricting which occurred between the two dates. While legislators from central city counties held about a third of Senate and House chairmanships in 1973 (a far larger portion than they held prior to 1965), their percentage of chairmanships was considerably less than their proportion of seats. (The legislative index for central city counties in the 1973 House is .67; for the 1973 Senate, it is .86.) [7]

In Delaware and New Jersey, states in which notable gains in representation occurred in suburban areas, reapportionment appears to be less closely linked with changes in the distribution of chairmanships than is the case in either Kansas or Tennessee. Review of the data in Table 4-1 indicates that the party in control, rather than quality of apportionment, is the critical determinant of the distribution of committee chairmanships among legislators from various types of constituencies. Before and after the major reapportionment activity of the mid-1960s, Democratic-controlled chambers in both states overrepresented central city counties (that is, established central city counties in New Jersey) in chairmanships on the population and legislative indices. Republican-controlled chambers overrepresented suburban areas on both scales. The two patterns are, of course, attributable to the relative strength of the central city and suburban components within each of the two parties, a pattern discussed in chapter three.

However, a close reading of the data in Table 4-1 reveals that apportionment exercises a detectable influence on the distribution of chairmanships beyond the impact of the party control factor. A comparison of the Democratic-controlled 1963 and 1965 sessions in Delaware, two sessions separated by major redistricting activity, shows clear-cut suburban gains. According to the population index, the suburban share of chairmanships relative to population more than doubled in both houses from 1963 to 1965. Likewise, comparisons of the Democratic-controlled 1962 and 1974 Assembly and 1966 and 1974 Senate in New Jersey display a similar pattern of suburban gains. Reapportionment has thus affected the spread of chairmanships across various constituency types, although not nearly as potently as has the changing of party majorities.

In the remaining two sample states of Oregon and South Dakota, where malapportionment was least severe, reapportionment apparently caused little change in the distribution of leadership positions on standing committees. In Oregon, central city representation in committee chairmanships for both chambers exceeded .75 on the population index prior to 1963; for 1963 and later years, the figure was sometimes higher than .75 (especially 1973), but also lower (the 1969 and 1971 House) as noted in Table 4-1. A similar pattern appears in the analysis of suburban representation in that the variation in share of chairmanships seems unrelated to reapportionment. Neither finding is surprising in light of the slight changes in distribution of seats by constituency type brought about by redistricting in Oregon over the period of 1959-74 (see Table 1-3 in chapter one).

The single central city county in South Dakota was actually overrepresented in committee chairmanships on both the population and legislative indices prior to the reapportionment of the mid-1960s. The overrepresentation continued until 1971. The decrease in central city representation in committee leadership in 1971 and 1973 is not attributable to reapportionment activity but rather to the two-party split in the Minnehaha delegation in 1971 and 1973. Prior to 1971 the delegation was almost invariably wholly Republican, with its strength therefore concentrated in the ruling party. (In 1971 the House delegation was divided, and in 1973 both Senate and House delegations were split between Republicans and Democrats.) As in Oregon, reapportionment had little effect on the distribution of committee chairmanships in South Dakota.

Analysis of the data on committee chairmanships indicates that in four of the states, excluding Oregon and South Dakota, reapportionment yielded some change in the distribution of committee chairmanships, generally in favor of those counties benefiting from increased representation. Equitable apportionment of seats, however, did not lead to an equitable distribution of chairmanships by constituency type. Even in Kansas and Tennessee, where changes in chairmanships are most evident, central city counties were underrepresented in chairmanships and nonmetropolitan areas overrepresented after reapportionment. Leadership selection procedures tend to dilute the impact of reapportionment on legislative power.[8] In Delaware and New Jersey, the influence of changing party control overshadowed the effect of reapportionment on the distribution of chairmanships. The structure of internal party power and party competition may dilute the impact of reapportionment on legislative power. This generalization also applies to Tennessee and South Dakota. In these two states, it appears that the fairly even division of central city seats between both parties has, in recent years, resulted in the underrepresentation of central cities in committee leadership regardless of the party controlling the chamber in question.

The Impact of Reapportionment on Chamber Leadership

Standing committee chairmen constitute one segment of legislative leadership. Another element in the legislative hierarchy is the formal chamber leadership which includes officials designated as president, president pro tempore, and speaker. A third division of leadership consists of majority and minority party chieftains. The three segments of legislative leadership are not separate but are highly interrelated. In most state legislatures, the top position in the formal chamber leadership is filled by a member of the majority party, by virtue of being chosen by the majority party caucus. The highest chamber official is ordinarily the top party chieftain in the majority party. The top chamber official, either alone or in consultation with others, often holds the power of assigning members of the chamber to standing committees and naming committee chairmen who usually come from the majority party as does the presiding officer.

The analysis of changes in official chamber leadership by constituency type over time thus provides some insight into the distribution of power within the chamber and the ruling party. In those chambers where the top chamber officer controls committee assignments, changes in chamber leadership help account for shifts in distribution of committee chairmanships over time.

Again, the key question to be answered in this examination is the effect of reapportionment on chamber leadership.

Table 4-2 reports constituency and party for the top chamber official in each house of the six sample legislatures from 1959 to 1974. Notice that "top official" is qualified by the words "internally-elected" meaning that he is chosen by the chamber and therefore a product and measure of political power within the chamber. In some state senates, such as that of South Dakota, the lieutenant governor is the presiding officer and is elected statewide. It is important to note that the top official listed in every chamber except those in the Kansas and South Dakota Senates controls committee appointments.

The data in Table 4-2 suggest that in most instances reapportionment has resulted in only slight changes in patterns of leadership selection. Only in Tennessee, where central city legislators assumed top positions twice in the Senate and once in the House in the period of 1965-73, does it appear that reapportionment unambiguously contributed to a break in past selection patterns. During the prereapportionment years of 1959-63, all Tennessee chamber leaders came from nonmetropolitan constituencies. Except for the 1973 Senate, nonmetropolitan legislators in Kansas controlled the top posts over the entire period of 1959-74 in spite of the substantial gains in central city and suburban representation resulting from reapportionment. This finding is not surprising in light of the continuing nonmetropolitan majority in the Kansas legislature and in the Republican party in particular. In Tennessee, nonmetropolitan forces are also a near majority and have greater representation than central city counties; suburban counties thus hold the balance of power (see Table 1-3 in chapter one). Given these facts, there is no reason to expect that reapportionment would necessarily result in more central city or suburban chamber leaders in either state, although the likelihood has increased as a result of reapportionment.

The substantial increase in suburban representation in Delaware due to reapportionment has raised the probability of the selection of suburban leadership which dominates the period of 1965-73 in both houses. (The one exception to this domination is the 1965 Senate.) However, suburban legislators presided over the House in 1959, 1961, and 1963 prior to reapportionment. Only in the Senate, in which leaders from 1959 to 1963 were nonsuburban, does reapportionment coincide with a change in leadership selection pat-

TABLE 4-2

Top Internally-Elected Officials for Upper and Lower Houses by Constituency Type and Party in the Six Sample States, 1959-74 [a]

Legislative Session Beginning	1959 (1960)	1961 (1962)	1963 (1964)	1965 (1966)	1967 (1968)	1969 (1970)	1971 (1972)	1973 (1974)
Delaware								
Senate[c]	NM(D)[g]	CC(D)[g]	NM(D)[g]	NM(D)[g]	S(D)[g]	S(R)[g]	S(R)[g]	S(R)[g]
House[f]	S(D)[g]	S(D)[g]	S(D)[g]	S(D)[g]	S(R)[g]	S(R)[g]	S(R)[g]	S(R)[g]
Kansas								
Senate[c]	NM(R)	NM(R)	NM(R)	NM(R)	NM(R)	NM(R)	NM(R)	S(R)
House[f]	NM(R)[g]	NM(R)[g]	NM(R)[g]	NM(R)[g]	NM(R)[g]	NM(R)[g]	NM(R)[g]	NM(R)[g]
New Jersey								
Senate[d]	NM(R)[g]	CC(R)[g]	NM(R)[g]	NM(D)[g]	S(R)[g]	S(R)[g]	NM(R)[g]	CC(D)[g]
Assembly[f]	CC(D)[g]	S(D)[g]	NM(R)[g]	CC(D)[g]	CC(R)[g]	S(R)[g]	CC(R)[g]	CC(D)[g]
Oregon								
Senate[d]	CC(D)[g]	NM(D)[g]	NM(D)[g]	NM(D)[g]	NM(D)[g]	NM(D)[g]	CC(D)[g]	NM(D)[g]
House[f]	NM(D)[g]	NM(D)[g]	NM(D)[g]	CC(R)[g]	CC(R)[g]	NM(R)[g]	NM(R)[g]	NM(D)[g]
South Dakota								
Senate[c]	NM(D)	NM(R)	NM(R)	NM(R)	NM(R)	NM(R)	NM(R)	NM(D)
House[f]	CC(R)[g]	NM(R)[g]	NM(R)[g]	NM(R)[g]	NM(R)[g]	NM(R)[g]	NM(R)[g]	NM(D)[g]
Tennessee								
Senate[e]	NM(D)[g]	NM(D)[g]	NM(D)[g]	NM(D)[g]	CC(D)[g]	CC(D)[g]	NM(D)[g]	NM(D)[g]
House[f]	NM(D)[g]	NM(D)[g]	NM(D)[g]	NM(D)[g]	NM(D)[g]	NM(R)[g]	CC(D)[g]	NM(D)[g]

Sources: The listing is compiled from sources described in Appendix B. Information on appointive power comes from The Book of the States, 1958-59 (Lexington, Ky.: Council of State Governments, 1958), p. 43.; The Book of the States, 1962-63 (Lexington, Ky.: Council of State Governments, 1962), p. 49; The Book of the States, 1964-65 (Lexington, Ky.: Council of State Governments, 1964), p. 51; The Book of the States, 1966-67 (Lexington, Ky.: Council of State Governments, 1966), p. 53; The Book of the States, 1968-69 (Lexington, Ky.: Council of State Governments, 1968), p. 57; The Book of the States, 1970-71 (Lexington, Ky.: Council of State Governments, 1970), p. 73; The Book of the States, 1972-73 (Lexington, Ky.: Council of State Governments, 1972), p. 67; The Book of the States, 1974-75 (Lexington, Ky.: Council of State Governments, 1974), p. 74.

[a]Key: CC - central city county (established central city county for New Jersey only)
S - suburban county
NM - nonmetropolitan county
(D) - Democrat
(R) - Republican

[b]Even-numbered years are for New Jersey only.

[c]President Pro Tempore of Senate (for Kansas Senate, top officer listed is President Pro Tempore, 1959-1971; President is listed for 1973).

[d]President of Senate.

[e]Speaker of Senate.

[f]Speaker of House (Assembly for New Jersey).

[g]Official appoints standing committees within chamber.

terns. Likewise, leadership selection in New Jersey reflects only a slight influence of reapportionment. As with committee chairmen, Democratic-controlled chambers have favored central city, that is, established central city legislators; Republican-controlled chambers have favored suburban or nonmetropolitan legislators. It appears likely that in the Senate, in which the reapportionment of the mid-1960s ended the one county, one senator scheme, the smaller nonmetropolitan counties have lost influence. In virtually every case, these counties have been combined with central city and suburban counties to create new senatorial districts as a result of various post-*Baker* reapportionments.

As expected, the modest redistricting activity in Oregon has yielded little discernible change in the patterns of leadership selection. Nonmetropolitan counties having a narrow legislative plurality have controlled leadership posts through most of the period, but central city counties have produced officers both before and after the reapportionment of the mid-1960s. In South Dakota, which was 86 percent nonmetropolitan in 1970, all leaders except one (1959 House speaker) have been nonmetropolitan during the period of 1959-74.

A review of leadership changes, as does the study of committee chairmanships, indicates with some clarity that the effects of reapportionment at the second level (in terms of the representation of constituency types) do not automatically translate into effects of equal potency at the third level (with regard to leadership selection). Significant gains in the proportion of seats held by central city counties in Kansas and Tennessee brought about less substantial increments in committee and chamber leadership positions; this pattern is largely due to the continued strength of nonmetropolitan elements. The dominance of party influences in Delaware and New Jersey in leadership selection procedures dwarfs the possible impact of the forces of reapportionment. As for Oregon and South Dakota, inconsequential second-level effects have yielded imperceptible third-level effects on leadership selection.

The Effects of Reapportionment upon Legislative Procedure: An Exploratory Analysis

While it might be expected that reapportionment would influence the distribution of leadership positions in legislatures, it is far less clear that redistricting should affect the rules of procedures by which legislatures operate. Only if reapportionment leads to the election of a significant number of legislators committed to procedural reform could reapportionment potentially affect the operational format of legislatures. Unless it can be shown that legislators from constituencies which gain representation from redistricting favor modification of procedures, it is impossible to conclude that reapportionment has played a role, even· when procedural reforms occur.

It may be, however, that the increased turnover temporarily produced by reapportionment created in many state legislatures a larger than normal group of new legislators receptive to procedural changes, if only because they felt little attachment to the old rules. Most states legislatures in the late 1960s and 1970s made major reductions in the number of standing committees, a reform perhaps stimulated by the infusion of new members as a result of the reapportionment of the mid-1960s. In 1963 twenty-nine states averaged more than twenty standing committees per legislative chamber. By 1975 the number of such states had fallen to just twelve.[9] The change is important because existing research has linked a reduced number of committees to better committee performance in writing and analyzing legislation.[10]

An analysis of changes in the number of standing committees in the six sample legislatures suggests that reapportionment may have contributed to the reduction of committees. As Table 4-3 shows, five of the six states, all but New Jersey, showed a decrease in the number of standing committees after the initiation of the major redistricting activity of the mid-1960s. Only in South Dakota did the reduction begin before reapportionment. That reductions occurred in Oregon and South Dakota, as well as in Delaware, Kansas, and Tennessee would seem to indicate that the redistribution of seats across central city, suburban, and non-metropolitan constituency types as a result of reapportionment is not the source of the reformist trend. (Very little redistribution occurred in Oregon and South Dakota.) The increase in new members as a result of reapportionment may have stimulated the reduction in committees. In the one state in which committees were not reduced in number after reapportionment, the absolute size of the legislature was increased by reapportionment. In New Jersey, the Senate expanded from twenty-one to forty members and the Assembly, from sixty to eighty members. Standing committees, which totalled twenty-four for both houses in 1964, numbered thirty-four in 1969 after the redistricting of the mid-1960s. In the

Number of Standing Committees by Chamber in the Six Sample Legislatures, 1959-74

(even years, N.J. only)	1959 (1960)	1961 (1962)	1963 (1964)	1965 (1966)	1967 (1968)	1969 (1970)	1971 (1972)	1973 (1974)
Delaware								
Senate	22	22	22	22	22	17	12	12
House	26	26	26	27	17	14	16	15
Kansas								
Senate	31	32	32	32	32	18	18	18
House	43	45	45	45	45	25	23	21
New Jersey								
Senate	12	12	12	13	16	17	10	10
Assembly	12	12	12	13	16	17	18	13
Oregon								
Senate	21	20	20	20	21	21	17	15
House	20	19	20	16	16	17	11	13
South Dakota								
Senate	26	17	16	16	16	16	14	14
House	26	23	23	25	25	25	14	14
Tennessee								
Senate	16	16	16	16	16	6	6	7
House	16	16	16	16	16	8	10	11

Sources: See Appendix B.

early 1970s, the New Jersey legislature reduced the number of committees to prereapportionment levels.

The preceding analysis suggests that with regard to the number of committees used in state legislatures, reapportionment may have had some impact on procedure. Reapportionment may have influenced other aspects of procedure, although the present analysis has accumulated little evidence in this regard. Two case studies of procedural reform involving two sample legislatures do, however, raise the possibility of an added impact of reapportionment.

In 1971 the Kansas legislature abandoned its Legislative Council which had been in operation since 1933. The council, composed of fifteen representatives and ten senators chosen by the House speaker and lieutenant-governor respectively, researched and prepared legislation between legislative sessions. It also helped establish the agenda for consideration of bills when the legislature met.[11] The 1971 legislature replaced the council with year-round standing committees and a new Legislative Coordinating Committee. Harder and Rampey note that the legislators themselves attributed the change at least partly to reapportionment. The Legislative Budget Committee reported,

> Still another reason [for abolition of the Legislative Council] was that in the period following reapportionment of the legislature, many new, younger members wanted to be more involved in the total legislative process and they challenged old institutions which they felt were obstacles to such involvement.[12]

A significant change in procedure also occurred in the New Jersey legislature in the early 1970s, although the change is not clearly tied to reapportionment. Until the reform of standing committee organization and procedure in the early 1970s, the majority party caucuses generally controlled the writing, flow, and passage of legislation in the New Jersey legislature. John Burns observed in 1970 that

> Standing committees seem to exist mostly on paper in New Jersey. Committees seldom meet or hold public hearings.... Committees do not develop, review, or report legislation to

their respective houses, nor do they carry on a systematic or thorough review of the programs of state agencies under their jurisdictions. Almost all committee activity is perfunctory in nature. More than 90 percent of all bills which spend money are declared to be "policy bills" and are remanded to the "conferences" (caucuses) for review. It is the majority conference (caucus) which then either kills the bill or recommends it for passage.[13]

During the 1970-71 session, the New Jersey Assembly expanded committee staff resources, increased the time allotted for committee meetings, and required attendance to be taken at committee meetings. In 1971 the Republican majority in the Assembly disbanded the caucus in favor of a bipartisan conference committee which, on appeal from a bill's sponsor, could remove legislation from a recalcitrant committee and bring it to the floor.[14] Prior to this change, the caucus might direct the committee to withhold legislation from the floor.[15] Rosenthal's account of developments in the Assembly does not suggest that committees are as yet strong and independent forces in the policy-making process. The increased resources and the reduced might of the majority party organization (changes continued under a Democratic majority in 1974), however, open the door for more autonomous committees.[16]

Whether reapportionment influenced the progress of committee reform in the New Jersey Assembly is not certain, although the influx of new members generated by the extensive redistricting activity of the late 1960s may have created a substantial block of legislators receptive to reform. It would seem that the committee system, as opposed to the party caucus, provides a better mechanism for distributing legislative influence across a large number of legislators anxious for a meaningful role in policy making. It may well be that the 1967 expansion of the Assembly from sixty to eighty members rendered the caucus unworkable; the expansion, of course, grew out of the requirement under court order to reapportion. It is important to note that the Senate, with only forty members (up from twenty-one prior to reapportionment), maintained the caucus system into 1974 (the year in which the period of this study ended).[17] As in the case of the Kansas Legislative Council, there is at least the hint of reapportionment's influence on the procedural changes in New Jersey.

Legislators' Perceptions of the Effects of Reapportionment on Legislative Leadership and Procedure

The questionnaire sent to 1973 legislators in the six sample states can provide some perspective on the analysis of the impact of reapportionment on leadership and procedure thus far advanced. The survey asked legislators if they believed reapportionment had had any impact on chamber organization and procedure. Legislators who responded affirmatively to this question were further asked to specify the changes they thought had been produced by reapportionment.[18] The format of the questions requires a caveat about the responses yielded. Because of the open-ended aspect of the follow-up question, many respondents who indicated they had perceived change did not elaborate. Secondly, legislators were asked not just about changes in organization and procedure but about those changes attributable to reapportionment. Undoubtedly, legislators would more accurately perceive changes than the causes of those changes. Thirdly, legislators could cite changes which have taken place without detailing the extent of the changes. The case of Oregon, as displayed in Table 4-4, may be evidence of the weaknesses in the format of the questions. Oregon legislators gave the second highest percentage of "yes" responses, despite the strong expectation that reapportionment should have little effect in that state as it was well apportioned before *Baker*. The other states' results fall roughly in line with expectations derived from previous analysis. Kansas, Delaware, Tennessee, and Oregon legislators gave at least 40 percent "yes" responses, while New Jersey and South Dakota totalled about 25 percent "yes" answers.

The elaboration by those who responded affirmatively follows rather closely the discussion in preceding sections. As Table 4-4 shows, nearly three-fourths of the Kansas "yes" respondents perceived increased central city and suburban representation in committee chairmanships. Nearly two-thirds of Delaware's positive respondents saw an increase in metropolitan chairmen attributable to reapportionment. In Tennessee, where central cities made less substantial gains in chairmanships relative to their total representation than central cities in Kansas, about a quarter of the respondents mentioned greater metropolitan control of committees. In Oregon, the largest block of elaborations (nearly 40 percent) notably focused on change in party control. The conversion to single-member districts prior to the 1972 elections may well have contributed to the Democratic takeover of both houses in

TABLE 4-4

Legislators' Elaborations of the Impact of Reapportionment on Chamber Organization and Procedure in the Six Sample Legislatures (Senate and House Responses Combined)

		Changes in Intra-Party Power[a]					Change in Party Ideology[a]				
	% of All Respondents Perceiving Change in Party	Greater Power in Metro Wing[b]	Greater Power in Central City Wing[c]	Greater Power in Suburban Wing[d]	Other Not Classified	No Elaboration	More Liberal	More Conservative	Other Not Classified	No Elaboration	Number Perceiving Change (N)
Delaware											
Dem.	55.6%	0%	0%	20.0%	0%	80.0%	60.0%	20.0%	0%	20.0%	(5)
Rep.	75.0	25.0	0	66.7	0	8.3	33.3	0	0	66.7	(12)
Kansas											
Dem.	60.0	80.0	0	0	13.3	6.7	40.0	0	13.3	46.7	(15)
Rep.	62.3	86.8	0	2.6	0	10.5	15.8	0	0	84.2	(38)
New Jersey											
Dem.	40.0	50.0	12.5	25.0	0	12.5	12.5	12.5	0	75.0	(8)
Rep.	62.5	53.3	0	20.0	0	26.7	20.0	0	0	80.0	(15)
Oregon											
Dem.	72.7	43.8	6.3	0	18.8	31.3	43.8	12.5	0	43.8	(16)
Rep.	23.5	25.0	0	0	25.0	50.0	50.0	0	0	50.0	(4)
South Dakota											
Dem.	61.9	76.9	0	0	0	23.1	38.5	0	0	61.5	(13)
Rep.	30.9	69.2	0	0	7.7	23.1	23.1	0	0	76.9	(13)
Tennessee											
Dem.	64.7	81.8	0	0	0	18.2	45.5	0	9.1	45.5	(11)
Rep.	64.0	50.0	0	6.3	0	43.8	12.5	0	12.5	75.0	(16)

Sources: Responses to 1973 survey of state legislators in six sample states. See question #7 in Appendix A.

[a] The elaborations are expressed as a percentage of those who perceived change, based on the number of cases in the last column. (See the "Yes" responses in Table C-7 in Appendix C.)

[b] General reference was made to urban or metropolitan areas, without specifying central city or suburban legislators.

[c] Specific reference was made to central city legislators only.

[d] Specific reference was made to suburban legislators only.

1973. About 40 percent of "yes" respondents in South Dakota also noted the switch in party control in 1973, but it is difficult to link this to reapportionment.

Fewer elaborations touched on the elements of procedure than on those of leadership. It is worth pointing out that in New Jersey one-third of the "yes" respondents attributed, at least partially, the strengthening of standing committees of reapportionment. (Keep in mind, however, that the one-third of affirmative respondents represents less than a tenth of the New Jersey survey.)

Legislators' Perceptions of Reapportionment's Impact On Internal Party Power

As noted earlier in this chapter, chamber leadership and committee leadership rest heavily on the distribution of power within the legislative parties and especially on that of the majority party. Legislators were asked whether they thought reapportionment had changed the distribution of power within their respective parties and, if so, to specify the change they thought had occurred.[19] Table 4-5 summarizes their responses. The format of the questions suffers from the same shortcomings as the one on procedure. The number of responses indicating the perception of change, however, strongly reinforces the foregoing analysis of data. A majority of legislators in both parties in Delaware, Kansas, and Tennessee attributed a shift in power to reapportionment. A majority of New Jersey Republicans (but not Democrats) and a majority of Oregon and South Dakota Democrats (but not Republicans in those states) perceived a modified distribution in internal party power attributable to reapportionment. In Delaware, the reapportionment of the mid-1960s led to a more suburban Republican party, an observation noted by two-thirds of the Republican "yes" respondents; at least one-third of the "yes" Republicans also viewed the shift as liberal. Delaware Democrats, to a lesser extent than Republicans, saw a more suburban orientation, but 60 percent of the Democrats who answered positively viewed the party as more liberal. Both Kansas Republicans and Democrats overwhelmingly viewed their parties as substantially more metropolitan, although Democrats were more than twice as likely as Republicans to see a liberal shift. This is perhaps attributable to the concentration of Democratic metropolitan gains in central cities, while Republicans have prospered in the more conservative suburbs. A pattern similar to that of Kansas prevails in Tennessee

TABLE 4-5

Legislators' Elaborations of the Impact of Reapportionment on the Distribution of Power within Their Respective Political Parties in the Six Sample Legislatures (Senate and House Combined)

| | % of All Respondents Perceiving Change in Party | Changes in Intra-Party Power[a] | | | | | Change in Party Ideology[a] | | | | Number Perceiving Change (N) |
		Greater Power in Metro Wing[b]	Greater Power in Central City Wing[c]	Greater Power in Suburban Wing[d]	Other Not Classified	No Elaboration	More Liberal	More Conservative	Other Not Classified	No Elaboration	
Delaware											
Dem.	55.6%	0%	0%	20.0%	0%	30.0%	60.0%	20.0%	0%	20.0%	(5)
Rep.	75.0	25.0	0	66.7	0	8.3	33.3	0	0	66.7	(12)
Kansas											
Dem.	60.0	80.0	0	0	13.3	6.7	40.0	0	13.3	46.7	(15)
Rep.	62.3	86.8	0	2.6	0	10.5	15.8	0	0	84.2	(38)
New Jersey											
Dem.	40.0	50.0	12.5	25.0	0	12.5	12.5	12.5	0	75.0	(8)
Rep.	62.5	53.3	0	20.0	0	26.7	20.0	0	0	80.0	(15)
Oregon											
Dem.	72.7	43.8	6.3	0	18.8	31.3	43.8	12.5	0	43.8	(16)
Rep.	23.5	20.0	0	0	40.0	40.0	40.0	0	0	60.0	(5)
South Dakota											
Dem.	61.9	76.9	0	0	0	23.1	38.5	0	0	61.5	(13)
Rep.	30.0	69.2	0	0	7.7	23.1	23.1	0	0	76.9	(13)
Tennessee											
Dem.	64.7	81.8	0	0	0	18.2	45.5	0	0	45.5	(11)
Rep.	64.0	50.0	0	6.3	0	43.8	12.5	0	12.5	75.0	(16)

Sources: Responses to 1973 survey of state legislators in six sample states. See question #7 in Appendix A.

[a] The elaborations are expressed as a percentage of those who perceived change, based on the number of cases in the last column. (See the "yes" responses in Table C-7 in Appendix C.)

[b] General reference was made to urban or metropolitan areas, without specifying central city or suburban legislators.

[c] Specific reference was made to central city legislators only.

[d] Specific reference was made to suburban legislators only.

with those who answered affirmatively from both parties (82 percent of Democrats and 50 percent of Republicans) noting a more metropolitan orientation. Again, nearly four times as many Democrats as Republicans perceived the change as liberal, apparently for reasons similar to those applied to Kansas.

New Jersey Republicans perceived a shift toward the metropolitan wing; nearly three-fourths of those who responded affirmatively noted a gain either for metropolitan power in general or suburban power in particular. Only 40 percent of New Jersey Democrats saw a shift in internal power, but the elaborations suggest a recognition of a growing suburban role.

In both Oregon and South Dakota, Democratic majorities replaced Republican majorities in both houses in 1973. Moreover, the Democratic gains occurred in part in central city counties which had traditionally voted Republican (for example, in Lane County in Oregon and Minnehaha in South Dakota). Democrats in both states viewed their parties as being more urban and liberal, while Republicans perceived little change. The role of reapportionment in stimulating the perceived changes is questionable, although single-member districting may have aided Democrats in Oregon.

The perceptions of intraparty change generally accord with the analysis of chapter three as well as with the examination of committee and leadership patterns reviewed earlier in this chapter.

Concluding Comments

The analysis of available quantitative data and legislators' perceptions indicates that reapportionment has had a detectable effect on the distribution of committee chairmanships and chamber leadership positions. This effect, however, is not as great as might be projected on the basis of second-level changes in the distribution of seats by constituency type. Central city gains in legislative representation led to a significant increase in the proportion of committees chaired by urban legislators in Kansas, but central city legislators in Tennessee were far less successful in gaining chairmanships. In Delaware and New Jersey, partisan factors rather than reapportionment accounted for most of the change in the distribution of chairmanships. Change in the distribution of chairmanships in Oregon and South Dakota could not be directly attributed to reapportionment. The examination of chamber leadership in all six states produced even less evidence of reapportionment-induced change than the review of committee chairmanships. Tentative research does indicate, however, that reapportionment has contributed to procedural changes such as the reduction in the number of standing committees and, in New Jersey, the relative power of committees.

Notes

1. The definitive study of state legislative standing committees is Alan Rosenthal, *Legislative Performance in the States: Explorations of Committee Behavior* (New York: Free Press, 1974).
2. Ibid., chap. 3, pp. 57-58. For a description of the major features of the legislative process in New Jersey prior to reapportionment, see John C. Wahlke et al., *The Legislative System: Explorations in Legislative Behavior* (New York: John Wiley & Sons, 1962), pp. 35-36. A current account of New Jersey legislative politics is Alan Rosenthal's "The Governor, the Legislature, and State Policy Making," in *Politics in New Jersey*, ed. Alan Rosenthal and John Blydenburgh (New Brunswick, N.J.: The Eagleton Institute of Politics, Rutgers University, 1975), pp. 141-74.
3. For a description of the legislative process in Oregon, see Lawrence C. Pierce, Richard G. Frey, and S. Scott Pengelly, *The Freshman Legislator: Problems and Opportunities*, State Legislative Service Program of the American Political Science Association (Eugene: Department of Political Science, University of Oregon, 1972); also Donald G. Balmer, "Oregon," in *Impact of Reapportionment on the Thirteen Western States*, ed. Eleanore Bushnell (Salt Lake City: University of Utah Press, 1970), pp. 241-62. On Kansas, see John G. Grumm, "The Kansas Legislature: Republican Coalition," in *Midwest Legislative Politics*, ed. Samuel C. Patterson (Iowa City: Institute of Public Affairs, University of Iowa, 1967), pp. 37-66; also Marvin Harder and Carolyn Rampey, *The Kansas Legislature: Procedures, Personalities, and Problems*, State Legislative Service Project of the American Political Science Association (Lawrence: The University Press of Kansas, 1972). On South Dakota, see Alan L. Clem, *Prairie State Politics: Popular Democracy in South Dakota* (Washington, D.C.: Public Affairs Press, 1967), pp. 98-114. On Tennessee, Jewell and Greene, *Kentucky and Tennessee Legislatures*, pp. 31-62, and Wahlke et al ., pp. 56-59.
4. Rosenthal rated standing committees in Delaware and New Jersey as "poorer performing" among all state legislative committee systems; Oregon, Kansas, South Dakota, and Tennessee were rated in the "medium-performing" category. Rosenthal, *Legislative Performance*, pp. 42-43.
5. Table C-6 in Appendix C provides a straightforward listing of the percentage distribution of chairmen by constituency and party.
6. The indices are taken from Hawkins, pp. 284-87.
7. Traditionally, both parties in the Tennessee legislature have shared in

the distribution of committee chairmanships. By the early 1970s, House Democrats had abandoned this practice and all chairmanships went to Democrats. (Lee S. Greene, Professor of Political Science, University of Tennessee, Knoxville pointed out this change to me in a letter, 16 June 1977.) The development is hardly attributable to reapportionment, although the more substantial Republican threat after reapportionment may have contributed to the change. In the other sample legislatures, chairmanship selection procedures regarding party remained stable throughout the period of this study. Delaware, Kansas, New Jersey (with the exception of 1972), and South Dakota followed the practice of assigning chairmanships only to majority party members. Oregon usually rewarded chairmanships to members of both parties. The partisan division of chairmanships in the six state legislatures over the period of 1959-74 is provided in Table C-6 in Appendix C.

8. Similar conclusions are reached in separate studies on Georgia and California. See Hawkins, pp. 284-87, and Alvin D. Sokolow and Richard W. Brandsma, "Partisanship and Seniority in Legislative Committee Assignments: California After Reapportionment," *Western Political Quarterly* 24 (1971), 740-60.

9. The figures on standing committees are derived from data in *The Book of the States, 1964-1965* (Lexington, Ky.: Council of State Governments, 1964), p. 51, and *The Book of the States, 1974-75* (Lexington, Ky.: Council of State Governments, 1974), p. 74. The averages presented do not include joint standing committees except in Connecticut, Maine, and Massachusetts where most or all standing committees are joint.

10. Rosenthal, *Legislative Performance*, pp. 44-48.

11. Grumm, "Kansas Legislature," pp. 45-47, and Harder and Rampey, pp. 79-83.

12. As quoted in Harder and Rampey, pp. 83-84.

13. John Burns and the Citizens Conference on State Legislatures, *The Sometime Governments: A Critical Study of the Fifty American Legislatures* (New York: Bantam Books, 1971), p. 261. Also see Wahlke et al., pp. 55-56, 62.

14. Rosenthal, *Legislative Performance*, pp. 110-45. Also see Walter D. Waggoner, "Assembly Votes to Open Meetings," *New York Times*, 1 February 1974, p. 64.

15. Rosenthal, *Legislative Performance*, p. 130n. Also see Wahlke et al., *Legislative System*, pp. 55-56.

16. Rosenthal, *Legislative Performance*, pp. 110-45.

17. "Senate Panel Plans Hearing on Rules," *New York Times*, 20 January 1974, p. 74.

18. See question 6 in the questionnaire reprinted in Appendix A. The simple distribution of "yes" and "no" responses to this question is reported in Table C-7 in Appendix C.

19. See question 7 in the questionnaire reprinted in Appendix A. The simple distribution of "yes" and "no" responses to this question is reported in Table C-8 in Appendix C.

Chapter Five

The Impact of Reapportionment on Legislative Conflict

Possible Effects of Reapportionment on Legislative Conflict

If reapportionment leads to significant changes in the legislative representation of population-based interests including urban and rural blocs or Republican and Democratic delegations, it may also contribute to alterations in the usual patterns of legislative conflict. In the absence of major shifts in legislative representation following reapportionment, there is little reason to expect changes in legislative conflict which can be attributed to reapportionment. Even when reapportionment produces notable modifications in urban-rural or partisan representation, however, patterns of legislative conflict need not change. For example, the conversion of a minority into a majority party may bring about only minor changes in patterns of conflict in a legislature in which party lines are irrelevant. In another instance, increased urban representation may not lead to greater urban-rural conflict in a legislature in which rural interests remain dominant; urban interests may, in this case, find it advantageous to avoid open urban-rural splits which would leave the urban forces hopelessly outnumbered.

The central point of this analysis is to suggest that reapportionment will lead to changes in patterns of legislative conflict only if there are major changes in the representation of population-based interests in the legislature. Major changes in representation, however, will not necessarily alter patterns of conflict. In the language of chapter one, second-level effects (changes in group representation) are necessary but not sufficient to produce third-level effects (legislative conflict). Previously established legislative customs and institutions for conflict resolution may significantly reduce the impact of reapportionment on conflict.

Before we can begin to consider the effects of reapportionment on conflict in the six sample legislatures, some attention must be focused on the problem of defining and measuring conflict. The literature on the legislative process has examined conflict in two ways: (1) legislators' perceptions of major sources of conflict[1] and (2) legislators' behavior measured by roll call voting as evidence of sources of conflict.[2] Perceptions may not accurately reflect reality, and roll call voting may not reveal the existence of conflict at lower stages of the law-making process. Despite these weaknesses, these two approaches offer perhaps the only quantifiable measures of conflict, although the two methods may yield contradictory findings.

Reapportionment and Changing Patterns of Conflict

The questionnaire sent to legislators in the six sample states asked respondents to rank the three most important sources of conflict in their respective chambers. The legislators could choose among eight given types of conflict including partisan, urban versus rural, urban versus suburban, big city versus small city, regional, liberal versus conservative, pro-governor versus anti-governor, pro-labor versus anti-labor; legislators also had the option to add other types of conflict.[3] Because prereapportionment studies by Wayne Francis and Wahlke et al. employed similar questions in analyzing the sample state legislatures, it is possible to obtain some indication of the nature of legislative conflict in these states both before and after reapportionment.[4] Comparing before and after responses can provide some indication of reapportionment-induced changes in legislative conflict.

Some difficulties emerge in the comparison of data from the questionnaire with the data of both Francis and Wahlke. The question format used here is more similar to that of Wahlke, who examined only two of the sample states (New Jersey and Tennessee). Wahlke's 1957 data and the 1973 data on New Jersey and Tennessee appear in Table 5-1. The only difference between the two data sets is the inclusion in the 1973 questionnaire of the items on urban versus suburban conflict and big city versus small city conflict. Data for 1973 only for the four states not covered by the Wahlke study are given in Table 5-2. Francis presented returns from all fifty state legislatures (1963), but he omitted partisan conflict from his questions and asked legislators to name the principal sources of legislative division. Furthermore, he reported only the source of division for each state named by more than half of the respondents in any legislature. The data of Francis and the 1973 data, which summarize the perceptions of legislators of types of conflict other than partisan, appear in Table 5-3.[5]

Because of the absence of readily comparable data on perceived partisan conflict in the Francis study, it is difficult to determine the changes in conflict between parties following reapportionment. Francis did, however, produce a measure of party conflict based on legislators' reports of sources of conflict on issues of major importance. These responses are summarized as composite percentages for all issues and indicate the level of partisan conflict in 1963, as well as the levels of intraparty factional conflict, regional conflict, and conflict involving pressure groups. Table 5-4 reproduces this data.[6]

The data in Tables 5-1 to 5-4, coupled with data introduced later, allow for considerable interpretative analysis on the effects of reapportionment in legislative conflict as perceived by state legislators. The following discussion examines each state legislature separately and in detail in order to determine postreapportionment changes in conflict.

Perhaps the most dramatic evidence of postreapportionment changes among the six sample states arises in Tennessee. As Table 5-1 indicates, the proportion of legislators in Tennessee who saw partisan conflict as important was about five times greater in 1973 than in 1957. In 1973, 90 percent of the Senators and 100 percent of the 1973 House members saw partisan conflict as important; the comparable figures for 1957 are 17 percent for the Senate and 23 percent for the House. This increase in perceived party salience should not be surprising in light of the dramatic Republican gains

TABLE 5-1

Legislators' Perceptions of Major Sources of Conflict in New Jersey and Tennessee by Chamber, 1957 and 1973 (in Percentages) [a]

New Jersey

	Senate		Assembly	
	1957 (N=20)	1973 (N=15)[b]	1957 (N=51)	1973 (N=29)[b]
Partisan	85	73.3	96	75.9
Urban-Rural	50	40.0	53	31.0
Urban-Suburban	--	60.0	--	41.4
Big City-Small City	--	0.0	--	13.8
Regional	40	26.7	18	17.2
Liberal-Conservative	25	40.0	22	48.3
Pro v. Anti-Governor	70	33.3	76	34.5
Pro v. Anti-Labor	15	13.3	18	20.7

Tennessee

	Senate		House	
	1957 (N=30)	1973 (N=10)[b]	1957 (N=83)	1973 (N=31)[b]
Partisan	17	90.0	23	100.0
Urban-Rural	63	90.0	91	80.6
Urban-Suburban	--	0.0	--	3.2
Big City-Small City	--	10.0	--	3.2
Regional	20	0.0	13	19.4
Liberal-Conservative	37	70.0	29	35.5
Pro v. Anti-Governor	96	20.0	89	29.0
Pro v. Anti-Labor	67	0.0	54	6.5

Sources: The 1957 data are taken from John C. Wahlke et al., The Legislative System: Explorations in Legislative Behavior. (New York: John Wiley & Sons, 1962), p. 425. The 1973 data are taken from the 1973 survey of state legislators in the six sample states. See question #3 in the questionnaire reprinted in Appendix A.

[a] Figures represent percentage of legislators ranking conflict first, second, or third most important source of legislative divisions.

[b] N for 1973 is the number of respondents who answered the particular question on conflict, not the total number responding to the questionnaire.

TABLE 5-2

Legislators' Perceptions of Major Sources of Legislative Conflict in Four Sample States by Chamber, 1973 (in Percentages) [a]

	Delaware		Kansas	
	Senate[b] (N=9)	House[b] (N=16)	Senate[b] (N=23)	House[b] (N=63)
Partisan	88.9	62.5	73.9	81.0
Urban-Rural	44.4	50.0	100.0	95.2
Urban-Suburban	33.3	18.8	0.0	4.8
Big City-Small City	0.0	0.0	17.4	17.5
Regional	33.3	37.5	13.0	19.0
Liberal-Conservative	77.8	75.0	39.1	28.6
Pro v. Anti-Governor	11.1	25.0	43.5	34.9
Pro v. Anti-Labor	3.8	0.0	1.1	9.5

	Oregon		South Dakota	
	Senate[b] (N=15)	House[b] (N=24)	Senate[b] (N=20)	House[b] (N=32)
Partisan	86.7	58.3	75.0	93.8
Urban-Rural	66.7	70.8	65.0	100.0
Urban-Suburban	13.3	8.3	15.0	0.0
Big City-Small City	0.0	12.5	10.0	3.1
Regional	26.7	20.8	45.0	37.5
Liberal-Conservative	80.0	79.2	70.0	53.1
Pro v. Anti-Governor	0.0	12.5	5.0	3.1
Pro v. Anti-Labor	13.3	25.0	15.0	3.1

Source: Responses to the 1973 survey of state legislators in the six sample states. See question #3 in Appendix A.

[a] Figures represent percentage of legislators ranking conflict first, second, or third most important source of legislative divisions.

[b] N is the number of respondents who answered the particular question on conflict, not the total number responding to the questionnaire.

TABLE 5-3

Legislators' Perceptions of Most Important Sources of Legislative Conflict Other Than Partisan for the Six Sample States, 1963 and 1973

	Most Important Source(s) of Conflict Other than Partisan, 1963[a]	Most Important Source(s) of Conflict Other than Partisan, 1973[b,c]
Delaware	Urban v. rural	Liberal v. conservative (76.0%)
Kansas	More v. less spending	Urban v. rural (96.5%)
New Jersey	More v. less spending	Urban v. suburban (47.7%) Liberal v. conservative (45.5%)
Oregon	More v. less spending Business v. labor	Liberal v. conservative (79.5%) Urban v. rural (69.2%)
South Dakota	More v. less spending	Urban v. rural (86.5%) Liberal v. conservative (59.6%)
Tennessee	Urban v. rural	Urban v. rural (82.9%)

Sources: The 1963 data are taken from Wayne L. Francis, Legislative Issues in the Fifty States: A Comparative Analysis (Chicago: Rand McNally, 1967), pp. 37-41. The 1973 data are derived from the 1973 survey of state legislators in the six sample states. See question #3 in Appendix A.

[a]The most important source listed is that one designated by 50% or more of sampled legislators (both houses), choosing from six options: "more spending versus less spending,""business versus labor," "profederal aid versus antifederal aid," "urban versus rural," "urban versus suburban," "big city versus small city."

[b]The most important source is based upon the percentage of legislators (both houses) who ranked the designated conflict either first, second, or third in significance. Except for New Jersey, only percentages over 50% are reported.

[c]For 1973, N=25 for Delaware; N=86 for Kansas; N=44 for New Jersey; N=39 for Oregon; N=52 for South Dakota; N=41 for Tennessee.

following the initial wave of reapportionment in the mid-1960s. As noted in chapter three, much of the Republican surge is attributable to reapportionment which aided Republican fortunes in metropolitan areas. Therefore, reapportionment is largely responsible for the increase in partisan conflict. While party conflict jumped from 1957 to 1973, conflict over gubernatorial programs and labor issues dropped precipitously. This might suggest that conflicts concerning the governor's program and labor questions, which were largely conflicts within the dominant Democratic party in 1957, had been subordinated to party-based battles in 1973 on gubernatorial and labor issues. Urban-rural conflict was ranked as highly significant in both 1957 and 1973, although the representation of urban-rural interests in 1973 differed substantially from the alignment in 1957. Given the fairly even division of urban and rural elements across both Democratic and Republican parties in

TABLE 5-4

Legislators' Perceptions of Sources of Conflict on Major Issues in the Six Sample States in 1963 [a]

	Partisan[b]	Factional[c]	Regional[d]	Pressure Group[e]
Delaware	.444	.296	.519	.407
Kansas	.139	.453	.384	.314
New Jersey	.512	.366	.244	.537
Oregon	.320	.600	.267	.493
South Dakota	.137	.490	.235	.451
Tennessee	.130	.584	.416	.507

Source: Wayne L. Francis, Legislative Issues in the Fifty States: A Comparative Analysis (Chicago: Rand McNally, 1967), pp. 44-45.

[a]Figures reported are percentages expressed as decimal fractions.

[b]Conflict between Republicans and Democrats.

[c]Conflict between factions within one party or both.

[d]Conflict between urban and rural, urban and suburban, or regional interests.

[e]Conflict among competing pressure groups.

1973 (see Table 3-1), it is possible that party loyalties served to moderate urban-rural divisions in 1973—an effect far more unlikely in the heavily Democratic legislature in 1957.

In Kansas, the sample state most similar to Tennessee in terms of population characteristics and degree of party competition, there were also several prominent shifts after reapportionment in the kinds of conflict perceived as significant by the legislators. About three-fourths of the Kansas legislators in 1973 viewed party conflict as important (see Table 5-2). This is an observation which appears to contrast with the Francis data in Table 5-4 on partisan conflict in Kansas in 1963. The extent to which partisan conflict may have increased after reapportionment is difficult to assess for Francis' data may understate the significance of party divisions in 1963. Zeller's data for 1951, for example, showed that Kansas legislators perceived party cohesion to be high.[7] A comparison of the data of 1973 with Grumm's survey of Kansas legislators in 1965 (when the Senate, but not the House, had undergone major redistricting) suggests that partisan conflict increased more notably in the House than in the Senate as a result of reapportionment.[8] Grumm's findings, which indicate the percentage of legislators who designated a given type of conflict as first in importance, are compared to the responses of 1973 in Table 5-5.

If the dimensions of change in partisan conflict in Kansas remain somewhat speculative, it seems certain that the postreapportionment Kansas legislature has experienced more urban-rural conflict. As Table 5-3 shows, Kansas legislators in 1973 were nearly unanimous in ranking urban-rural conflict as important. This view is in contrast to that of legislators in 1963 who viewed increased spending as the most significant division (excluding partisan conflict). Comparison of responses made in 1973 with data of 1965, noted in Table 5-5, indicates a sharp rise in the percentage of legislators who saw urban-rural conflict as the most important source of conflict. In 1973, 65 percent of the senators and 57 percent of 1973 representatives rated urban-rural conflict first, up from 41 percent in the Senate and 37 percent in the House in 1965. The gain in central city representation, one suspects, has led to this more divisive pattern. The rise in urban-rural conflict may help account for the apparent rise in partisan conflict in light of the fact that Democrats held half of the central city seats in the Senate, and nearly three-fifths of the central city seats in the House in 1973.

The decline in the conflict between supporters and opponents of increased spending, which is roughly comparable to liberal versus conservative in 1973 (see Tables 5-2 and 5-3), may be accounted for by the increase in partisan and urban-rural conflict. In 1971 Harder and Rampey found that Kansas Republican legislators were far less sympathetic to increases in welfare expenditures than were Democratic legislators. Urban Democrats were three times more likely to support higher appropriations than were Republicans and over two times more likely to support higher appropriations than were rural Democrats.[9]

The evidence from Tennessee and Kansas indicates rather significant reapportionment-induced changes in patterns of legislative conflict. Data on legislative conflict in New Jersey and Delaware suggest less substantial, but still measurable changes in conflict. In Delaware, partisan conflict remained prominent after reapportionment (see Table 5-2), just as it had been before reapportionment

TABLE 5-5

First Most Important Source of Conflict Perceived by Kansas Legislators, 1965 and 1973 (in Percentages)

	Senate		House	
	1965	1973 (N=23)	1965	1973 (N=63)
Urban-rural	41	65.2	37	57.1
Partisan	18	21.7	21	31.7
Liberal-Conservative	17	0	23	4.8
Pro-Anti-Governor	2	13.0	8	1.6

Sources: The 1965 data are taken from John G. Grumm, "The Kansas Legislature: Republican Coalition," in Midwest Legislative Politics, ed. Samuel C. Patterson (Iowa City: Institute of Public Affairs, University of Iowa, 1967), p. 62. The 1973 data are taken from the 1973 survey of state legislators in the six sample states.

(see Table 5-4). However, comparison of the data for both 1973 and 1963 in Table 5-3 leads to the conclusion that urban-rural conflict has declined following reapportionment. Nonmetropolitan seats, which constituted three-fifths of the legislative seats in 1961, represented only three-tenths of the seats in 1973. The drop in urban-rural conflict may derive from the reduced size of the rural bloc and, concomitantly, from the growth of the suburban block which is neither urban nor rural. The emergence of liberal-conservative conflict after reapportionment may have resulted from the expanded representation of the Republican party after the mid-1960s. Reapportionment, we can speculate, has led to a more purely suburban and conservative Republican party. If this explanation were accurate, it would account for the decline of urban-rural conflict, the rise in liberal-conservative conflict, and the persistence in partisan conflict.

New Jersey displays a pattern of postreapportionment conflict which is in some ways close to that of Delaware. Partisan conflict remained high in 1973, as Table 5-1 reveals, but there is evidence of some decline in partisan conflict in both houses. As in Delaware, urban-rural conflict in New Jersey apparently declined after reapportionment. One suspects that this is because of the reduced strength of rural elements (see Table 1-3). There is some ambiguity about change in urban-suburban conflict since the data of 1957 do not list the urban-suburban division. It is possible that the sample in 1957 included urban-suburban conflict in the urban-rural category. Assuming this to be the case, we can judge changes in 1973 by the combined conflict of urban versus suburban and rural in the later years. Only four out of thirty-one legislators who mentioned either urban-rural or urban-suburban conflict as important listed both among the top three sources of division in 1973. This might indicate that the proportion who ranked urban versus suburban and rural conflict as important might be 80 percent in the Senate and about 65 percent in the Assembly. Both of these figures are substantially higher than the levels for urban-rural conflict in 1957. It would seem that most of the increase could be attributed to a rise in urban-suburban conflict; the rise in urban-suburban conflict could in turn be attributed to the increase in suburban representation produced by reapportionment.

Apart from the rise in urban-suburban conflict, several other shifts in conflict in the postreapportionment legislature deserve mention. A comparison of the 1957 and 1973 data on New Jersey in Table 5-1 clearly suggests a decline in conflict over gubernatorial programs. However, the high level of gubernatorial conflict in 1957 grew out of the fact that the party which controlled one or both houses in the legislature was different from the party of the governor. In 1973 one party held control of both the legislature and the governorship.

The noticeable rise in liberal-conservative conflict between 1957 and 1973, from 25 percent to 40 percent in the Senate and from 22 percent to 48 percent in the Assembly (see Table 5-1), appears to have occurred prior to reapportionment. Francis' questionnaire shows conflict over more versus less spending, roughly equivalent to liberal versus conservative conflict, to have been an important division in 1963.

In sum, a review of prereapportionment and postreapportionment data on New Jersey indicates a gain in urban-suburban conflict largely attributable to reapportionment. Other changes in conflict patterns are better accounted for by factors other than reapportionment. A final observation on New Jersey is that partisan conflict, while still very high in 1973, declined over the period 1957 (85 percent and 96 percent in the Senate and Assembly, respectively) to 1973 (73 percent in the Senate and 76 percent in the Assembly). In the Assembly, this drop probably was caused, in part, by the abandonment of the caucus system in the early 1970s. This abandonment, in turn, may have resulted from increases in legislative membership adopted under reapportionment (see chapter four).

Changes in patterns of conflict in the two remaining sample states are much more difficult to assess than those of the first four states in terms of reapportionment-induced changes. In neither Oregon nor South Dakota did reapportionment produce major shifts in the balance of either metropolitan-nonmetropolitan representation or partisan representation. Still, Table 5-3 suggests that urban-rural conflict increased notably in both states from 1963 to 1973, an effect which would normally be associated with reapportionment if reapportionment significantly modified urban-rural representation. However, evidence presented earlier in Table 1-3 argues against the interpretation that reapportionment stimulated the greater level of urban-rural conflict in either Oregon or South Dakota.

An alternative explanation for heightened urban-rural conflict is related to changes in partisan representation in the two legislatures. In South Dakota, Democrats made inroads into Republican strength in Minnehaha County, the only metropolitan county in 1971 and 1973. Democrats held 80 percent of the Minnehaha House seats in 1973—the first instance of Democratic majority control of this delegation during the period of this study (see Table 3-1). In 1973 Democrats dominated both House and Senate delegations from Pennington County which contains Rapid City, the state's second largest city. The rise in urban-rural conflict may thus be partly attributable to the correspondence of Democratic and Republican representation to urban-rural divisions; this pattern emerged in the early 1970s, and it is not attributable to reapportionment. If this explanation were accurate, perceived partisan conflict would probably also rise in response to this correspondence and to the greater overall Democratic control of the legislature. Notice in Table 5-2 that 75 percent of senators and 94 percent of representatives rank partisan conflict as important. This is in sharp contrast to the relative low weight given to partisan conflict in 1963 as noted in Table 5-4.

In Oregon, similar forces appear to be at work. Republicans in the Oregon House made steady gains in nonmetropolitan areas and suffered steady losses in metropolitan areas from 1959 to 1973. In the latter years, Republicans held 70 percent of nonmetropolitan seats, but only one-third of the metropolitan seats (see

Table 3-1). The situation in the Senate is less clear, since Republicans lost metropolitan strength from 1959 to 1973, but gained suburban strength, and their strength in nonmetropolitan areas fluctuated (see Table 3-1). Within the parties, however, certain patterns are evident. House Republicans, two-thirds of whom were central city (52%) and suburban (15%) in 1959, were two-thirds suburban (15%) and nonmetropolitan (52%) in 1973. In 1959 House Democrats were two-thirds suburban (9%) and nonmetropolitan (58%), but were more than 80% central city (52%) and suburban (30%) in 1973. Senate Republicans, three-fourths of whom were suburban (18%) and nonmetropolitan (55%) in 1959, were more than 80% suburban (50%) and nonmetropolitan (33%) by 1973. Finally, Senate Democrats, nearly 60% of whom were suburban (11%) and nonmetropolitan (47%) in 1959, were two-thirds central city (61%) and suburban (6%) in 1973. In short, the parties over the period of 1959-73 came to represent increasingly distinctive urban and rural constituencies, thus enhancing urban-rural conflict and also exacerbating partisan conflict. A comparison of the data in Table 5-2 on partisan conflict in Oregon (87 percent in the Senate and 58 percent in the House in 1973) with data in Table 5-4 on partisan conflict in 1963 reveals the rise in partisan divisions. Changes in patterns of conflict in Oregon, as in South Dakota, grew out of the homogenizing of party constituencies along urban-rural lines, a development not attributable to reapportionment. It is also probable that the split in party control of the governorship and legislature increased party conflict. The low level of conflict over gubernatorial programs (see Table 5-2), however, minimizes the import of this account.

Legislators' Perceptions of Reapportionment's Impact

Up to this point, the analysis has attempted to assess reapportionment's impact on patterns of legislative conflict by comparing legislators' perceptions of conflict before and after reapportionment. Differences in prereapportionment and postreapportionment perceptions have been analyzed, and an attempt has been made to explain the contribution of reapportionment to the changes which occurred. A different approach would have allowed legislators themselves to assess the impact of reapportionment on conflict. The 1973 questionnaire asked legislators to indicate whether reapportionment had increased, decreased, or had no effect on the types of conflict discussed above.[10] (See Tables 5-1 and 5-2.) In at least one way this approach seems a less dependable guide to reapportionment's impact than does the analysis of the preceding section. While most legislators have probably given some thought to the lines of conflict within their chambers and can readily provide observations on that conflict, it seems likely that few have considered the underlying forces such as reapportionment which may alter the levels of various conflicts over time. A measure of this absence of recognition is the fact that almost 80 percent of New Jersey legislators responding to the questionnaire did not answer any of the given items on the impact of reapportionment on conflict. For other states, the comparable figures are much lower (averaging about 10 percent), but the problem of uninformed answers and of answers which do not reflect careful thought remains. This difficulty would be more apparent in types of conflict which legislators do not regard as salient. Therefore, legislators' perceptions on reapportionment's impact are reported only for the three most significant conflicts in each chamber.[11]

Perceptions of legislators in Kansas provide the greatest support for the analysis of the preceding section. More than 90 percent of respondents in both chambers agreed that reapportionment heightened urban-rural tensions, while a slight majority believed that reapportionment had intensified partisan conflict.

In Tennessee, responses also tend to confirm the above discussion. Solid majorities of 60 percent or more in both houses believed that reapportionment had increased partisan, urban-rural, and liberal-conservative conflict. Senators were notably less certain than representatives about the effect of reapportionment on partisan conflict and urban-rural conflict. (Sixty percent of the senators pointed to increased partisan and urban-rural conflict, while more than three-fourths of the representatives believed that these types of conflict had increased.) At least part of the disparity between chambers on perceived partisan conflict is attributable to the smaller proportion of Republicans in the Senate than in the House.

In Delaware, clear majorities ranging from 71 percent to 87 percent for both houses perceived increased liberal-conservative and urban-rural conflict due to reapportionment; only about 38 percent of the senators and 47 percent of the representatives, however, believed that reapportionment had led to increased partisan conflict. (About 13 percent of the representatives saw decreased partisan conflict resulting from reapportionment—an observation that finds partial support in a roll call analysis discussed later in this chapter.) The perceptions of increased urban-rural conflict contra-dict the earlier evidence that urban-rural tensions declined in Delaware after reapportionment. The disparity can be reconciled by recognizing the possibility that urban-rural conflict could increase but decline in relative importance if other conflicts became more prominent.

About three-fourths of the respondents in Oregon in both houses attributed increased urban-rural and liberal-conservative conflict to reapportionment. While only 43 percent of the senators believed that reapportionment had enhanced partisan conflict, 63 percent of the representatives saw increased partisan conflict re-sulting from reapportionment. These perceptions generally parallel the actual changes in levels of conflict after reapportionment (discussed in the first section of this chapter), but it is questionable that the changes themselves can be attributed to reapportionment as noted earlier. In the same way, in South Dakota, legislators attributed changes in conflict to reapportionment (78 percent of senators and 93 percent of representatives perceived increased urban-rural conflict). These changes in conflict, however, seem better accounted for by factors other than reapportionment.

Reconciling data from New Jersey with the earlier analysis pre-sents special problems not present in the other states. The questionnaire sent to legislators in all sample states mistakenly omitted the item on reapportionment's impact on urban-suburban conflict. As a result, in the case of New Jersey, we are left with a gap in the data on perceived impact on one of the three major sources of conflict. (New Jersey is the only state in which urban-suburban conflict ranked in the top three.) It is significant that about 10 percent of the legislators in both chambers in New Jersey volunteered that reapportionment increased urban-suburban conflict, a perception which supports the earlier discussion. Likewise, the general tendency to discount the effect of reapportionment on partisan conflict and to see a slight increase in liberal-conservative conflict resulting from reapportionment is consistent with the judgment of the preceding section.

Reapportionment and Roll Call Voting

The present study does not undertake any original analyses of roll call voting. It relies instead on existing research in the sample states in order to round out the assessment of the impact of reapportionment on legislative conflict as developed up to this point.

Prereapportionment and postreapportionment studies of roll call voting have been done for the sample states of Kansas, South Dakota, and Tennessee. Comparable, though partial, prereapportionment and postreapportionment roll call data are also available for the New Jersey legislature. (Postreapportionment here refers to the period following the initial court-ordered changes of the mid-1960s.) A postreapportionment analysis of the Delaware House of Representatives has been conducted, but there is no comparable prereapportionment study. For Oregon, there are no postreapportionment studies available.

Glen T. Broach's roll call analysis of the 1961 and 1967 Tennessee legislatures provides rather solid support for the conclusions on reapportionment's impact based on the review of legislators' perceptions.[12] Examining roll calls in the lower house only, Broach found a dramatic increase in the extent of partisan conflict from 1961 to 1967; partisan conflict in the 1967 Tennessee House was more significant than partisan conflict in the traditionally two-party Indiana House for the same year. Broach, who used Guttmann scale analysis, noted a rise in the mean correlation between legislators' party affiliation and scale score from .303 in the 1961 Tennessee legislature to .581 in 1967. The comparable correlation for the 1967 Indiana legislature was .491. Over the same period, Broach found a slight decline in the importance of urban-rural divisions at the roll call stage. Using a definition of urban and rural which is roughly equivalent to the metropolitan-nonmetropolitan dichotomy used in the present study, Broach noted a drop in the correlation between urbanization of legislators' constituencies and roll call scores from .190 in 1961 to .177 in 1967. This information corresponds to the decline in the proportion of House members who perceived urban-rural conflict as important; 81 percent in 1973 versus 91 percent in 1957 saw urban-rural conflict as important (see Table 5-1). Of greater interest is Broach's finding that partisan conflict, as it had developed by 1967, emerged on a wide range of issues, while urban-rural conflict in both 1961 and 1967 arose on only a few issues.[13]

Consistent with the earlier review of legislators' perceptions, the roll call analysis suggests that increased Republican representation led to increased party conflict in the House and the submergence of other conflicts, such as urban-rural, in partisan divisions. It is valuable to recall that in the upper house of Tennessee, Republicans were less well represented than in the lower house. In 1973 senators perceived more urban-rural and less partisan conflict than their colleagues in the lower house. In the absence of hard evidence, we can speculate that partisan divisions would have been less relevant on Senate roll calls than on House roll calls and that urban-rural conflict would have been more salient in Senate roll calls.[14]

The Broach analysis, in summary, reinforces the previous description of the impact of reapportionment on legislative conflict in the Tennessee legislature. Reapportionment is tied to the sharp rise in partisan conflict which was perceived by legislators and evidenced by roll call divisions. While reapportionment apparently contributed to an increase in perceived urban-rural conflict in the Senate, the strong partisan divisions in the House muted urban-rural conflict there. It is worth noting that the adoption of single-member districting in House elections in 1966 may have played a major role in raising the level of partisan conflict and reducing the extent of urban-rural conflict. As the analysis in chapter three showed, single-member districting in central city counties led to a sharp increase in the number of Republican legislators. Jewell's analysis of roll call voting by Shelby (Memphis) and Davidson (Nashville) County representatives in 1965 and 1967 found that cohesion within the Shelby delegation dropped markedly from 1965 when the delegation was wholly Democratic to 1967 when the delegation was one-third Republican; cohesion in the Davidson County delegation, which in 1965 and 1967 was completely Democratic, was high in both years.[15] Single-member districting contributed to Republican gains and to party conflict in the legislature. At the same time, it divided some central city county delegations and thus reduced urban bloc voting and presumably the extent of simple urban-rural conflict.[16]

Roll call studies of the Kansas legislature help to remove some of the ambiguities clouding the earlier analysis of legislators' perceptions of conflict before and after reapportionment. There are problems of comparability of the prereapportionment and postreapportionment roll call studies which are due to differences in technique and reporting. However, a sifting of the evidence indicates little change in the overall importance of either partisan or urban-rural conflict at the voting stage of the legislative process. Roll call research on the 1957 and 1959 Kansas legislature indicates that party majorities opposed one another rather infrequently, although party division emerged as the most salient conflict during those two sessions. John Grumm's cluster bloc analysis of the 1957 and 1959 Senate and the 1959 House uncovered primarily partisan-oriented blocs. Party divisions largely over-shadowed urban-rural splits, although the dominant Republican party suffered some internal urban-rural schism.[17] Harder and Rampey's cluster bloc study of the 1971 Kansas legislature deviates little from Grumm's prereapportionment findings. In both houses in 1971, the dominant voting blocs followed party lines although the Republican majority again displayed some urban-rural factionalism. However, there were few votes (13 percent for both houses) on which party majorities opposed one another; but on upwards of three-quarters of all votes, both parties maintained rather high rates of cohesion (that is, over 75 percent of party members voted together) in the Senate and House.[18]

Roll call data seem to indicate that conflict patterns have changed little in the Kansas legislature in the wake of reapportionment. The earlier examination of legislators' perceptions, however, suggested that urban-rural conflict had increased significantly following reapportionment. It appears likely that much of the perceived urban-rural conflict corresponds to partisan conflict involving a Democratic party which was increasingly dominated by central city interests and a predominately suburban and rural Republican party. This does not mean that urban-rural conflict has not increased, but rather that it has been channelled to a greater degree than before through partisan divisions at the roll call stage. Reapportionment, it can be concluded, has exacerbated urban-rural conflict, but existing patterns of party cohesion have moderated the overall impact of this change. That party conflict has not in turn increased significantly is probably attributable to the limited relevance of urban-rural conflict for a broad range of issues and the continuing dominance of the Republican party. The dominance of the Republicans reduces the necessity for cohesion within their party and renders futile the drive for Democratic cohesion.

In contrast to the discussions of conflict in Tennessee and Kansas, analysis of roll call voting in South Dakota before and after reapportionment does little to clarify the picture of reapportionment's impact derived from legislators' perceptions. LeBlanc uncovered a relatively high level of partisan cohesion in the 1959 South Dakota Senate.[19] High partisan conflict in that year is largely attributable to Democratic control of the Senate, a circumstance not again repeated in either house until 1973 when Democrats won the House. More typical of conflict patterns in the South Dakota legislature are the findings of Alan Clem's studies of roll call voting in the 1965 (prereapportionment) and 1969 (post-reapportionment) legislatures. In 1965 Democratic and Republican cohesion in the Senate approached the 1959 levels in that each party averaged 56 percent cohesion, but party cohesion in the House was considerably lower (about 46 percent for both parties). Only 31 percent of nonunanimous roll calls in the Senate and 41 percent in the House produced party majorities opposing one another.[20] In 1969 party lines were even less salient (although a precise comparison with 1965 is not possible) as Republicans outnumbered Democrats by three and one-half to one.[21] Clem did not examine directly the level of urban-rural conflict in either 1965 or 1969, although his cluster bloc analysis of the 1969 legislature isolated no persistent urban and rural voting blocs. This lends credence to the earlier assertion that reapportionment was not responsible for the high level of urban-rural conflict perceived by legislators in 1973. If reapportionment were the cause, some urban-rural bloc voting ought to have emerged by 1969 after most of the major districting changes had already occurred. The conclusion that the level of urban-rural conflict perceived in 1973 derived from Democratic gains in Minnehaha and Pennington Counties gains added support. As noted previously, partisan divisions in 1973 enhanced urban-rural divisions and these divisions in turn stimulated party splits. Partisan conflict intensified because of the fairly even division of seats between the parties. On the basis of the roll call studies of earlier years, we would expect party voting to increase as the size of the working majority declines. None of these developments of 1973 can be properly attributed to reapportionment.

Limited evidence from roll call voting for New Jersey tends to substantiate the earlier assertion based on legislators' perceptions that partisan conflict has declined following reapportionment. LeBlanc, who examined divided roll calls in the New Jersey Senate in 1960, found average Democratic cohesion to be 79 percent and average Republican cohesion to be 65 percent. Comparable data for roll calls in the 1972-73 Senate, as reported by Rosenthal, showed Democratic cohesion averaging 44.3 percent and Republican cohesion as 40.7 percent. (Note that cohesion levels in both parties in the 1972-73 Assembly exceeded Senate levels. This pattern corresponds to the results of the 1973 questionnaire, in which Assembly respondents reported slightly higher partisan conflict than did Senate respondents. See Table 5-1.) [22] It may be that the expansion of the membership of the Senate and Assembly and the demise of the caucus system in the Assembly (discussed in chapter four) has assured that party allegiance will be a less dominant force in organizing conflict in postreapportionment legislatures than in prereapportionment legislatures, especially in the Assembly. Based on legislators' perceptions, we would expect less party voting and cohesion in postreapportionment legislatures than the impressive levels LeBlanc found in his analysis of roll call voting of the 1959 New Jersey Senate. By doubling the size of the Senate and increasing the size of the Assembly by a third, reapportionment has probably contributed to the abandonment of the caucus in the Assembly and made party discipline more difficult to enforce in both chambers. Thus, reapportionment has led to a slight decline in the prominence of partisan conflict and to the growing relevance of other types of conflict such as urban-suburban conflict.

In general, roll call studies of the Tennessee, Kansas, South Dakota, and New Jersey legislatures have reinforced the earlier interpretations of the impact of reapportionment on legislative conflict. In the case of Delaware, existing roll call research is less supportive, although its nature hinders the analysis of reapportionment's effects. John S. Isaacs examined roll call voting in the Delaware House from 1965 to 1970, a period following major redistricting changes.[23] Unfortunately, there is no comparable prereapportionment analysis of the Delaware House, although LeBlanc studied roll calls in the 1959 Senate.[24]

Isaacs' analysis does not report on overall levels of cohesion among identifiable groups such as Republican or Democratic and urban or rural. Instead, the research divides legislators into high support and low support categories based on their votes for bills on four areas of policy. Isaacs defined high support as voting for at least 70 percent of the bills in a category and low support as voting for less than 70 percent. During the period of 1965-70, the percentage of Democrats receiving high support scores consistently exceeded the percentage of Republicans with high support scores in the areas of welfare policy, employment policy, civil liberties and housing policy, and assistance to the major city of Wilmington. Majorities in both parties, however, had high support scores. It is significant that the difference in the proportion of metropolitan Republicans (central city and suburban) and of nonmetropolitan Republicans with high scores was greater than the difference between the proportion of Republican and Democratic high scorers for all four policy categories. This finding implies a significant degree of metropolitan-nonmetropolitan (urban-rural) conflict in the Republican party. Moreover, Isaacs' data suggests the emergence of a cross-party alliance of Democrats and metropolitan Republicans on a limited basis at least.[25] If this were the case, the earlier assertion that urban-rural conflict in the postreapportionment legislature had been submerged in Democratic-Republican conflict would seem misguided. The previous interpretation may hold true for the Senate in which 89 percent of the legislators perceived partisan conflict as important and only 44 percent saw urban-rural conflict as important (see Table 5-2). For the House, just 63 percent of legislators perceived partisan conflict as important, while 50 percent judged urban-rural conflict to be important. One might hypothesize, on the basis of the roll call evidence and the analysis of perceptions, that higher urban-rural conflict is linked to lower partisan conflict in Delaware and that the Senate, with less urban-rural conflict than the House, is more partisan-oriented.[26]

The roll call data imply that the discussion of changes in legislators' perceptions of conflict overstated the decline in urban-rural divisions following reapportionment. It is significant that 81 percent of the representatives and 71 percent of the senators in Delaware in 1973 believed that reapportionment had increased urban-rural conflict. It would appear that reapportionment produced rather slight changes in the patterns of conflict in the Delaware legislature and that prereapportionment levels of partisan and urban-rural conflict remained high after reapportionment. The rise in liberal-conservative conflict as perceived by legislators may be tied to the persistence of both partisan and urban-rural conflicts, either of which can assume liberal-conservative overtones.

Although no roll call studies are available for postreapportionment Oregon, a comment on changes in conflict patterns in that state may be made. Reapportionment in Oregon yielded only minor changes in legislative representation. Therefore, it is unlikely that reapportionment significantly altered patterns of conflict, although the analysis of perceptions indicates that the postreapportionment Oregon legislature has experienced more partisan and urban-rural conflict.

Conclusions

In light of the analysis of reapportionment's impact on patterns of legislative conflict, it is worthwhile to return to some of the theoretical considerations raised in chapter one. Only in the case of Tennessee were major first-level changes in legislative membership (high turnover) and second-level changes in the representation of population-based interests (partisan and metropolitan) translated into significant third-level changes in patterns of conflict. Reapportionment contributed to the formation of two-party politics in the Tennessee legislature. In Kansas, where first-level and second-level changes were extensive, third-level changes in patterns of conflict were less prominent in the face of continuing one-party dominance and established party cohesion. Fairly extensive first-level and second-level changes in Delaware but less consequential changes in New Jersey resulted in smaller modifications in conflict in those states than occurred in either Tennessee or Kansas; partisan loyalties, though perhaps diminished, continued to overshadow other types of conflicts. The South Dakota and Oregon legislatures, which experienced little second-level impact, underwent slight alterations in conflict attributable to reapportionment. The evidence presented supports the proposition laid out in chapter one that third-level effects are likely only when reapportionment produces major shifts in group representation and that even then established patterns of legislative conflict and organization may mute the total effect of reapportionment-induced changes.

Notes

1. Two of the most important studies employing this approach are Francis, the major portion of which is devoted to legislators' perceptions of conflict, and Wahlke et al., pp. 424-27.
2. Published studies on state legislative roll call voting are far too numerous to list. Among those that address the question of the impact of reapportionment on legislative conflict are the following: Broach, "Comparative Dimensional Analysis;" Frank M. Bryan, "The Metamorphosis of a Rural Legislature," *Polity* 1 (1968): 191-212; Furness, "Response of Colorado Assembly;" C. Richard Hofstetter, "Malapportionment and Roll-Call Voting in Indiana, 1923-1968: A Computer Simulation," *Journal of Politics* 33 (1971): 92-111; Robeck, "Legislative Partisanship;" and Ira Sharkansky, "Reapportionment and Roll Call Voting: The Case of the Georgia Legislature," *Social Science Quarterly* 51 (1970): 129-37. Also see the prereapportionment studies of David R. Derge, "Metropolitan and Outstate Alignments in Illinois and Missouri Legislative Delegations," *American Political Science Review* 52 (1958): 1051-65; and Robert S. Friedman, "The Urban-Rural Conflict Revisited," *Western Political Quarterly* 14 (1961): 481-95. For summaries of the roll call studies relating to reapportionment, see

Samuel C. Patterson, "Political Representation and Public Policy," paper presented at the Social Science Research Conference on the Impacts of Public Policies, St. Thomas, U.S. Virgin Islands, 3-5 December 1971, pp. 17-21; and Timothy G. O'Rourke, "Impact of Reapportionment," pp. 70-87.

3. See question 3 in the questionnaire reprinted in Appendix A.
4. See Francis, pp. 37-41 and Wahlke et al., pp. 424-25.
5. Ibid.
6. Francis, pp. 15-17, 44-45.
7. Belle Zeller, ed., *American State Legislatures: Report of the Committee on State Legislatures of the American Political Science Association* (New York: Thomas Y. Crowell Co., 1954), pp. 190-91. Zeller's data, as adapted by Austin Ranney, are the basis for the classification of legislative party cohesion in Tables 1-1 and 1-2 above. See Ranney, "Parties in State Politics," in *Politics in the American States,* ed. Herbert Jacob and Kenneth N. Vines (Boston: Little, Brown & Co., 1965), p. 88.
8. Grumm, "Kansas Legislature," p. 62.
9. Harder and Rampey, pp. 34-35. Harder and Rampey followed the Census Bureau's definition of urban (a place of 2500 or more population) in designating urban and rural legislators.
10. See question 4 in the questionnaire reprinted in Appendix A.
11. These data are given in detail in Table C-9 in Appendix C.
12. Broach, pp. 911-21. The remainder of the paragraph is a summary of Broach's findings concerning Tennessee.
13. While partisan divisions are now more apparent in roll call voting in the Tennessee legislature, Lee S. Greene, a noted observer of Tennessee politics, suggests that true party voting has occurred infrequently and that the respondents to the 1973 questionnaire survey might have overestimated the importance of partisan conflict. Letter from Lee S. Greene, 16 June 1977.
14. It is worth noting that the Democratic majority in the House in 1973 assigned all committee chairmanships to Democrats, a break with tradition that could be regarded as further evidence of greater party salience. (See n. 7 in chapter four.)
15. Jewell, *Metropolitan Representation,* pp. 37-40.
16. It is interesting that rural legislators in Tennessee pushed for the inclusion of single-member districts in the reapportionment plans of the mid-1960s in order to divide central city legislative delegations and to gain suburban allies. Neal R. Pierce, *The Border South States* (New York: W. W. Norton & Co., 1975), p. 310.
17. Grumm, "Kansas Legislature," pp. 58-62. Also see the following articles by Grumm: "The Systematic Analysis of Blocs in the Study of Legislative Behavior," *Western Political Quarterly* 18 (1965): 350-62; "The Means of Measuring Conflict and Cohesion in the Legislature," *Southwestern Social Science Quarterly* 44 (1964): 377-88; and "A Factor Analysis of Legislative Behavior," *Midwest Journal of Political Science* 7 (1963): 336-56.
18. Harder and Rampey, pp. 131-46.

19. Hugh L. LeBlanc, "Voting in State Senates: Party and Constituency Influences," *Midwest Journal of Political Science* 13 (1969): 36.
20. Alan L. Clem, "Roll Call Voting Behavior in the South Dakota Legislature," *Public Affairs,* no. 25, 15 May 1966, pp. 1-8.
21. Alan L. Clem, "Party and Bloc Voting in the 1969 South Dakota Legislature," *Public Affairs,* no. 38, 15 August 1969, pp. 1-6.
22. LeBlanc, p. 36; Rosenthal, "Governor, Legislature, and State Policy Making," p. 168.
23. John S. Isaacs, II, "An Analysis of Voting Behavior in the Delaware House of Representatives, 1965-1970" (Master's thesis, University of Delaware, 1971).
24. LeBlanc, p. 36.
25. Isaacs, pp. 56-67.
26. Paul Dolan, Professor of Political Science, University of Delaware, letter of 17 June 1977. A long-time observer of the Delaware legislature, he expressed the view that partisan divisions in both houses may be less relevant now than previously.

Chapter Six

The Effects of Reapportionment on State Policies

Reapportionment and Policy: An Overview

The theoretical framework set out in chapter one leads to the expectation that reapportionment would have a substantial impact upon policy in relatively few states. The link between changes in patterns of legislative districting and alterations in policies adopted by legislatures is a tenuous and distant one. Reapportionment, in order to affect policy (fourth-level effects) would have to produce substantial legislative turnover (first-level effects) leading to a significant modification in the balance of interests such as urban and rural or Democratic and Republican in the legislature (second-level effects). Whether the altered balance of interests proved meaningful for policy would depend on further changes in the legislative process including changes in chamber and committee leadership and patterns of legislative conflict (third-level effects). Beyond this, pressures for policy change encounter constraints imposed by such factors as revenues and the difficulty of modifying established administrative operations. Thus, reappor-

119

tionment does not impinge on policy directly; it initiates a series
of modifications in the legislative process which may culminate in
altered policy priorities and policy outcomes.

The analysis of the sample states as thus far outlined has not
led to firm expectations of the impact of reapportionment on policy. Chapter one, however, argued that the policy impact of reapportionment would be relatively small in most states. In Oregon
and South Dakota, where malapportionment was comparatively
slight prior to *Baker* v. *Carr*, reapportionment did little to modify
the balance of interests in the legislatures and, therefore, cannot
be viewed as a major stimulant to policy changes which may have
occurred after reapportionment. The examination of legislative
conflict, which showed that legislators in Oregon and South Dakota perceived much greater levels of urban-rural divisiveness
after reapportionment, warns against the prediction that reapportionment would have no effect on policy.

In Delaware and New Jersey, redistricting in the mid-1960s and
early 1970s led to added suburban representation which in turn
aided Republican ascendancy in the short run following reapportionment. In neither state, however, could the Republican takeover
of the legislature be attributed solely or even largely to reapportionment as the party made gains in all constituency types in the
late 1960s. (This point is discussed in chapter three.) Furthermore,
in both Delaware and New Jersey, legislative policy making is
predominantly party policy making. Even before the major redistricting activity of the mid-1960s, suburban interests dominated
the Republican party in both states, and reapportionment only
enhanced that domination. In the Democratic party in both states,
suburban influences grew as a result of reapportionment, but the
locus of party leadership remained nonsuburban (that is, central
city in New Jersey and central city and nonmetropolitan in Delaware). Still, the significant increase in Delaware in the legislative
representation of New Castle County and the continuing high
level of urban-rural divisions raise the possibility that policies
may have been influenced by redistricting. In New Jersey as well,
the increase in central city representation in the Senate and the
gains for suburban representation in both houses may have led to
policy changes.

It was in Kansas and Tennessee that reapportionment yielded
the most substantial changes in the distribution of seats among
the categories of central city, suburban and nonmetropolitan
constituencies. While central city representation quadrupled as a

result of the redistricting in the mid-1960s in Kansas, nonmetropolitan legislators continued to constitute both a legislative majority and a majority in the dominant Republican party. While this circumstance diminishes the expectation of a major shift in policy in Kansas, the sharp jump in urban-rural conflict perceived by Kansas legislators suggests that the impact of reapportionment on policy would not be inconsequential. The situation in Tennessee may offer the prospect of greater policy changes in the wake of reapportionment. Representation of central city counties doubled as a result of reapportionment. Coupled with suburban legislators, central city legislators by the early 1970s constituted a Senate and House majority, a majority in the Senate wing of the Democratic party, a majority in both Senate and House Republican delegations, and a near majority in the House Democratic delegation. The analysis in chapter four showed, however, that nonmetropolitan legislators continued to dominate positions of chamber leadership and committee chairmanships after reapportionment. This would suggest that the operative strength of metropolitan legislators was notably less than the apparent representational strength. As in Kansas, however, the high level of perceived urban-rural conflict and the rise of partisan conflict in the case of Tennessee indicate that reapportionment may have modified policies ultimately adopted in Tennessee.

The Impact of Reapportionment on the Distribution of State Expenditures in the Six Sample States

Many of the previous attempts to analyze the effects of apportionment patterns on policy outputs have focused on the possible association between the quality of apportionment and total or per capita state expenditures in various policy areas. (These studies are discussed at length later in the chapter.) Among other influences, overall expenditure levels depend heavily on the revenue resources of the state, past budgetary decisions, and requirements of federal aid programs and thus may not be the most accurate indicators of the impact of reapportionment, especially given the small number of states to be examined.[1] The present study relies instead on the distribution of state expenditures among the several categories of constituencies within the states. Presumably, areas gaining added representation in the legislatures as a result of reapportionment would receive a larger proportion of state expenditures. In the following analysis, attention will be devoted to only two aspects of state expenditures: (1) the distribution of state aid to all local governments in metropolitan counties and (2) the distribution of state aid to the largest municipal governments. Examination of these two variables is sufficient, however, to provide a partial answer to the question of whether reapportionment has modified the distribution of state expenditures in the six sample states.

Regarding the first variable, Tables 6-1 and 6-2 provide data on the distribution of state intergovernmental aid to local governments in metropolitan counties in the six sample states before and after reapportionment. Table 6-1 displays the proportion of total state aid to local governments which was channelled to local governments in central city and suburban counties in each of the six states in 1962 and 1971-72. The table also shows the proportion of legislative seats (that is, the average for both chambers) held by these categories of counties in 1961 and in 1971. In Table 6-2, the data on aid and seats are expressed in relation to each category's proportion of state population.

Several observations emerge from the data in Tables 6-1 and 6-2. First, areas victimized by severe underrepresentation in the legislature in 1962 generally fared far better in terms of proportion of aid received than in terms of proportion of legislative seats. For example, in 1962 New Castle County in Delaware, which had less than three-fifths of the representation to which it would have been entitled on the basis of population, received more than 90 percent of its aid entitlement expressed in terms of population.[2] (See Table 6-2.) In 1962 central city counties in Kansas, having about a fourth of the legislative representation justified by their population, received about 86 percent of their population-based share of aid. Suburban counties in Kansas also held a larger proportion of state aid than of legislative representation. In South Dakota, in 1962 Minnehaha County received about 92 percent of its population-based share of aid, but had only two-thirds of its population-based share of seats. Central city counties in Tennessee held a little more than half of the seats to which they were entitled, but received more than 80 percent of their population-based proportion of aid. (Suburban counties, which were slightly overrepresented in the legislature on the basis of population, received about 100 percent of their population-based share of aid.) New Jersey's established central city counties got more than their population-based share of aid in 1962, although they possessed only about 95 percent of their entitlement to legislative seats. Suburban counties in New Jersey were underrepresented in seats and more so in aid—an exception to the general pattern described thus far. Only in Oregon, do the 1962 figures show a fairly close fit between proportion of seats and proportion of aid at least in the case of central city counties, which were slightly shortchanged in both seats and aid. Suburban counties in Oregon, which were underrepresented in seats but not in aid, fit the more common pattern. In summary, the 1962 data for all six states do show an apparent association between underrepresentation in the legislature and underrepresentation in share of state aid, but representation patterns hardly account for all variations in the distribution of aid.

Not unexpectedly, the change in the share of state aid directed to a given category of constituency between 1962 and 1971-72 generally does not match the change in legislative representation between 1962 and 1972. Though central city counties in all six states received a larger share of state aid in relation to population in 1971-72, the percentage gain in aid for central city counties in every state except Oregon fell short of the percentage gain in legislative representation. While the proportion of aid to central city counties rose over the decade 1962-72, the ratio of aid to population in suburban counties either remained fairly constant as in Oregon and Tennessee or declined as in Kansas and New Jersey. Paradoxically, suburban counties in Kansas, Oregon, and New Jersey and new central city counties in New Jersey received increased legislative representation but either suffered a decline in the share of state aid (as did suburban counties in Kansas and New Jersey and new central city counties in New Jersey) or failed to gain (as did Oregon's suburban counties). This trend would suggest that factors other than legislative representation exercised a dominant influence on changes in the distribution of state expenditures.[3]

Although reapportionment probably contributed to the increase in aid directed to central city counties, recognition by the states of the "urban crisis" together with federal matching grants for urban revitalization might have played a more important role in increasing aid. Greater sensitivity to urban problems seems particularly relevant to the explanation of expenditure data for New Jersey. A succession of legislative acts favorable to central cities emerged during the period of 1967-71 which included both Democratic control of the governorship and legislature (1967-69) and Republican control of the executive and legislature (1970-71). Urban programs which won approval include the following: state aid for urban

TABLE 6-1

Proportion of Total State Aid to Local Governments Distributed to Metropolitan Counties in the Six Sample States, 1961-62 and 1971-72

State	County Type	1961 % of Seats in Legislature [a]	1962 % of State Aid	1971 % of Seats in Legislature [a]	1971-72 % of State Aid
Delaware	Central City (Suburban) County: New Castle	42.1	63.4	68.8	70.4
Kansas	Central City Counties: Sedgwick, Shawnee, Wyandotte	8.6	26.4	29.8	38.0
	Suburban Counties: Butler, Johnson	4.5	6.7	11.1	8.5
New Jersey	Established Central City Counties: Atlantic, Essex, Hudson, Mercer, Passaic	36.9	41.3	39.4	46.7
	New Central City Counties: Cumberland, Middlesex, Monmouth[b]	(13.8)	(14.8)	15.0	14.4
	Suburban Counties: Bergen, Burlington, Camden, Gloucester, Morris, Salem, Union, Warren	34.9	34.4	43.2	32.1
Oregon	Central City Counties: Lane, Marion, Multnomah	39.2	39.5	44.2	43.8
	Suburban Counties: Clackamas, Washington only	10.0	12.4	12.5	13.2

South Dakota	Central City County: Minnehaha	8.2	11.5	11.7	12.6
Tennessee	Central City Counties: Davidson, Hamilton, Knox, Shelby	23.2	34.6	42.4	39.3
	Suburban Counties: Anderson, Blount, Sumner, Wilson	7.3	5.4	7.6	5.8

Sources: Figures on state aid were computed from data in the following references: U.S., Department of Commerce, Bureau of the Census, Census of Governments: 1962, vol. 4, no. 4, Compendium of Government Finances, table 46, pp. 76-126, table 53, pp. 302-610; vol. 5, Local Government in Metropolitan Areas, tables 11-12, pp. 188-281; U.S., Department of Commerce, Bureau of the Census, Census of Governments: 1972, vol. 4, no. 5, Compendium of Government Finances, table 46, pp. 76-126; vol. 5, Local Government in Metropolitan Areas, tables 11-12, pp. 245-378. Figures on state legislative representation are taken from Table 1-3 (in chapter one), although some modifications have been made in suburban Oregon for which data on aid do not include all counties in that category of districts.

[a] Figures on legislative representation are for the 1961-62 and 1971-72 legislative sessions for all states except New Jersey. Figures for New Jersey refer to the 1960-61 and 1970-71 sessions.

[b] Data on new central city counties, recognized after 1970, are given in parentheses for 1961-62.

TABLE 6-2

Relationship between Legislative Representation and Population and Share of State Aid and Population for Metropolitan Counties, 1961-62 and 1971-72

State	County Type	1961 Ratio of Seats to 1960 Population[a]	1962 Ratio of Aid to 1960 Population	1971 Ratio of Seats to 1970 Population[a]	1971-72 Ratio of Aid to 1970 Population
Delaware	Central City (and Suburban) County	.61	.92	.98	1.00
Kansas	Central City Counties	.28	.86	.97	1.23
	Suburban Counties	.54	.80	.97	.75
New Jersey	Established Central City Counties	.95	1.06	1.14	1.35
	New Central City Counties[b]	(.96)	(1.03)	.93	.89
	Suburban Counties	.87	.86	1.06	.79
Oregon	Central City Counties	.86	.87	1.00	.99
	Suburban Counties	.86	1.07	1.00	1.06
South Dakota	Central City County	.65	.91	.82	.92
Tennessee	Central City Counties	.55	.81	.98	.91
	Suburban Counties	1.43	1.06	1.38	1.05

Sources: Ratios are computed, with some modifications, from data in Tables 1-3 and 6-1. The attempt here to relate changes in legislative representation to changes in state aid to metropolitan counties is similar to earlier efforts by Robert E. Firestine, "The Impact of Reapportionment upon Local Government Aid Receipts within Large Metropolitan Areas," Social Science Quarterly 54 (September 1973): 394-402, and by H. George Frederickson and Yong Hyo Cho, "Legislative Reapportionment and Fiscal Policy in the American States," Western Political Quarterly 27 (March 1974): 5-37. Also see n. 3 and n. 21 at the end of this chapter.

[a]Figures on legislative representation are for the 1961-62 and 1971-72 legislative sessions for all states but New Jersey. Figures for New Jersey refer to the 1960-61 and 1970-71 sessions.

[b]Data on new central city counties, recognized after 1970, are given in parentheses for 1961-62.

renewal (1967); approval by voters of bond issues for mass transit and low-income housing (1968); state takeover of most local welfare costs in 1968 (saving Newark alone $7 million initially); provision of nearly $28 million for low-income housing, aid to the disadvantaged for education and health, and urban renewal (1969); $50 million in aid and tax authorizations for Newark (1970); and the doubling of aid to large cities for redevelopment (1971). The aid package for Newark, enacted in 1970, succeeded with the support of a Republican governor and a suburban-dominated Republican legislative majority. However, especially in the Senate, opposition came from Democrats from the central city who represented cities other than Newark.[4] Expanded aid to urban areas in New Jersey appears to be more the result of a general commitment by both parties to address the problems of central cities than of representational changes induced by reapportionment. This conclusion is reinforced by the fact that in terms of representation, suburban areas ultimately benefited most from reapportionment in New Jersey. Despite the substantial increase in suburban representation in Delaware, postreapportionment legislative sessions there as in New Jersey brought several new programs favorable to central city Wilmington. These programs included state aid for housing and urban redevelopment and state assumption of local welfare costs in the late 1960s. The data in Table 6-3 summarize state aid to the largest cities for the six sample states and reveal the emerging commitment in New Jersey and Delaware to central city problems. In both states, the largest cities received an increasing proportion of state municipal aid even as their percentage of municipal population declined.[5]

While the evidence suggests that changes in the distribution of state aid in Delaware and New Jersey are only weakly related to reapportionment, redistricting during the mid-1960s seems to account for much of the shift in expenditure patterns in Kansas. Central city counties, as Table 6-1 shows, enjoyed an increase of nearly 12 percent in share of state expenditures. With a gain of .58 in the ratio of seats to population, central city counties experienced an increase of .37 in the ratio of aid to population as noted in Table 6-2. The proportion of state aid to municipalities directed to the state's largest cities also expanded from 51 percent to 57 percent between 1962 and 1972. (See Table 6-3.) The substantial shift in aid to central city counties derived from such legislative actions as the modification of state aid-to-education policy beginning in 1965, the alteration of the distribution formula for motor fuel tax revenues, and provision for state support of urban renewal and sewerage treatment (1969-70). These developments are at least partially attributable to reapportionment.[6]

It might be expected that reapportionment in Tennessee would produce changes in expenditure patterns as substantial as those in Kansas, but the evidence indicates otherwise. Central city counties were the major beneficiaries of redistricting in Tennessee and increased their share of state aid in relation to population from .81 to .91 between 1962 and 1972. It is difficult, however, to judge the contribution of reapportionment to this gain. Substantial increases in overall appropriations, especially in educational expenditures, contributed to the more favorable share of aid for central city counties. There is, however, no indication that postreapportionment legislatures between 1969 and 1972 or afterward actively

TABLE 6-3

Proportion of Total State Aid to Municipalities Distributed to Cities of the Largest Population Category in the Six Sample States, 1962 and 1971-72

	Population Category	No. of Cities in Category	1962		1971-72	
			% of State's Municipal Population	% of All State Aid to Municipalities	% of State's Municipal Population	% of All State Aid to Municipalities
Delaware	50,000 - 99,999	1[a]	54.4	81.9	43.6	89.2
Kansas	100,000 +	3[b]	32.2	51.4	33.0	56.7
New Jersey	100,000 +	6[c]	27.5	43.1	24.4	60.5
Oregon	100,000 +	1[d]	38.5	33.1	32.4	31.0
South Dakota	50,000 - 99,999	1[e]	16.4	13.9	17.6	24.2
Tennessee	100,000 +	4[f]	53.3	61.5	56.8	69.8

Sources: U.S., Department of Commerce, Bureau of the Census, Census of Governments: 1962, vol. 4, no. 3, Finances of Municipal and Township Governments, table 16, pp. 36-137. U.S., Department of Commerce, Census of Governments: 1972, vol. 4, no. 4, Finances of Municipal and Township Governments, table 17, pp. 36-139.

[a] Wilmington (New Castle County).

[b] Kansas City (Wyandotte), Topeka (Chawnee), Wichita (Sedgwick).

[c] Camden (Camden), Elizabeth City (Union), Jersey City (Hudson), Newark (Essex), Paterson (Passaic), Trenton (Mercer).

[d] Portland (Multnomah).

[e] Sioux Falls (Minnehaha).

[f] Chattanooga (Hamilton), Knoxville (Knox), Memphis (Shelby), Nashville (Davidson).

sought or enacted legislation to bring about modification of state aid formulas in order to shift a greater portion of aid to central city counties or to central cities.[7] An academic expert on Tennessee politics, who requested anonymity, indicated in a 1977 conversation that "as a general proposition, reapportionment has not helped cities." The observer suggested that the source of the legislature's unresponsiveness to cities is a growing division within metropolitan areas between central city and suburban legislators. While the data in Table 6-3 show a rise in the percentage of all municipal aid directed to the four largest cities from 62 percent to 70 percent, some portion of this increase is attributable to educational funds included in the aid totals of the larger cities but not in those of the smaller ones. Thus, reapportionment did not produce the dramatic shift in state expenditures toward central city counties and central cities that might have been expected on the basis of representational change.

In Oregon and South Dakota, where representational changes resulting from reapportionment were less pronounced than those in the other four states, it is expected that reapportionment would yield slight if any modifications in the distribution of state aid. In South Dakota, the central city county experienced virtually no gain in its share of state aid between 1962 and 1972 (see Tables 6-1 and 6-2). The more favorable position of Sioux Falls with respect to state aid to municipalities (Table 6-3) cannot be attributed to conscious legislative attempts to distribute aid more favorably to larger cities. It is not surprising that reapportionment appears to have had little effect on state aid policies in South Dakota.

Compared to the figures for South Dakota, the data on the distribution of state aid in Oregon pose more difficult problems of interpretation. The percentage of state aid directed to central city counties rose about four points between 1962 and 1972 (Table 6-1), although this change represented a gain of .12 in terms of expenditures in relation to population (Table 6-2). The city of Portland actually suffered a decline in its share of state municipal aid over the same period (Table 6-3). The more favorable position of central city counties in 1972 may have resulted from the enactment of property tax relief in 1965 and a modification in the formula for distributing highway tax revenues to county and city governments in 1967 (both of these actions occurring prior to post-*Baker* reapportionment). Legislation following reapportionment included state assumption of county welfare costs in 1969 which saved Multnomah County nearly $6 million, a series of laws authorizing governmental reorganization in metropolitan Portland in 1969, support for sewerage treatment facilities in 1969, and new property tax relief legislation in 1971.[8] The legislation following reapportionment, although beneficial to metropolitan areas, can hardly be judged detrimental to nonmetropolitan areas. The legislative developments of the late 1960s and early 1970s and the ambiguous data on changes in expediture patterns lead to the conclusion that reapportionment has not contributed to significant changes in legislative policy making in Oregon.

While this brief examination of patterns of expenditures before and after reapportionment must be regarded as only suggestive, the data on state aid to local governments in metropolitan counties indicate that reapportionment has clearly influenced the distribution of expenditures in only one of the six sample states. Impressive changes in policy occurred in Kansas, where central cities and central city counties made dramatic gains in legislative representation as a consequence of reapportionment. It is perhaps surprising that the major representational changes in Tennessee, although similar to those that occurred in Kansas, did not lead to significant modifications in the distribution of state funds to metropolitan areas. Reapportionment in New Jersey and Delaware probably contributed to the enactment of numerous appropriations oriented toward central cities in the late 1960s and early 1970s, but reapportionment hardly emerges as the primary factor accounting for these policy changes. Finally, in Oregon and South Dakota, the minor representational alterations resulting from reapportionment appear to have caused no notable shifts in expenditure patterns. Enhanced metropolitan representation in Oregon, however, may have contributed to the passage of several programs especially beneficial to major population centers. While examination of other expenditure areas would undoubtedly provide a more complete picture of the effects of reapportionment, the expenditures reviewed convey the general dimensions of the impact of reapportionment on expenditure policy.[9]

Legislators' Perceptions of Policy Changes Induced by Reapportionment

While expenditure data can provide readily quantifiable measures of policy change during the period before and after reapportionment, a variety of other policies not revealed by expenditure data may be affected by reapportionment. The responses of legislators to the 1973 questionnaire provide added insight into the policies affected by reapportionment. (Again, the reader is cautioned about the reliability of responses to questions which require legislators not only to identify changes in policy but to recognize the causes of those changes.)

In response to the general questions of whether reapportionment had affected legislation introduced and adopted, legislators in the six states produced a varied pattern of responses.[10] One half or more of the respondents in both houses of the legislatures in Kansas, Oregon, and South Dakota agreed that reapportionment had influenced the legislation introduced and the legislation adopted. In Delaware, a clear majority of both houses believed reapportionment had affected legislation adopted, but only 44 percent believed it had affected legislation introduced. In Tennessee and New Jersey, the upper and lower houses displayed divergent responses. While half or more of the Tennessee senators answered that reapportionment had affected legislation introduced and legislation adopted, less than half the House members indicated this. It is notable that in the lower house, members who recognized an impact outnumbered those who saw no effect of reapportionment on legislation introduced and legislation adopted. It is possible that the closer partisan division prevailing in the lower house in the late 1960s and early 1970s neutralized policy initiatives that may have emerged in the more solidly Democratic Senate. In New Jersey, a majority of senators attributed to reapportionment an impact on legislation introduced and legislation adopted, but in the Assembly those who saw no effect outnumbered those who perceived an impact. Reapportionment more profoundly altered representational patterns in the Senate than in the Assembly (see Table 1-3). In all six states and among all legislators who believed reapportionment had influenced legislation that was introduced and/or adopted, those who elaborated on the nature of the impact most often indicated that the effect of reapportionment had been the production of more liberal and metropolitan-oriented policies. The data on legislators' elaborations appear in Table 6-4.

More specific data on the perceptions of legislators of the impact of reapportionment on policy are contained in Table 6-5 which summarizes legislators' listings of issues affected by reapportionment.[11] Except for the area of education, noted by 51 percent of Kansas legislators, no issue domain acquired support from a majority of legislators in any state. Most respondents in every state mentioned several policy areas which they judged to have been influenced by reapportionment; but, as the data make obvious, little consensus emerged with respect to specific issues affected by redistricting. In general, the perceptions of the legislators again confirm the difficulty of isolating and measuring the effects of reapportionment on policy. Although the responses varied considerably among the six states, distribution of state aid to

TABLE 6-4

Elaborations of Legislators Who Believed Reapportionment Had Affected Legislation Introduced or Adopted in the Six Sample Legislatures (Senate and House Combined)

State	Legislation Introduced[a]						Legislation Adopted[b]					
	% of All Respondents Perceiving Change (N)	More Liberal	More Conser-vative	More Metro-politan Oriented[d]	More Suburban Oriented[d]	Miscel-laneous or No Elabora-tion	% of All Respondents Perceiving Change (N)	More Liberal	More Conser-vative	More Metro-politan Oriented[d]	More Suburban Oriented[d]	Miscel-laneous or No Elabora-tion
Delaware	44.0% (11)	27.3%	18.2%	45.5%	9.1%	18.2%	68.8% (17)	52.9%	5.9%	41.2%	5.9%	5.9%
Kansas	61.6 (53)	20.8	0	45.3	0	35.8	68.6 (59)	20.3	0	61.0	0	22.0
New Jersey	38.6 (17)	17.6	0	17.6	0	64.7	47.7 (21)	23.8	4.7	19.0	4.7	52.3
Oregon	61.5 (24)	41.7	4.2	16.7	0	41.7	58.9 (23)	39.1	4.3	21.7	0	34.8
South Dakota	51.9 (27)	37.0	0	33.3	3.7	37.0	57.7 (30)	33.3	0	36.7	0	30.0
Tennessee	38.1 (16)	56.3	0	25.0	0	25.0	52.4 (22)	40.9	0	40.9	0	22.7

Source: Responses to the 1973 survey of state legislators in the six sample states. See questions #9 and #10 in the
questionnaire reprinted in Appendix A.

aThe elaborations are expressed as a percentage of those who perceived change, given in the first column under Legislation
Introduced. (See the "Yes" responses in Table C-10 in Appendix C.) Percentages may not add to 100 due to multiple responses.

bThe elaborations are expressed as a percentage of those who perceived change, given in the first column under Legislation
Adopted. (See the "Yes" responses in Table C-11 in Appendix C.) Percentages may not add to 100 due to multiple responses.

cResponses referred to more urban-oriented policy, but no distinction was made between central city-oriented and suburban-
oriented policy.

dSpecific reference was made to suburban-oriented policy.

TABLE 6-5

Legislators' Perceptions of Issues Affected by Reapportionment in the Six Sample Legislatures [a]

	Delaware (N=25)	Kansas (N=86)	New Jersey (N=44)	Oregon (N=39)	South Dakota (N=52)	Tennessee (N=42)
Agriculture	0.0%	4.7%	6.8%	5.1%	11.5%	0.0%
Business and Labor	12.0	7.0	2.3	10.3	17.3	7.1
Civil Rights and Consumer Protection	4.0	10.5	4.5	10.3	9.6	16.7
Distribution of State Aid to Localities	28.0	37.2	31.8	17.9	1.9	40.5
Education	20.0	51.2	22.7	12.8	17.3	2.4
Environment	8.0	4.7	25.0	41.0	13.5	2.4
Government Reorganization	24.0	4.7	2.3	10.3	13.5	4.8
Highway Construction	8.0	17.4	11.4	20.5	1.9	2.4
Legislative Reform	0.0	11.6	4.5	2.6	0.0	9.5
Morals and Crime	24.0	17.4	0.0	0.0	1.9	7.1
Taxation	28.0	23.3	18.2	38.5	44.2	19.0
Welfare	8.0	18.6	18.2	20.5	9.6	2.4

Source: Responses to the 1973 survey of state legislators in the six sample states. See question #5 in Appendix A.

[a] Figures are percentages of all legislators responding to questionnaire.

localities was noted by more than a fourth of the respondents in all states except Oregon, where about a fifth of the legislators mentioned it, and South Dakota, where only 2 percent noted the issue. Taxation garnered a significant share of responses ranging from 18 percent in New Jersey to 44 percent in South Dakota. Legislators also mentioned education in substantial numbers ranging from 13 percent in Oregon to 51 percent in Kansas; in Tennessee, however, only 2 percent listed that issue.

The relatively large proportion of legislators who pointed to distribution of state aid to localities lends credence to the earlier emphasis on the analysis of the distribution of state expenditures. It is important to note that in Kansas, where the clearest shifts in aid distribution occurred, about 37 percent of legislators mentioned this issue. In Tennessee, where the expected shift in the distribution of expenditures failed to materialize, almost 41 percent of the legislators cited the issue of state aid; this might suggest that greater conflict had occurred without the development of major policy changes. It is interesting that 32 percent of the New Jersey respondents and 24 percent of the Delaware respondents mentioned the specific issue of urban funding. (The analysis of expenditures showed that an increasing portion of aid to municipalities and total state aid went to these states' central cities and central city counties after reapportionment, although representational changes do not fully account for the shift.)

It is difficult to determine the importance of the large number of legislators who mentioned taxation. Most of the notations referred generally to taxation or tax reform rather than to specific issues of taxation. The nature of the impact of reapportionment on tax policy does not emerge from the kind of responses given, although it is well to recall that Delaware, Oregon, and South Dakota legislators perceived an increase in liberal versus conservative conflict in their respective legislatures after reapportionment. Controversy may have arisen over increasing taxes between liberals who supported increases and conservatives who opposed them. (All six states raised levels of taxation between 1964 and 1974, but reapportionment is certainly not the only or even primary explanation for the hikes.)

With the exceptions of Kansas and New Jersey, the generality of the legislators' responses similarly impedes analysis of the effects of reapportionment on educational policy. In Kansas, 48 percent of the legislators mentioned the issue of financing public education. (The percentage is a composite of responses categorized under "Distribution of State Aid" and "Education" in Table 6-5.) The legislators' responses apparently referred to legislation which was eventually enacted and which nearly doubled the contribution of the state to local school districts in order to remedy wide variations in local capabilities to pay the costs of education.[12] Although several Kansas legislators suggested that the legislation most benefited the large cities, it is debatable that reapportionment played more than a small part in its adoption since a state District Court in Kansas had mandated a revision in the state's educational finance system.[13] Urban promotion of the legislation is questionable in light of Harder and Rampey's 1971 survey of Kansas legislators which showed that both Republican and Democratic urban legislators were less supportive of increased state aid to education than rural legislators of both parties; overall, three-fourths of both parties favored an increase.[14] In New Jersey, about half of the 23 percent of legislators who referred to education cited the specific question of the state's role in school finance, but here again, state court rulings on the system of school funding probably affected the emergence of this issue far more than redistricting.

Apart from the policy areas drawing prominent support among all six states, several other policy areas frequently noted in individual states merit attention in those instances in which the responses were sufficiently elaborate to allow for meaningful interpretation. In Kansas, 19 percent of the legislators cited welfare as a policy area affected by reapportionment. Many specifically noted reform of the welfare system and the 1973 legislation providing for a complete state takeover of welfare costs. Given the heavier concentration of poor in central cities, the legislation probably benefited central city counties (since welfare is a county-level function) more substantially than other counties. It is thus reasonable to conclude that reapportionment may have influenced the outcome of welfare reform. Among the 17 percent of Kansas legislators who noted moral issues, most referred to the adoption of legislation providing for a liquor-by-the-drink referendum. Liquor-by-the-drink is ordinarily favored by large city interests and opposed by rural elements. Because reapportionment benefited the large cities, it thus probably influenced the fate of the issue. References to environmental issues in New Jersey and Oregon may reflect the greater concern about pollution and land use planning in postreapportionment legislatures with a greater proportion of metropolitan legislators; [15] one-fourth of all Oregon respondents cited the particular issue of land use planning. The large number of references (17 percent) to highway construction in Kansas might be attributed to the modification in the formula for distributing gasoline tax revenues as noted earlier and to possible changes in general highway appropriations. An even larger percentage (21 percent) of Oregon legislators mentioned the issue of highway construction, although the comments did not specify the nature of reapportionment's influence.[16]

While the discussion thus far has focused on particular policies affected by reapportionment, it may be useful to look at another measure of policy change, that is, shifting patterns in interest group pressure. Reapportionment may alter the policy-making climate to the extent that existing policies are jeopardized and proposed policies may have greater chance for success. Shifts in interest group activity may reflect this. The 1973 questionnaire asked legislators to indicate what groups had increased or decreased pressure as a result of reapportionment; their responses are summarized in Table 6-6.[17] In no state did any interest group catego-

TABLE 6-6

Legislators' Perceptions of Interest Groups Increasing or Decreasing Lobbying Pressure as a Consequence of Reapportionment (Groups Mentioned by 5% or More of Respondents in Each of the Sample States)

	Interest Groups Perceived as Increasing Pressure (% of Legislators Perceiving Increase)	Interest Groups Perceived as Decreasing Pressure (% of Legislators Perceiving Decrease)	(N)
Delaware	Education (16.0%) Labor (8.0%)	None	(25)
Kansas	Agriculture(7.0%) Business (7.0%) Education (7.0%) Labor (4.7%)	None	(36)
New Jersey	Citizens' Lobbies (4.5%) Education (4.5%) Environmental (4.5%) Labor (4.5%)	None	(44)
Oregon	Citizens' Lobbies (15.4%) Labor (12.8%) Agriculture (7.7%) Business (7.7%) Environmental (7.7%) Urban Interests (5.1%)	None	(39)
South Dakota	Labor (19.2%) Education (11.5%) Agriculture (9.6%) Urban Interests (5.8%)	None	(52)
Tennessee	Education (7.1%) Business (4.8%) Labor (4.8%)	None	(12)

Source: Responses to the 1973 survey of state legislators in the six sample states. See question #8 in Appendix A.

ries attract as many as a fifth of the respondents, but the results are at least suggestive. In every state, 5 percent or more of the legislators cited increased pressure from labor, partly attributable in all states to diminished rural representation leading to a more favorable legislative climate for urban-based labor interests. The centrality of education in state policy, coupled with the rise of the issue of the state's share of state and local education expenditures, may account for the citation of increased educational interest group pressure in every state but Oregon. To the extent that distribution of state aid to education looms large, reapportionment may have influenced the pattern of pressure.

It is significant that legislators in three states, Kansas, Oregon, and South Dakota, cited greater pressure from agricultural interests. This may reflect a postreapportionment legislative climate less receptive to rural, agricultural interests. The frequency of mentions of increased pressure from citizen lobbies in Oregon and New Jersey may be due to a more metropolitan orientation of the postreapportionment legislatures, although this is questionable. The citation of increased pressure from urban interests by legislators in Oregon and South Dakota is more easily attributed to reapportionment.

As noted earlier, the responses of legislators on the effects of reapportionment on policy reinforces the conclusions derived from the analysis of the distribution of state expenditures. The responses provide the basis for forming more general conclusions about policy as well. The legislators believed that reapportionment had pushed policy in a more liberal direction—not a surprising conclusion in view of the expectation that additional central city or suburban representatives would be more liberal than the rural legislators whom they displaced. The responses also suggest that the impact of reapportionment is greater or more detectable in some policies than others. To the extent that reapportionment alters policy by affecting metropolitan-nonmetropolitan or central city-suburban balance in the legislature, the effects of reapportionment would be more evident in a limited set of policies for which urban-rural or similar divisions are relevant. With respect to the distribution of state aid to localities and, to a lesser extent, with regard to taxation, education, and certain moral issues, urban-rural divisions may loom large. This line of reasoning not only accounts for the differential impact of reapportionment on various policies, but also it accounts for legislators' perceptions of great urban-rural conflict in states such as Kansas, Tennessee, Oregon,

and South Dakota in the face of evidence which shows that urban-rural conflict does not generally emerge from roll call analysis
(see chapter four).

Turning from an examination of the impact of reapportionment
on issues to a review of the impact of reapportionment in different states, it appears that Kansas is the state most affected. Differ-
entiation among the other sample states in terms of the policy
impact of reapportionment is difficult, although reapportionment
apparently influenced policy to some degree in all five states.

One state deserves particular attention. In Oregon, where it was
expected that reapportionment would influence policy only
slightly, a surprising number of legislators believed reapportionment has affected such policy areas as the environment, taxation,
welfare, and highway construction. This might call for revision of
the common sense proposition that little change in reapportionment would lead to little change in policy. In situations in which
legislative interests are fairly evenly balanced, as in the case of
metropolitan and nonmetropolitan legislators in Oregon, marginal
changes in legislative representation may evoke considerable policy change. However, the data on distribution of state expenditures and the earlier examination of the impact of reapportionment on legislative organization and conflict would seem to
indicate that reapportionment has had a less significant impact on
policy than that which has been attributed to it by Oregon
legislators.

The data on legislators' perceptions of the impact of reapportionment on interest group activity suggests that postreapportionment legislatures have received greater pressure from labor and
education interests. These interest groups are perhaps seeking to
capitalize on the more liberal legislative climate. In several states,
agricultural interest groups have increased their activity; this may
be attributed to the need to lobby more strenuously in a less
favorable legislative environment.

The Policy Impact of Reapportionment: A Look at Previous
Research and Some Conclusions

The findings of the present study can be integrated with the
conclusions of prior research on the policy impact of malapportionment and reapportionment produced by a series of quantitative studies published in the 1960s and early 1970s. The first
quantitative studies focusing on the policy effects of legislative

districting attempted to determine the impact of malapportionment prior to *Baker* v. *Carr* on states' policies. In separate studies published between 1962 and 1967, Herbert Jacob, David Brady and Douglas Edmonds, Richard I. Hofferbert, and Thomas R. Dye found that various measures of malapportionment in state legislatures accounted for little of the variation in states' expenditure patterns, especially after controlling for socioeconomic development in the states.[18] If malapportionment did not account for policy differences among the states, the studies implied that reapportionment would produce little change in states' policies. Allan G. Pulsipher and James L. Weatherby's regression analysis of the effects of malapportionment on expenditures led to a dissenting claim that malapportionment influenced total per capita expenditures, total education expenditures, total welfare expenditures, as well as several other output measures.[19] Likewise, Jack L. Walker's study of state legislative innovation uncovered a link between fair apportionment and a composite innovation score for each state based on eighty-eight policy areas.[20]

While the studies mentioned thus far examined the relationship between malapportionment and policy, H. George Frederickson and Yong Hyo Cho looked at the association between reapportionment measured by the change in indices of apportionment from 1962 to 1967 or 1969 and changes in state expenditure patterns. Among their most important findings, Frederickson and Cho noted that drastic apportionment change and greater representation of metropolitan constituencies after reapportionment correlated strongly with a reduction in discrimination against metropolitan areas in the distribution of state aid and a faster growth in total state taxes.[21] (The linking of greater metropolitan representation with increased taxation supports the presentation in this study of legislators' perceptions which indicated that reapportionment influenced tax policies in all six states.) In general, Frederickson and Cho found that reapportionment change was more highly related to state spending policies in 1967-69 than malapportionment to state policies in 1962.[22] This would support the contention that studies before *Baker* of malapportionment may have underestimated the effects of reapportionment.

The research of Frederickson and Cho on the policy impact of reapportionment together with previous studies on the policy effects of malapportionment [23] generally affirm the findings on the policy impact of reapportionment in the six sample states: legislative districting, whether viewed in terms of apportionment at a fixed point in time or in terms of apportionment change (that is, reapportionment), affects policy outcomes, although the impact is subtle and more evident on some policies than others; and the impact varies according to the state and its political and economic setting. Two important elements require special emphasis. First, apportionment does affect policy.[24] Some authors, having found that socioeconomic variables account for a greater amount of variation in state policies than do political variables such as apportionment or party competition, have tended to discount the effects of apportionment. Dye, for example, found a link between apportionment and several expenditure measures after controlling for socioeconomic development, but his conclusions focused on the relatively small explanatory value of apportionment.[25] The second essential point is that the effects of apportionment on policy are generally rather weak. This is hardly surprising in light of the myriad factors affecting policy. Revenue limitations, past appropriations, and federal aid stipulations all serve to constrain legislative activity in state budgetary policy. As the discussion in chapter four indicated, legislative institutions and procedures tend to affect or reduce the representational impact of reapportionment. It may well be that the full effects of reapportionment on policy will not be realized until enough time has elapsed to allow changes in legislative representation to permeate positions of chamber and committee leadership.[26]

Notes

1. For evidence on the influence of past budgetary allocations on present state expenditures, see Ira Sharkansky and Richard I. Hofferbert, "Dimensions of State Policy," in *Politics in the American States: A Comparative Analysis,* 2d. ed., edited by Herbert Jacob and Kenneth N. Vines (Boston: Little, Brown & Co., 1971), pp. 324-26. For a discussion of the impact of the federal government on state policies, see Douglas D. Rose, "National and Local Forces in State Politics: The Implications of Multi-Level Analysis," *American Political Science Review* 67 (1973): 1162-73.
2. Relating percentage of aid to percentage of population is not intended to imply that under an equitable system of distribution the two percentages should be identical. Population, although important, is only one of many factors upon which formulas for the distribution of state aid are based.
3. Robert E. Firestine, "The Impact of Reapportionment upon Local Government Aid Receipts within Large Metropolitan Areas," *Social Science Quarterly* 54 (1973): 394-402. Firestine examined the impact of reapportionment on the distribution of state aid to ninety-seven cen-

tral city and suburban counties in the thirty-eight largest SMSAs. He found that reapportionment had "a barely detectable positive effect upon state distributed intergovernmental aid to local governments in the nation's largest metropolitan areas" (quoted p. 402). Also see Michael C. LeMay, "The States and Urban Areas: A Comparative Assessment," *National Civic Review* 61 (1972): 542-48. This article provides an excellent summary of urban-oriented legislation enacted by postreapportionment legislatures during 1969-70 in all fifty states.

4. See Ronald Sullivan, "$50 Million Newark Aid Plan Is Voted by Jersey Legislature," *New York Times*, 19 December 1970, p. 20.

5. The figures in Table 6-3 should be viewed with some caution because in Delaware, New Jersey, and Tennessee, very large cities may receive public school funds which in smaller cities would go to separate school districts. Very large cities may thus receive aid to education which smaller cities do not receive. However, the figures presented do provide a general indication of changes in the distribution of state aid over time.

6. To say a "shift" in state expenditures favorable to major population centers is misleading to the extent that it implies a withdrawal of funds from nonmetropolitan areas. Kansas State Senator Donn J. Everett has described legislative changes as efforts "to tailor" new or expanded appropriations to the needs of central city counties without reducing expenditures in nonmetropolitan counties. His remarks were made in a telephone interview on 16 September 1977.

7. Commenting on the 1969 legislative session, William Bennett wrote, "The session was 45 days of frustration for those who had hoped that reapportionment and the reality of a strong two-party system would vastly improve the legislative image." William Bennett, "Special Interest Groups Dominated Assembly," *The Commercial Appeal* (Memphis), 11 May 1969, p. 4.

8. See especially A. McKoy Rich and Donald E. Carlson, "Oregon Laws Aid Municipal Areas," *National Civic Review* 58 (1969): 422-23.

9. Existing research generally supports the conclusions presented here. In a survey of city executives (either the city mayor or city manager in all U.S. cities over 10,000 population) conducted in the late 1960s, 51 percent of city executives believed that reapportionment had helped make their respective state legislature more sympathetic to the problems of urban areas. Kansas was among fifteen states in which more than half of the city executives thought that reapportionment had made the legislature more sympathetic; Tennessee was among six states in which city executives were equally divided over the question of whether or not reapportionment had made the legislature more sympathetic; New Jersey and Oregon were among eleven states in which a majority of city executives believed the state legislature's attitude toward urban areas had been unaffected by reapportionment. (Eighteen states were not classified because of an insufficient number of responses.) See Morley Segal and A. Lee Fritschler, "Emerging Patterns of Intergovernmental Relations," in *The Municipal Yearbook: 1970* (Washington, D.C.: International City Management Association, 1970), pp. 13-14, 32-35.

10. See questions 9 and 10 in the questionnaire reprinted in Appendix A. These data are reported in detail in Tables C-10 and C-11 in Appendix C.
11. See question 5 in the questionnaire reprinted in Appendix A.
12. For a thorough description of this legislation and the litigation which prompted it, see "Comment: The Inequality of Equality: Ruminations on the 1973 Kansas School District Equalization Act," *University of Kansas Law Review* 22 (Winter 1974): 229-62.
13. The legal issue is whether heavy reliance on local property taxation to finance public schools by producing irregularities in school expenditures among schools in high and low valuation areas violates national and/or state constitutional provisions that guarantee equal protection. The question was first addressed by the California State Supreme Court in *Serrano* v. *Priest* (1971). For a thorough analysis of the issue, see U.S. Advisory Commission on Intergovernmental Relations, *Financing Schools and Property Tax Relief—A State Responsibility* (Washington, D.C.: U.S. Government Printing Office, 1973). An up-to-date report on litigation appears in *The Book of the States, 1976-77* (Lexington, Ky.: Council of State Governments, 1976), pp. 314-17.
14. Harder and Rampey, pp. 34-35.
15. See LeMay.
16. Tentative evidence indicates that in both Kansas and Oregon, metropolitan counties received a larger share of state highway expenditures spent on state-administered highways after reapportionment. Supporting data are found in Table C-12 in Appendix C. However, the data on expenditures do not indicate when legislative commitments have been given for construction projects so that it is not possible to gauge the effects of reapportionment on changing patterns of appropriations. See the discussion of the effects of malapportionment on state highway expenditures by Robert I. Friedman, "State Politics and Highways," in *Politics in the American States: A Comparative Analysis*, 2nd ed., pp. 498-99.
17. See question 8 in the questionnaire reprinted in Appendix A. For a similar analysis of the impact of reapportionment on interest group activity, see Hawkins, pp. 282-83.
18. Herbert Jacob, "The Consequences of Malapportionment: A Note of Caution," *Social Forces* 43 (1964): 256-61; Thomas R. Dye, "Malapportionment and Public Policy in the States," *Journal of Politics* 27 (1965): 586-601; Richard I. Hofferbert, "The Relation between Public Policy and Some Structural and Environmental Variables in the American States," *American Political Science Review* 60 (1966): 73-82; David Brady and Douglas Edmonds, "One Man, One Vote—So What?" *Trans-action* 4 (1967): 41-46. For a more detailed review of the policy studies relating to apportionment, see Bicker, pp. 151-201, and Timothy G. O'Rourke, "Impact of Reapportionment," pp. 52-69.
19. Allan G. Pulsipher and James L. Weatherby, Jr., "Malapportionment, Party Competition, and the Functional Distribution of Governmental Expenditures," *American Political Science Review* 62 (1968): 1207-19.
20. Jack L. Walker, "The Diffusion of Innovation in the American

States," in *State and Urban Politics: Readings in Comparative Public Policy,* pp. 377-412, but especially pp. 381-390. This article originally appeared in the *American Political Science Review* 63 (1969): 880-99.

21. H. George Frederickson and Yong Hyo Cho, "Legislative Reapportionment and Fiscal Policy in the American States," *Western Political Quarterly* 27 (1974): 5-37, but especially 30-32. Also see by the same authors, "Sixties' Reapportionment: Is It Victory or Delusion?" *National Civic Review* 60 (1971): 73-78, and "The Effects of Reapportionment: Subtle, Selective, Limited," *National Civic Review* 63 (1974): 357-62. See also Firestine, "Impact of Reapportionment upon Local Government." pp. 394-402. Another attempt to assess the policy impact of reapportionment through quantitative analysis of forty-eight states is Roger Hanson and Robert Crew, "The Effects of Reapportionment on State Policy Out-Puts," in *The Impact of Supreme Court Decisions: Empirical Studies,* 2d ed., edited by Theodore L. Becker and Malcolm M. Feeley (New York: Oxford University Press, 1973), pp. 155-74.

22. Frederickson and Cho, "Legislative Apportionment," p. 25.

23. All of the quantitative studies suffer from serious shortcomings and their conclusions cannot be accepted uncritically. Perhaps the most telling weakness is that the studies rely on measures of apportionment which are largely arithmetical indices of population equality among legislative districts. (An example is the Dauer-Kelsay Index mentioned in chapter one.) The indices generally do not account for the underrepresentation or overrepresentation of political interests, such as urban or rural or Republican or Democrat interests, and therefore do not fully quantify the political consequences of apportionment. The David-Eisenberg Index, mentioned in chapter one, does measure to some extent the representation of interests, but it is not precisely comparable among all states. For a fuller treatment of this issue, see Bicker, "Effects of Malapportionment," pp. 161-71 and Timothy G. O'Rourke, "Impact of Reapportionment," pp. 9-33. The impact studies also suffer from a failure to consider intervening legislative variables such as party control of the legislature, distribution of committee chairmanships according to constituency, and legislative professionalism; presumably these factors may mediate the effect of apportionment on policy. Frederickson and Cho in "Legislative Apportionment," however, do introduce a number of such variables into their analysis (see especially pp. 14-15 and 36-37). In this regard, see the study by Edward G. Carmines, "The Mediating Influence of State Legislatures on the Linkage Between Interparty Competition and Welfare Policies," *American Political Science Review* 68 (1974): 1118-24; also Uslaner and Weber, "Electoral Impact," especially pp. 1-9; and chapter four above.

24. Further support of this view appears in William R. Cantrall and Stuart S. Nagel, "The Effects of Reapportionment on the Passage of Nonexpenditure Legislation," *Annals of the New York Academy of Sciences* 219 (1973): 269-79. This study is notable for its attempt to deal with nonbudgetary policy. The authors found significant relationships between apportionment and state policies in the areas of

racial and sexual equality and highway safety prior to *Baker* and *Reynolds*. Reapportionment change significantly correlated with modifications in laws concerning public accommodations, divorce, and driver education. Also see Yong Hyo Cho and H. George Frederickson, "Apportionment and Legislative Responsiveness to Policy Preferences in the American States," *Annals of the New York Academy of Sciences* 219 (1973): 248-67.

25. Dye, "Malapportionment and Public Policy," pp. 595-601.
26. Frederickson and Cho ("Legislative Apportionment," p. 30) found in their research that

> "... more drastic change in apportionment tended to be associated with slower spending growth rates, and longer legislative experience after reapportionment tended to be associated with faster spending growth rates. These results provide strong evidence substantiating the temporal argument of reapportionment consequence, in showing that positive policy responses to public need satisfaction could not be expected to immediately follow [sic] reapportionment."

Also see Alvin D. Sokolow, "Legislative Pluralism, Committee Assignments, and Internal Norms: The Delayed Impact of Reapportionment in California," *Annals of the New York Academy of Sciences* 219 (1973): 291-313.

Chapter Seven

The Impact of Reapportionment: Summary and Conclusions

This investigation of the impact of reapportionment in the six sample states has followed two interrelated lines of analysis. One line of analysis has focused on the relationship between legislative districting and the total legislative process. Proceeding on the foundations of the theoretical framework advanced in chapter one, the examination has attempted to determine the impact of reapportionment upon various elements in the legislative process ranging from legislator-constituency relations and partisan fortunes to legislative conflict and policy outputs. The classification of levels of effect has been employed to distinguish the effects of reapportionment at various stages of the legislative process and to account for the sequence of changes stimulated by reapportionment beginning with higher turnover, for example, and culminating in modified policy outputs. In addition to the examination of the interaction of redistricting and the legislative process, the research has been concerned with a second line of analysis: the impact of reapportionment on the politics of each of the sample states. Specifically, the study has tried to determine how reapportionment has modified the structure of political representation, conflict, and policy making in the individual states. Until now, the two lines of analysis have been presented together, but it may be useful in summarizing the research to separate the two approaches and the conclusions that emerge from each.

The Levels of Reapportionment Effects: Conclusions

The examination of reapportionment in six states has generally confirmed the expectations outlined in chapter one. Some changes (first-level effects) almost always are associated with legislative redistricting, while other changes, such as partisan gains (second-level effects), depend upon the distribution of population-based interests which vary independently of apportionment patterns. Changes in legislative organization and conflict (third-level effects) rise from first-level and second-level effects, but established rules, customs, and patterns of conflict tend to reduce the impact of changes at the third level. Policy changes (fourth-level effects) derive from changes at the three lower levels but are also minimized by a variety of restraints from such factors as revenue limitations and past policy commitments.

With respect to first-level effects, the analysis of chapter two indicated that in all six sample states, modification of legislative districts by reapportionment caused some changes in legislator-constituency relations; reapportionment was associated with higher than normal legislative turnover in all states except Tennessee, where "normal" turnover as well as turnover in reapportionment years was exceedingly high. Although the extent of first-level effects varied from one state to another, it is notable that even in Oregon and South Dakota, states which were fairly well apportioned prior to *Baker* and *Reynolds*, certain effects such as higher turnover were associated with reapportionment. Legislators in all six states were extremely sensitive to the effects of alterations in legislative districts. A review of legislators' perceptions and independent analysis indicates that reapportionment produced (1) higher than normal legislative turnover in all states except Tennessee as a result of subdivision, consolidation, and other modifications of existing districts; (2) alterations in individual electoral fortunes as the result of changes in existing districts evidenced by the number of incumbents who readily noted the extent to which reapportionment had aided or hindered their chances of reelection; (3) modified campaign opportunities as noted, for example, by Oregon legislators who felt that smaller legislative districts made for more manageable campaign expenses; (4) closer legislator-constituency relations in those instances in which reapportionment subdivided populous districts or more difficult legislator-constituency contact in geographically expanded districts created by the consolidation of less populous rural constituencies; and (5) in selected states, changes in legislator characteristics such as age and experience.

The nature, if not the extent, of first-level effects was similar among all six sample states, but second-level effects, which depend on the distribution of population-based interests, were far more diverse. The most extensive second-level changes occurred in each of the three sample states (Delaware, Kansas, and Tennessee) in which malapportionment had created huge nonmetropolitan majorities in the legislature although metropolitan areas contained a majority or nearly a majority of the population of the state. In New Jersey, malapportionment had discriminated against central city counties in the Senate and to a slight degree against suburban areas in both chambers, but a metropolitan majority had been retained in both houses; second-level changes there were less profound and more ambiguous than those in Delaware, Kansas, and Tennessee. Second-level changes were almost nonexistent in the well apportioned states of Oregon and South Dakota. A catalogue of the second-level effects which appeared in the six sample states would include the following: (1) an increase in the central city/county representation in the legislature (most significantly in Tennessee and Kansas); (2) an increase in suburban representation in the legislature (most dramatically in Delaware, but also in New Jersey); (3) an increase in the number of black legislators as a result of greater central city representation and subdistricting of central city counties (Tennessee, Kansas and New Jersey); (4) a decline in the percentage of farmers in the legislature as a result of reduced nonmetropolitan representation (Kansas, Tennessee, and probably Delaware); (5) the emergence of viable two-party competition for legislative control as a result of reapportionment which favored the minority party's areas of greatest strength (Tennessee and, to a lesser extent, Kansas); (6) a shift in partisan control of the legislature (perhaps Delaware and New Jersey, although reapportionment was not the only influence at work; also Tennessee, one house only); (7) an increase in the success of the minority party in some counties as a result of subdistricting of county-wide multimember districts (Tennessee and New Jersey);

(8) a change in intraparty legislative majorities from nonmetropolitan to metropolitan (both parties in Tennessee and the Democratic party in Kansas); and (9) a reduction in the power of county party chairmen to control slating of legislative candidates as a result of subdistricting of county-wide districts (New Jersey and Tennessee).

Generally, the impact of changes at the third level of effects did not match the strength of changes at the second level because second-level changes were diluted by the influence of institutional forces in the legislature. In Tennessee, for example, the increases in central city representation in standing committee chairmanships fell far short of central city gains in legislative representation. Internal party factors played a greater role in determining committee chairmen in Delaware and New Jersey than did the relative representation of central city, suburban, and nonmetropolitan constituencies after reapportionment. However, it is evident that reapportionment did lead to a number of third-level changes including the following: (1) an increase in central city representation in committee chairmanships (Kansas especially, but also Tennessee); (2) an increase in suburban representation in committee chairmanships (Kansas, Delaware, and New Jersey); (3) an increase in the number of chamber leaders from central city areas (Tennessee); (4) a reduction in the number of standing committees (all sample states except New Jersey); (5) a modification of standing committee power (New Jersey) or interim committee power (Kansas); (6) an increase in urban-rural conflict in the legislature after reapportionment (Kansas, perhaps Oregon and South Dakota); (7) an increase in urban-suburban conflict (New Jersey); (8) an increase in partisan conflict (Kansas, but especially Tennessee, where the postreapportionment surge in Republican legislative representation led to a sharp rise in the salience of partisan divisions); (9) a slight decline in partisan conflict (perhaps Delaware and New Jersey, where partisan conflict was extremely high prior to reapportionment (expansion of legislative membership, the influx of new members, and changes in urban-rural and urban-suburban conflict may have reduced party cohesion in postreapportionment legislatures); and (10) the elimination of the party caucus (New Jersey Assembly—this may have contributed to the decline in partisan conflict).

Examination of third-level effects has indicated that the distribution of legislative leadership positions among legislators from central

city, suburban, and nonmetropolitan constituencies and the patterns
of legislative conflict underwent less substantial change than might
have been expected on the basis of second-level effects. In Kansas,
nonmetropolitan legislators continued to constitute a majority in the
dominant Republican party and controlled most leadership positions
in committees and chambers after reapportionment, despite strong
central city and suburban gains. Central city legislators in Tennessee
experienced some difficulty in obtaining a fair share of leadership
positions after reapportionment; it is also likely that partisan splits
among metropolitan legislators helped neutralize potential metropolitan-nonmetropolitan divisions in the Tennessee legislature. Despite
some apparent reduction in party conflict after reapportionment,
partisan divisions continued to dominate legislative conflict in Delaware and New Jersey into the early 1970s; in addition, party leadership in both parties tended to come from the same constituency areas
before and after reapportionment. In neither Oregon nor South
Dakota did notable shifts appear in legislative power or conflict as a
result of reapportionement.

On the basis of the analysis of third-level effects in the six
sample states, one might expect that fourth-level effects would
have been rather limited. In all six sample states many legislators
surveyed in 1973 believed that reapportionment had affected a
wide array of policies; their observations do not, however, provide
a measure of the effect of reapportionment relative to other factors affecting policy. The evidence presented suggests that reapportionment has affected selected policies in all sample states, but
that the overall influence of reapportionment on policy has been
rather limited and immeasurable. Among the fourth-level effects
noted in the analysis were the following: (1) a distribution of state
expenditures more favorable to central city counties (most clearly
in Kansas); (2) a distribution of state expenditures more favorable
to central cities (Kansas, perhaps Delaware, New Jersey, South
Dakota, and Tennessee); (3) generally more liberal policies (for
example higher taxes perhaps) which are possibly attributable to
the displacement of nonmetropolitan legislators by metropolitan
legislators (all six states); (4) a modification of regulatory policies
with respect to liquor, for example (Kansas); (5) possibly, a less
favorable climate for agricultural interests (Kansas, Oregon, and
South Dakota); and (6) possibly, a more favorable climate for labor interests (all states).

Reapportionment in the Six Sample States: Conclusions

Reapportionment produced the most extensive changes in Tennessee and Kansas, the two states in which malapportionment had severely discriminated against metropolitan areas which included a near majority of the population. In both states, reapportionment was associated with very high turnover (although not higher than usual in Tennessee), a decline in the percentage of farmer-legislators, an increase in the number of black legislators, and an increase in the legislative representation of the minority party (the Republican party in Tennessee and the Democratic party in Kansas) as a result of expanded central city county representation. In Tennessee, the gains of the Republican party following reapportionment marked the emergence of viable two-party competition for control of the legislature. The impact of reapportionment on party competition in Kansas was less dramatic partly because competitive metropolitan constituencies accounted for a lesser proportion of the legislature in Kansas than in Tennessee. The metropolitan population of Kansas is more suburban than the metropolitan population of Tennessee, and Republican gains in suburban Kansas helped to offset Democratic gains in central cities.

It is important to note that both Democrats and Republicans in Kansas and Tennessee became more central city-oriented after reapportionment. In Tennessee, central city counties accounted for about the same proportion of representation within each party's legislative delegation (more than 40 percent). In contrast, the dominant Republican party in Kansas remained solidly nonmetropolitan after reapportionment. Within the Democratic party, however, a metropolitan majority emerged after reapportionment. These patterns of intraparty representation apparently influenced the nature of legislative conflict in both states. Partisan conflict in Tennessee increased substantially following reapportionment largely because of the greater number of Republicans. Urban-rural conflict as perceived by the legislators rose in the Senate and declined in the House after reapportionment. It seems likely, however, that given the distribution of urban and rural elements between the two parties and the perceived intensity of partisan conflict, party divisions moderated urban-rural splits at least in the House. In Kansas, it appears that both urban-rural and Democratic-Republican divisions intensified after reapportionment because the two patterns of conflict reinforced one another.

Regarding legislative procedure and organization, reapportionment brought about greater representation of central city legislators in standing committee chairmanships in both states, although to a greater extent in Kansas than in Tennessee. Reapportionment contributed to the election of three central city chamber leaders after 1965 in Tennessee, but chamber leadership in Kansas remained wholly nonmetropolitan after reapportionment. In both states, reapportionment may have been related to the reduction in the number of standing committees and, in Kansas, to the elimination of the Legislative Council.

As noted in the previous chapter, reapportionment apparently produced a more liberal policy environment in the Kansas and Tennessee legislatures in the view of legislators. In particular in Kansas, according to data on expenditures and legislative activity, reapportionment resulted in central city counties receiving a larger share of state aid to local governments and in central cities receiving a larger portion of state aid to municipalities. The expected major changes in the distribution of state expenditures in Tennessee did not materialize, although slightly higher percentages of state aid were directed to central city counties and central cities after reapportionment. Changes in other specific policy areas were difficult to pinpoint, although reapportionment apparently altered some regulatory policies (for example liquor-by-the-drink), highway policy, and welfare policy in Kansas.

As in Kansas and Tennessee, malapportionment had resulted in a significant level of metropolitan underrepresentation in the Delaware legislature. Although central city counties benefited most from reapportionment in Kansas and Tennessee, a suburban majority replaced a nonmetropolitan one following reapportionment in Delaware. Reapportionment in Delaware created higher legislative turnover, partly because of the expansion in the membership of both the Senate and the House and probably contributed to the reduction in the number of farmer-legislators. In a state already strongly two-party, Republicans appeared to be the immediate beneficiaries of expanded representation for the suburbs as they won control of the legislature in the late 1960s. Internally, the Republican party changed little since reapportionment made a predominately suburban delegation even more suburban. Reapportionment had little effect on the Democratic party, although suburban representation increased slightly.

With respect to legislative organization, reapportionment had far less effect on the distribution of committee and chamber leadership positions among various constituency types than did changes in party control of the legislature but reapportionment did result in a greater percentage of suburban committee chairmen. An analysis of roll call data and legislators' perceptions suggests that suburban and central city legislators of both parties may have been closer on some issues than were metropolitan and nonmetropolitan legislators within parties in the sessions following reapportionment. This pattern, if accurately described, would lend support to other bits of evidence hinting at a slight decline in partisan conflict, at least in the House, following reapportionment; it would less easily explain the observed decline in urban-rural conflict although this could be attributed to the diminished strength of nonmetropolitan representation.

The effects of reapportionment on policy change in Delaware are rather obscure. While Delaware legislators in 1973 believed reapportionment led to more liberal policies, this opinion was expressed by legislators in all six sample states. The dramatic shift in the distribution of state funds which occurred in Kansas after reapportionment did not materialize in Delaware partly because neither New Castle County nor Wilmington City were significantly underfunded in relation to population prior to reapportionment. However, an increasing percentage of state urban aid went to the city of Wilmington in the late 1960s and early 1970s even as the city came to represent a smaller proportion of the state's municipal population and suffered a decline in legislative representation. While the growing bloc of suburban legislators may have been more sympathetic to the problems of the central city of Wilmington than the nonmetropolitan legislators whom they displaced, it is more likely that national and state concern with the "urban crisis" rather than with reapportionment promoted the policy changes. It is also possible that durable two-party competition in Delaware, where each party could win seats in central city, suburban, and nonmetropolitan constituencies and where a party's chances of controlling the legislature depended on success in all three areas, contributed to a fairly even-handed and responsive distribution of state aid before and after reapportionment.

In New Jersey, where malapportionment did not overrepresent nonmetropolitan areas to the extent noted in Delaware, reapportionment produced mixed effects including some changes in policy. Established central city counties benefited from increased Senate representation following reapportionment in the mid-1960s while suburban areas made slight gains in the Senate and more substantial gains in the Assembly. As later reapportionment activity brought legislative districts in line with more current population figures, established central city counties suffered a decline in representation—a circumstance especially evident in post-1970 apportionment plans—while suburbs continued to gain. The enhanced legislative representation of suburban areas contributed to a Republican resurgence in the late 1960s, but was by no means the sole factor which contributed to the success of the Republicans. Many of the most important changes associated with reapportionment were exacerbated by the expansion in the membership of both the Senate and Assembly. Among the effects magnified by the expansion were the very high turnover, the reduction in level of legislators' experience, an enlarged number of standing committees, and a decline in legislative party cohesion. Subdistricting of populous counties contributed to the election of a greater number of black legislators and to a diminution in the control of county party organizations over legislative candidates—a development perhaps related to the reduced legislative party cohesion. Reapportionment may have contributed to the strengthening of standing committees by producing a huge influx of reform-oriented and younger legislators. As in Delaware, the distribution of committee and chamber leadership positions in New Jersey was little affected by reapportionment. Neither did reapportionment alter the dominance of suburban interests within the Republican legislative delegation nor the orientation of the Democratic party toward the central city. Regarding policy, reapportionment produced no major changes. This is not surprising in light of the absence of significant internal changes in the two major parties. Reapportionment may have liberalized policy by reducing the percentage of nonmetropolitan legislators. It may have also altered the distribution of aid, although this is not clear. Established central city counties gained a greater share of aid in the face of declining representation, while suburban areas gained a greater share of legislative seats but received a smaller portion of aid. The nature of party competition in New Jersey probably mandates that both parties cast broad-based appeals to all constituencies, and this leads to a pattern of aid distribution not strictly accounted for by the representative strength of various constituencies in the legislature. This explanation is in accord with the proposition in chapter one that reapportionment would have less impact on two-party states than on one-party states.

In Oregon and South Dakota, the two sample states in which malapportionment was least severe, reapportionment produced less extensive changes than those evidenced in the other four states. Reapportionment led to higher turnover in the short run, but did not produce significant alterations in partisan fortunes, intraparty power, or chamber and committee leadership. Higher turnover may have created a legislative membership more sympathetic to some reforms such as the reduction in the number of standing committees. While Oregon and South Dakota legislators perceived greater urban-rural conflict after reapportionment, it is doubtful that reapportionment resulted in more than slight variations in traditional patterns of legislative conflict. Legislators in both states believed reapportionment had liberalized policy, and there is evidence that reapportionment produced a slight modification in the distribution of state expenditures. A final point of note is that the conversion in 1972 to single-member districting in central city counties in Oregon apparently expanded the opportunities for legislative candidacies, but it did not bring expected Republican gains in Multnomah County (Portland).

Reapportionment: Final Considerations

A review of the impact of reapportionment in the six sample states requires some comment about the implications of this study of six states for all states in general. The examination of the sample states has reinforced the major propositions about the effects of reapportionment as set out in chapter one. It is not surprising that the impact of reapportionment apparently has been more extensive in those states more severely malapportioned prior to *Baker* and *Reynolds* than in states less severely malapportioned. An analysis of the six sample states confirms the White-Thomas thesis that reapportionment would have its strongest impact in those states in which malapportionment had created an artificial rural majority in the legislature (although the present research dealt with metropolitan and nonmetropolitan areas rather than urban and rural areas and thus deviated from the White-Thomas analysis). An important refinement of their general proposition would recognize that the impact of reapportionment among those states in which urban interests were severely underrepresented by malapportionment has apparently been greater in those states in which central city areas were more prominently underrepresented than suburban areas (for example, Kansas and Tennessee) as opposed to those states in which suburban areas were more severely discriminated against (for example, Delaware).

This study of the sample states also suggests that reapportionment has led to less profound changes in two-party states such as Delaware than in modified one-party states such as Kansas and Tennessee. This holds true even when the two-party and one-party states compared exhibited similar degrees of malapportionment prior to 1962. This pattern tends to underline the mediating and moderating influence of two-party politics on the impact of reapportionment. It is possible that two-party politics itself signals that a broad range of diverse political interests are already represented in government and makes it less likely that reapportionment will bring interests to the political arena which are not already represented. The experience of Kansas and Tennessee suggests that in some modified one-party states reapportionment has produced a wider representation of interests which has led to more competitive party politics. The fact that two-party states tended to be *less* severely malapportioned prior to *Baker* and *Reynolds* (as noted in chapter one) points to the possible link between fair apportionment and party competition.

It could be argued, however, that reapportionment has proved more significant in closely competitive two-party states, in which redistricting enabled the minority party to win control of the legislature by gaining a few additional seats than in a modified one-party or solid one-party state where even a substantial increase in seats for the minority party left it short of control of the legislature. The cases of two-party Delaware and New Jersey constitute evidence against this view. While reapportionment may have aided Republican ascendancy in both state legislatures in the late 1960s, other forces, including the Nixon tide and statewide issues favorable to Republicans contributed perhaps more substantially to the success of the GOP. Reapportionment conferred no permanent advantage on Republicans, however, as Democrats gained strength in the suburbs and returned to control of the legislatures in the mid-1970s. Finally, the evidence on policy changes in these two states indicates that reapportionment led to less substantial modifications in patterns of expenditures than in a modified one-party state such as Kansas.

A second issue relating party competition and reapportionment concerns not the varying effects of redistricting on one-party and two-party states, but the possible influence of future reapportionment activity on two-party politics in general. Slumping Republican fortunes in Congress, state legislatures, and governorships may decline even further if the Democratic party maintains its present control over state legislatures and governorships into the early 1980s.[1] Democrats would then be in a position to extend their dominance by drawing favorable districting plans for both congressional and state seats in the legislatures during reapportionment activity which will follow the 1980 census. Of course, the actual electoral advantage which will accrue to the party in command of the redistricting process varies with political circumstances and may change significantly in the next few years. Nevertheless, the prospect of Democratic-dictated reapportionment for most congressional and state seats in the legislatures must be a matter of deep concern for Republican leaders.

Apart from these residual considerations concerning reapportionment and party competition, a final issue must be addressed. An examination of the impact of reapportionment ultimately touches on the larger question of whether the United States Supreme Court's entry into the "political thicket" of state legislative apportionment has been justified by the results produced. Has the "reapportionment revolution," described by the late Chief Justice Earl Warren as the most significant set of decisions during his tenure on the Court,[2] been worth the time and effort involved in implementation and the high cost in terms of state autonomy within the federal system? Nathan Glazer, drawing on the work of Ward E. Y. Elliott,[3] has answered this question in the negative.

> At first it was believed that a strict reapportionment of electoral districts on the basis of one man to one vote would shift some power to the cities or to the minorities who lived in them. Quite early it became clear it would not—at best it would help the conservative suburbs. In the event it turned out that it had almost no consequence at all. An ideological exercise was nevertheless carried out by those who thought they knew better, or who simply wanted to clean up the messiness of history . . . unfortunately at the cost of stripping away the last shred of pretense that states had some degree of sovereignty, and by losing great stores of respect for the neutrality and objectivity of the courts.[4]

In contrast to Glazer, Robert B. McKay has argued that malapportionment prior to *Baker* and *Reynolds* jeopardized "the integrity of representative government in many instances." McKay suggested in 1968 that reapportionment of state legislatures had contributed to perceivable changes in state policies including "increased aid for schools, greater home rule, increased consumer protection, stronger civil rights legislation, curbs on air and water pollution, and reform of criminal justice." [5]

A common element in the opinions of Glazer and McKay is the view that judicial involvement in state legislative apportionment can be partly justified to the extent that the "one man, one vote" principle has led to discernible, presumably salutary changes in the legislative process.[6] Reapportioned legislatures ought to be more responsive, at least more equally responsive to all voters and policies adopted by legislatures ought to be better, or at least different from those adopted by malapportioned legislatures. Whatever the abstract constitutional validity of "one man, one vote," implementation of the equal-population standard is a worthwhile enterprise only if it has practical political consequences. The individuals and groups initiating suits against malapportioned legislatures were less concerned with the assertion of a principle than with the achievement, through court-ordered reapportionment, of real political gains—initially greater legislative representation, ultimately more favorable legislative enactments. Reapportionment surely has involved the assertion of the Supreme Court that equal influence at the polls is a fundamental constitutional right. But if the right is truly fundamental and thus important, the securing of the right in cases in which it was previously abridged should lead to perceivable changes in the governing process.

The research presented here has attempted to address the consequences of reapportionment. In addition, the findings bear on the questions of whether reapportionment has been worth the trouble or whether "one man, one vote" is, in Alexander Bickel's words, "at best a triviality." [7] The evidence indicates that reapportionment has affected legislative politics in the six states studied, although all states have not been affected equally or similarly. In no state examined did redistricting yield political changes of the sort that would justify the characterization of "reapportionment revolution."

However, the full impact of the so-called reapportionment revolution is yet to be realized. Because the Supreme Court's rulings in *Baker, Reynolds,* and subsequent cases mandate periodic redistricting to bring legislative districts in line with population changes, legislative apportionment in the coming years can provide little protection to those political interests which suffer a declining population base. This situation is in sharp contrast to the half century before *Baker* when malapportionment entrenched conservative and rural elements in the face of adverse population trends. The gains to central cities in states such as Delaware and New Jersey manifested in the first wave of redistricting following *Baker* and *Reynolds* have already been undermined by suburban gains in more recent reapportionment plans. The Court's decisions, which require continual adjustment of legislative districts, have added an element of continual change and uncertainty to the politics of state legislatures.

Notes

1. In 1977 Democrats controlled both state legislative chambers in thirty-six states, governorships in thirty-seven states, and both the legislature and the governorship in twenty-one states. Republicans controlled both legislative chambers in five states, only one of which had a Republican governor. Matt Pinkers, "Democrats Still Control Most State Legislatures," *Congressional Quarterly Weekly Report* 34 (1976): 3162-63. In the 1978 elections, Republicans made inroads into the Democratic dominance of state legislatures. "The gains ... gave the GOP control of thirteen legislatures plus one-house majorities in eleven more—enough to provide gerrymander insurance in nearly half the nation overnight." Quoted from "The New Tilt," *Newsweek* 92 (November 20, 1978): 46.
2. "Warren Calls Vote Rulings Most Important," *New York Times,* 27 June 1969, pp. 1, 17.
3. Elliott, esp. pp. 166-70. Elliott argues that the Supreme Court's decisions dealing with reapportionment suffer from an ideological imposition of a simplistic doctrine, "one man, one vote," on the extremely complex process of representation. He recognizes that the worst cases of malapportionment required judicial intervention, while he rejects the general intervention into virtually every legislative situation (Congress, state legislatures, and local governing boards) compelled by the equal vote principle as defined by the Supreme Court. For related views, see esp. Raoul Berger, *Government By Judiciary: The Transformation of the Fourteenth Amendment* (Cambridge, Mass.: Harvard University Press, 1977), pp. 69-98, 263-64, 419-27. Amassing evidence on the intent of the framers of the Fourteenth Amendment, Berger asserts that the Warren Court wrongly construed the "equal protection" clause to embrace problems of apportionment.
4. Nathan Glazer, "Towards an Imperial Judiciary?" *The Public Interest,* no. 41 (Fall 1975): pp. 120-21.
5. Robert B. McKay, "Reapportionment: Success Story of the Warren Court," *Michigan Law Review* 67 (1968): 223-36, as quoted pp. 226

and 230-31. See also Carl A. Auerbach, "Commentary," in *Reapportionment in the 1970s,* pp. 74-90.

6. Chief Justice Warren himself believed that a beneficial consequence of court-ordered reapportionment was the prospect that redistricted state legislatures would be more responsive to the problems of cities. "Warren Calls Vote Rulings Most Vital," p. 17.

7. Alexander Bickel, "The Supreme Court and Reapportionment," in *Reapportionment in the 1970s,* p. 69.

Appendix A

The 1973 Questionnaire Survey of State Legislators

The questionnaire on reapportionment, together with a cover letter explaining the purpose of the survey, was sent to every legislator serving in the six sample state legislatures in 1973.[1] About three weeks after the initial mailing, legislators who had not responded to the questionnaire were sent a follow-up postcard repeating the request for their participation in the survey.

The questionnaire asked legislators to indicate their perceptions of the effects of reapportionment on their respective legislatures regarding the areas of concern treated in the text. The questionnaire approached reapportionment as a single process beginning with redistricting activity stimulated by the Supreme Court's rulings of the early 1960s and continuing through the redistricting activity of the early 1970s. Generally, responses to the questionnaire indicated that this conception of reapportionment is a valid one in the sense that it elicited meaningful replies. Of greater methodological significance is the problem of addressing the questionnaire only to members of the 1973 legislatures. While a large number of 1973 legislators would not have served in the legislatures at the height of the reapportionment activity in the 1960s, it was assumed that they could at least claim direct familiarity with the post-1970 activity. In addition, they would have an informed awareness of the implications of the implementation of the "one man, one vote" mandate of the 1960s. (Just over half of the respondents in Delaware, New Jersey, South Dakota and Tennessee had served three years or less in the legislature; for Kansas and for Oregon the figure was about 44 percent. The percentage of legislators with seven or more years of experience ranged between 22 percent and 31 percent for all states except Oregon, from which about 4 percent of the respondents had served seven or more years.) Although the inclusion of both past and current legislators for the entire period of 1959-74 would have enhanced the merit of the survey, it also would have made the project prohibitively costly. There is reason to believe, moreover, that a survey of former legislators would have been unproductive. In Best's 1969 survey of Washington state legislators, the response rate of former legislators was less than half the rate for legislators in office.[2]

The response rates for all of the sample states appear in Table A-1; the rates vary from a high of 53 percent in Kansas to a low of 33 percent in Tennessee. The use of some open-ended questions probably contributed to the survey's achievement of a modest overall response rate of 43 percent.[3] However, the open-ended questions also produced occasional perceptive and detailed replies from obviously thoughtful observers of the legislature's activities.[4] Because this study focuses on the effects of reapportionment, as opposed to legislators' perceptions of its effects, the quality of responses weighs more heavily in the analysis than the sheer number of responses.

The questionnaire on reapportionment is reprinted on the following pages.

Coding No._____

Questionnaire on Reapportionment

The following questions attempt to elicit your perceptions of changes which may have taken place in your legislature as a result of reapportionment activity since the application of the "one man, one vote" standard in the mid-sixties. Even if you have been in the legislature for only a short time and may feel unqualified to talk about changes which might have occurred prior to your elec-

TABLE A-1

Response Rates to Mail Questionnaire on Reapportionment

	Total Number of Seats in Legislature	Total Responses[a]	Response Rate[a]
Delaware	62	26	42%
Kansas	165	87	53%
New Jersey	120	45	38%[b]
Oregon	90	39	43%
South Dakota	105	53	50%
Tennessee	132	43	33%[c]

[a]Usable questionnaires numbered 25 in Delaware, 86 in Kansas, 44 in New Jersey, 39 in Oregon, 52 in South Dakota, and 42 in Tennessee.

[b]Only 117 members were listed for the New Jersey Legislature at the time the questionnaire was sent. Percentage is based on 117.

[c]Only 129 members were listed in the Tennessee General Assembly when the questionnaire was sent. Percentage is based on 129.

tion, your responses are still very valuable because of your overall familiarity and association with your state's politics.

"Reapportionment," within the context of this questionnaire, refers to all redistricting changes which have taken place in your legislature since 1962. It is meant to include redistricting done in the 1960s, as well as the redistricting action following the 1970 Census. In this regard, I hope you will pay particular attention to question #11.

1. What year were you first elected to this house of the legislature?_____

2. In your opinion, has reapportionment had any effects on this legislature since the *Baker* v. *Carr* decision? If yes, please indicate the changes that have occurred as a result of reapportionment? If you believe that reapportionment has pro-

duced little or no change, please indicate why it has had little effect? (Use back if needed.)

3. What are the three most important sources of differences in your chamber, in rank-order? (1=most important; 3=least important)

_____Republicans v.   _____Region v. Region
Democrats
_____Urban v. Rural   _____Liberal v. Conservative
Legislators
_____Urban v. Suburban   _____Pro-Governor v. Anti-
Governor
_____Big City v. Small City _____Pro-Labor v. Anti-Labor
_____Other (please specify)_____ _

4. What effect, if any, has reapportionment had upon the various kinds of differences within your chamber? Please check appropriate boxes.

	Greatly Increased	Some Increase	No Effect	Some Decrease	Greatly Decreased
Partisan					
Urban-Rural					
Big City-Small City					
Regional					
Liberal-Conservative					
Pro v. Anti-Governor					
Pro v. Anti-Labor					
Other (specify)					

5. What legislative issues, if any, have been affected by reapportionment? List.

   1. _____   3. _____
   2. _____   4. _____

6. Has reapportionment had any effect upon procedure or organization within your chamber? (e.g., committee organization, selection of committee chairmen)
   Yes_____ No_____ Don't Know_____
   If yes, can you indicate the changes that have taken place?

7. Has reapportionment had any effect upon the distribution of influence within your party?
   Yes_____ No_____ Don't Know_____
   If yes, can you indicate the changes? (e.g., more influence for the urban wing or liberal wing of party, etc.)

8. Has reapportionment led to increased or decreased pressure on you from interest groups? (e.g., urban-based interests, labor interests, etc.)
   Increased_____ Decreased_____ No Change_____ Don't Know_____
   If increased, can you name any of the groups that have increased pressure?
   1. _____   2. _____
   If decreased, can you name any of the groups that have decreased pressure?
   1. _____   2. _____

9. Do you believe that reapportionment has had any observable effect upon the kinds of legislation *adopted* in your chamber?
   Yes_____ No_____ Don't Know_____
   If yes, what effect have you observed?

10. Do you believe that reapportionment has had any observable effect upon the kinds of legislation *introduced* in your chamber?
    Yes_____ No_____ Don't Know_____
    If yes, what effect have you observed?

11. Has the redistricting which took place after the 1970 Census had any effects different from the redistricting activity of the mid-sixties?
    Yes_____ No_____ Don't Know_____
    If yes, can you elaborate?

12. Were you an incumbent in the most recent state legislative elections?
    Yes_____ No_____

If yes, did the redistricting which took place following the Census affect your chances for reelection? (e.g., perhaps by altering your district, affecting competition in primary or general election, etc.)

Yes_____ No_____ Don't Know_____

If yes, can you elaborate?

Notes

1. Addresses for legislators were obtained from *The Book of the States, 1972-73; Supplement I: State Elective Officials and the Legislatures* (Lexington, Ky.: Council of State Governments, 1973), pp. 31-32, 49-51, 86-88, 101-3, and 112-15.
2. Best, "Impact of Reapportionment on Washington," p. 152.
3. Other analyses employing multistate mail surveys of state legislators include the following: Wayne Francis, *Legislative Issues;* Cory M. Rosen, "Legislative Influence and Policy Orientation in American State Legislatures," *American Journal of Political Science* 18 (1974): 681-92: Douglas C. Chaffey, "The Institutionalization of State Legislatures: A Comparative Study," *Western Political Quarterly* 23 (1970): 180-96; and Eric M. Uslaner and Ronald E. Weber, *Patterns of Decision-Making in State Legislatures* (New York: Praeger Special Studies, 1977). Response rates ranged from 58 percent in Rosen's four-state study to 38 percent in the Uslaner-Weber fifty-state analysis.
4. On this point, see Rosenthal, *Legislative Performance*, pp. 40-41.

Appendix B

Sources for Data on the Six Sample State Legislatures

The following listing provides a complete breakdown of state documents used in compiling the tables analyzing the impact of reapportionment in the six sample states. For each state, citations are organized according to the type of information provided. The categories of information include the following:

1. District Classification (that is, central city, suburban, non-metropolitan), also including partisan divisions (Tables 1-3, 3-1, 3-2, 4-1, 4-2, 6-1, 6-2, C-1, C-5, C-6)
2. Membership Turnover, including legislative experience (Tables 2-1, 2-2, and C-3)
3. Biographical Data (Table C-4)
4. Standing Committee Chairmen, including number of committees (Tables 4-1, 4-3, C-6)
5. Chamber Leadership (Table 4-2).

Apart from the state documents noted below, data for the district classification were obtained from John Clements, *Taylor's Encyclopedia of Government Officials: Federal and State*, vol. 4, 1973-74 (Dallas: Political Research, Inc., 1973), pp. 68-69, 88-89, 120-21, 136-37, 146-47, and 148-49; and National Municipal League, *Ap-*

portionment in the Nineteen Sixties, rev. ed. (New York: National Municipal League, 1970), sections on Delaware, Kansas, New Jersey, Oregon, South Dakota, and Tennessee.

Delaware

District Classification, Membership Turnover, and Chamber Leadership

Arden Ellsworth Bing, Delaware Blue Book, 1957-58 (Milford, Del.: Milford Chronicle Publishing Co., 1958), p. 130-69.

Delaware, Secretary of State, Delaware State Manual: 1959, pp. 9-10..(Subsequent references are cited as Manual.)

Manual: 1962, pp. 9-10.

Manual: 1963, pp. 9-10.

Manual: 1965, pp. 9-10.

Manual: 1967, pp. 9-11.

Manual: 1969, pp. 9-11.

Manual: 1971-72, pp. 14-16.

Manual: 1973-74, pp. 20-36.

Delaware, State Legislature, Senate, Journal of the State Senate, 1961 Session, p. 2. (Subsequent references are cited as Senate Journal.)

Senate Journal, 1965 Session, p. 2.

Senate Journal, 1967 Session, p. 2.

Senate Journal, 1969 Session, p. 2.

Senate Journal, 1971 Session, p. 2.

Delaware, State Legislature, House of Representatives, Journal of the State House of Representatives, 1959 Session, p. iv. (Subsequent references are cited as House Journal.)

House Journal, 1961 Session, pp. iii-iv.

House Journal, 1965 Session, p. iii.

House Journal, 1967 Session, pp. iii-iv.

House Journal, 1969 Session, pp. 3-4, 9-10.

House Journal, 1971 Session, pp. 5-6.

Biographical Data

Bing, Delaware Blue Book: 1957-58, pp. 130-69.

Manual: 1973-74, pp. 20-36.

Standing Committee Chairmen

(Note: An asterisk indicates that the citation was provided by the Delaware Legislative Council which also supplied a list of Senate Standing Committee Chairmen for 1965 and 1971.)

Senate Journal, 1959 Session, pp. 27-28.*

Senate Journal, 1961 Session, pp. 23-24.

Senate Journal, 1963 Session, pp. 10-11.*
Senate Journal, 1967 Session, pp. 19-20.
Senate Journal, 1969 Session, pp. 6-7.
Senate Journal, 1973 Session, pp. 10-11.*
House Journal, 1959 Session, pp. v-vi.
House Journal, 1961 Session, pp. v-vi.
House Journal, 1963 Session, pp. vii-viii.*
House Journal, 1965 Session, pp. v-vi.
House Journal, 1967 Session, pp. 5-6.
House Journal, 1969 Session, pp. 11-16.
House Journal, 1971 Session, prefatory pages.
House Journal, 1973 Session, pp. 3-4.

Kansas

District Classification, Membership Turnover, Biographical Data, Standing Committee Chairmen, and Chamber Leadership
   Kansas, State Legislature, *Proceedings of the Legislature,* 1955 Session, pp. vii, xxxiii-xxxv.
   Kansas, Secretary of State, *Kansas Directory: 1957-1958,* pp. 38-41. (Subsequent references are cited as *Directory.*)
   Kansas, State Legislature, Senate, *Proceedings of the Senate,* 1959 Session, pp. vi-viii, xxi-xxii. (Subsequent references are cited as *Senate Proceedings.*)
   Senate Proceedings, 1961 Session, pp. vi-vii, xxi-xxii.
   Senate Proceedings, 1963 Session, pp. vi-vii, xxi-xxii.
   Senate Proceedings, 1965 Session, pp. vi-vii, xxi-xxii.
   Senate Proceedings, 1967 Session, pp. vi-vii, xxi.
   Senate Proceedings, 1969 Session, pp. vi-vii, xxi.
   Senate Proceedings, 1971 Session, pp. vi-vii, xxvii.
   Senate Proceedings, 1973 Session, pp. vi-vii, xxi.
   Kansas, State Legislature, House, *Proceedings of the Senate,* 1959 Session, pp. xxx-xxxvi, xlix-1. (Subsequent references are cited as *House Proceedings.*)
   House Proceedings, 1961 Session, pp. xxxii-xxxviii-li-lii.
   House Proceedings, 1963 Session, pp. xxxii-xxxviii, lii-liii.
   House Proceedings, 1965 Session, pp. xxxii-xxxix, liii-liv.
   House Proceedings, 1967 Session, pp. xxxi-xxxvii, lxiii-lxiv.
   House Proceedings, 1969 Session, pp. xxxii-xxxv, l-li.
   House Proceedings, 1971 Session, pp. xxxiii-xxxviii, lxiv-lxv.
   House Proceedings, 1973 Session, pp. xxxii-xxxvi, lxii-lxiii.
District Classification Only
   Directory: 1959-1969, pp. 120-24.

Directory: 1961, pp. 120, 123-24.
Directory: 1963-64, pp. 130-35.
Directory: 1967-68, pp. 149-60.
Directory: 1973, pp. 179-90.

New Jersey

District Classification, Membership Turnover, Biographical Data, Standing Committee Chairmen, and Chamber Leadership
New Jersey, State Legislature, Manual of the Legislature of New Jersey: 1960, pp. 162-205, 360-408, 725-33. (Subsequent references are cited as Manual.)
Manual: 1962, pp. 179-226, 388-435, 772-80.
Manual: 1964, pp. 187-219, 392-439, 793-800.
Manual: 1966, pp. 157-84, 360-410, 754-59.
Manual: 1968, pp. 166-67, 172-75, 353-418, 810-17.
Manual: 1970, pp. 169-70, 193-97, 374-440, 812-18.
Manual: 1972, pp. 171-72, 197-98, 368-432, 868-72.
Manual: 1974, pp. 176-183, 342-403, 888-90, 894-98.

Oregon

District Classification, Membership Turnover, and Biographical Data
Oregon, Secretary of State, Oregon Blue Book: 1959-60, pp. 24-33. (Subsequent references are cited as Blue Book.)
Blue Book: 1961-62, pp. 22-31, 39.
Blue Book: 1963-64, pp. 22-32.
Blue Book: 1965-66, pp. 22-32.
Blue Book: 1967-68, pp. 55-65.
Blue Book: 1969-70, pp. 74-84.
Blue Book: 1971-72, pp. 83-94.
Blue Book: 1973-74, pp. 82-92.
Standing Committee Chairmen and Chamber Leadership
Oregon, Legislative Assembly, Journals and Calendars of the Senate and House, 1959 Regular Session, pp. 4-8. (Subsequent references are cited as Journals.)
Journals, 1961 Regular Session, pp. 3-7.
Journals, 1963 Regular Session, pp. 4-10
Journals, 1965 Regular Session, pp. 7-11.
Journals, 1967 Regular Session, pp. 7-9, 11-14.
Journals, 1969 Regular Session, pp. 7-9, 13-16.

Journals, 1971 Regular Session, pp. 7-10, 12-15.
Journals, 1973 Regular Session, pp. vii-ix, viii-xv.

South Dakota

*District Classification, Membership Turnover, Biographical Data
and Chamber Leadership*
South Dakota, Department of Finance, *South Dakota Legislative
Manual: 1959,* pp. 456-95. (Subsequent references are cited as
Manual. Beginning in 1971, the *Manual* was published by South
Dakota Department of Administration.)
Manual: 1961, pp. 435-74.
Manual: 1963, pp. 427-67.
Manual: 1965, pp. 109-47.
Manual: 1967, pp. 132-70.
Manual: 1969, pp. 284-322.
Manual: 1971, pp. 107-43.
Manual: 1973, pp. 139-74.
Standing Committee Chairmen and Chamber Leadership
(Note: An asterisk indicates that the citation was supplied by
the South Dakota State Legislative Research Council.)
South Dakota, State Legislature, Senate, *Proceedings of the Sen-
ate,* 1959 Session, pp. 33-34.* (Subsequent references are cited as
Senate Proceedings.)
Senate Proceedings, 1961 Session, pp. 2-4, 28-29.
Senate Proceedings, 1963 Session, pp. 2-3, 18-19.
Senate Proceedings, 1965 Session, pp. 32-33.*
Senate Proceedings, 1967 Session, pp. 13-14.*
Senate Proceedings, 1969 Session, pp. 2-3, 5-12.
Senate Proceedings, 1971 Session, pp. 2-3, 17, 51-52.
Senate Proceedings, 1973 Session, pp. 2-3, 12, 19-21.
South Dakota, State Legislature, House, *Proceedings of the
House,* 1959 Session, pp. 41-43.* (Subsequent references are
cited as *House Proceedings.)*
House Proceedings, 1961 Session, pp. 4, 56-58.
House Proceedings, 1963 Session, pp. 2-4, 21-23.
House Proceedings, 1965 Session, pp. 34-36.*
House Proceedings, 1967 Session, pp. 26-28.*
House Proceedings, 1969 Session, pp. 3-5, 7, 39-41.
House Proceedings, 1971 Session, pp. 2-4, 7, 13-15.
House Proceedings, 1973 Session, pp. 2-4, 9, 17-18.

Tennessee

District Classification, Membership Turnover, Biographical Data, and Chamber Leadership
Tennessee, Secretary of State, *Tennessee Blue Book: 1960*, pp. 20-55. (Subsequent references are cited as *Blue Book*.)
Blue Book: 1961-62, pp. 20-55.
Blue Book: 1963-64, pp. 19-54.
Blue Book: 1965-66, pp. 19-54.
Blue Book: 1967-68, pp. 12-46.
Blue Book: 1969-70, pp. 10-11, 15-49.
Blue Book: 1971-72, pp. 10-11, 15-50.
Blue Book: 1973-74, pp. 10-11, 15-62.
Standing Committee Chairmen
Tennessee, General Assembly, Senate, *Senate Journal*, 1959 Session, pp. 23, 32, 82, 85-88. (Subsequent references are cited as *Senate Journal*.)
Senate Journal, 1961 Session, pp. 68-69.
Senate Journal, 1963 Session, pp. 27, 55-57.
Senate Journal, 1965 Session, pp. 47-49.
Senate Journal, 1967 Session, pp. 46-48.
Senate Journal, 1969 Session, pp. 54-55.
Senate Journal, 1971 Session, prefatory pages.
Senate Journal, 1973 Session, prefatory pages.
Tennessee, General Assembly, House of Representatives, *House of Representatives Journal*, 1959 Session, pp. 32, 99, 104-7. (Subsequent references are cited as *House Journal*.)
House Journal, 1961 Session, pp. 60-62.
House Journal, 1963 Session, pp. 37-38, 61-63.
House Journal, 1965 Session, pp. 44, 49-52.
House Journal, 1967 Session, pp. 64-67.
House Journal, 1969 Session, pp. 80-81, 103.
House Journal, 1971 Session, pp. 117-18.
House Journal, 1973 Session, pp. 111-13.

Appendix C

Supplementary Data on the Impact of Reapportionment on the Six Sample State Legislatures

The following tables provide supporting data for the analysis in the main text. Table C-1 summarizes apportionment activity in the six sample states over the period of analysis. Six of the tables (C-2, C-7 through C-11) report legislators' perceptions of the impact of reapportionment, as revealed in the 1973 questionnaire survey of legislators in the six sample states. Tables C-3 and C-4 supply data on the legislative experience and racial, sexual, age, and occupational characteristics of state legislators in the sample states over the period of 1959-74; these data are discussed in chapter two. Table C-5, referred to in chapter three, displays changes in the metropolitan and nonmetropolitan character of legislative parties in the sample states for 1959-74. The raw data on the distribution of committee chairmanships among constituency categories in the sample legislatures—used to develop the indices in Table 4-1—appear in Table C-6. Table C-12 contains data on highway expenditures in the sample states which are judged to be too ambiguous for inclusion in chapter six on the impact of reapportionment on policy.

A final word is in order with regard to the reliability of certain kinds of data. Tables involving the district classification scheme of central city, suburban, and nonmetropolitan are necessarily imprecise, for the reasons set out in chapter one. The data in Tables C-5 and C-6 below and in Tables 1-3, 3-1, 4-1, 4-2, 6-1, and 6-2 should be viewed with the limitations of the classification system in mind. Especially in the case of New Jersey, the established central city category by encompassing both central city and suburban areas in the named counties masks some important demographic and political developments in the state. As a group, the established central cities, but not the counties in which they were located, actually lost population between 1960 and 1970. Thus, the decline in legislative representation of these cities in the early 1970s is actually more profound than the data in Table 1-3, for instance, reveal. Concomitantly, the growth in legislative representation for suburban areas of New Jersey, a part of it occurring in counties labeled established central city, is more significant than the data indicate. (See n. 22 on p. 77.)

Data on the characteristics of legislators, as in Table C-4, are influenced by the relative completeness and clarity of information available; figures on the occupational characteristics of legislators, for example, reflect judgments involving the primary occupation of legislators who list several vocations. Of course, data on legislators' perceptions, derived from the 1973 survey, suffer from the limited number of responses and the difficulties of interpreting some replies; these problems are treated in the text and in Appendix A.

TABLE C-1

Reapportionment Activity in the Six Sample States, 1960-73

State	Last Reapportionment Prior to 1960	Reapportionment 1960-1973	Chambers Affected	Reapportioning Agency
Delaware	1897	1964	House & Senate	Legislature
		1967	House & Senate	Legislature
		1971	House & Senate	Legislature
Kansas	1947 (Senate only)	1961	House	Legislature
	1959 (House only)	1964	House & Senate	Legislature
		1966	House	Legislature
		1968	Senate	Court
		1972	House	Legislature
			Senate	Court
		1973	House	Legislature
New Jersey	1941 (House only)	1961	House	Gov./Sec. of State
		1965	Senate	Legislature
		1966	House & Senate	Constitution
		1969	House & Senate	Court
		1971	House & Senate	Board
		1973	House & Senate	Board, Court
Oregon	1954	1961	House & Senate	Legislature
		1967	House	Legislature
		1971	House & Senate	Court/Sec. of State

TABLE C-1 (continued)

South Dakota	1951			
	1961	House & Senate	Legislature
	1965	House & Senate	Legislature
	1971	House & Senate	Legislature

Tennessee	1901			
	1962	House & Senate	Legislature
	1963	House & Senate	Legislature
	1965	House & Senate	Legislature
	1966	House & Senate	Constitution
	1972	House & Senate	Legislature
	1973	House & Senate	Legislature

Sources: The Book of the States, 1962-63 (Lexington, Ky.: Council of State Governments, 1962), pp. 58-62; The Book of the States, 1964-65 (Lexington, Ky.: Council of State Governments, 1964), pp. 62-66; The Book of the States, 1966-67 (Lexington, Ky.: Council of State Governments, 1966), pp. 64-67; The Book of the States, 1968-69 (Lexington, Ky.: Council of State Governments, 1968), pp. 66-67; The Book of the States, 1970-71 (Lexington, Ky.: Council of State Governments, 1970), pp. 82-83; The Book of the States, 1972-73 (Lexington, Ky.: Council of State Governments, 1972), pp. 64-65; The Book of the States, 1974-75 (Lexington, Ky.: Council of State Governments, 1974), pp. 66-67; National Municipal League, Apportionment in the Nineteen Sixties, rev. ed. (New York: National Municipal League, 1970); National Legislative Conference and the Council of State Governments, Reapportionment in the States (Lexington, Ky.: National Legislative Conference and the Council of State Governments, 1972), pp. 32-90. Also see references, Appendix B.

TABLE C-2

Percentage of Legislators in the Six Sample States Citing the Effects of Reapportionment with Regard to Single-Member Districts and Size of Legislative Districts

	Percentage Referring to Single-Member Districts	Percentage Referring to Size of Legislative Districts	(N)
Delaware	0	4.0	(25)
Kansas	1.2	9.3	(86)
New Jersey	18.2	6.7	(45)[a]
Oregon	46.2	15.4	(39)
South Dakota	1.9	5.8	(52)
Tennessee	2.4	11.9	(42)

Source: Responses to the 1973 survey of state legislators in the six sample states. See question #2 in the questionnaire reprinted in Appendix A.

[a]Total N for New Jersey is 45 for this question only; except as noted, N for New Jersey for all other questions is 44.

TABLE C-3

Percentage of Legislators with Four or More Years Experience in the Six Sample States by Chamber, 1959-74

Legislative Session Beginning[a]	1959 (1960)	1961 (1962)	1963 (1964)	1965 (1966)	1967 (1968)	1969 (1970)	1971 (1972)	1973 (1974)	Average for Non-Reapportionment Years	Average for Reapportionment[b] Years
Delaware										
Senate[c]	29.4	35.3	47.1	33.3*	44.4	42.1*	57.9	52.4*	42.8	42.6
House[c]	20.0	20.0	31.4	28.6*	17.1	15.4*	20.5	22.0*	21.8	22.0
Kansas										
Senate[c,e]	(30.0)	55.0	(45.0)	32.5*	(42.5)	52.5*	(47.5)	52.5*	55.0	45.8
House[c]	33.6	35.2*	36.8*	43.2*	32.0*	32.8	52.8	44.8*	39.7	38.4
New Jersey										
Senate[c,f]	71.4	76.2	66.7	34.5*	15.0*	(27.5)	47.5*	17.5*	71.4	28.6
Assembly[c]	18.3	38.3*	40.0	41.7	10.0*	15.0*	26.3*	12.5*	33.3	20.4
Oregon										
Senate[d]	56.7	70.0	76.7*	76.7	86.7	86.7	80.0	83.3*	76.1	80.0
House[d]	16.7	45.0	36.7*	41.7	43.3*	45.0	38.3	30.0*	37.3	36.7
South Dakota										
Senate[d]	28.6	51.4	40.0*	28.6	37.1*	37.1	31.4	31.4*	35.4	36.2
House[d]	41.3	41.3	34.7*	37.3	30.7*	30.7	36.0	41.4*	37.3	35.6
Tennessee										
Senate[d,g]	21.2	39.4	39.4*	51.5*	39.4*	39.4*	66.7	78.8*	42.4	49.7
House[d]	26.3	20.2	26.3*	21.2*	20.2*	20.2	23.2	30.3	22.5	24.5

Sources: See Appendix B.

[a] Years in parentheses are for New Jersey which begins post-election sessions in even-numbered years.

[b] Years in which the legislative houses had been elected under a new apportionment plan are designated by asterisks.

[c] Figures are percentages of total chamber members who served four or more consecutive years in the chamber.

[d] Figures are percentages of chamber members who have served four or more consecutive years in either house of the legislature.

[e] Figures in parentheses are for non-election years and are not averaged in column nine.

[f] Until 1965, New Jersey used staggered four-year terms for senators. However, all senators stood for election from 1965 on, except in 1969 when no Senate seats were up for election. The cumulative data in columns nine and ten include all years except 1970.

[g] Until the 1968 election, Tennessee used two-year terms for senators. In 1968, all Senate seats were up for election with staggered four-year terms to be phased in by the 1972 elections. The cumulative data in columns nine and ten embrace all years, including 1971 and 1973 when only about half of the seats were up for election.

TABLE C-4

Characteristics of Legislators in the Six Sample States by Chamber, 1959-74

Delaware (Senate/House)

Legislative Session Beginning	1959	1961	1963	1965	1967	1969	1971	1973
Average age (Years)	Not Available (NA)							
Age 35 or Under (%)	NA	NA	NA	NA	NA	NA	NA	NA
Women (%)	0/2.9	5.9/0	5.9/NA	11.1/5.7	11.1/5.7	5.3/7.7	5.3/10.3	9.5/14.6
Black (%)	NA	NA	NA	NA	5.6/5.7	0/5.1	5.3/5.1	4.8/4.9
Occupations (%)	NA	NA	NA	NA	NA	NA	NA	NA

Kansas (Senate/House)

Legislative Session Beginning	1959	1961	1963	1965	1967	1969	1971	1973
Average Age (Years)	NA	NA	NA	NA				
Age 35 or Under (%)	NA	NA	NA	NA				
Women (%)	0/2.4	0/1.6	0/1.6	2.5/3.2	2.5/0.8	2.5/0.8	0/1.6	2.5/3.2
Black (%)	NA	NA	NA	NA	7.5/0.8	0/2.4	0/2.4	2.5/3.2
Occupations (%)								
Agriculture	20.0/40.0	15.0/42.4	17.5/40.8	22.5/40.0	20.0/25.6	15.0/23.2	15.0/24.0	15.0/23.2
Attorney	47.5/15.2	45.0/13.6	42.5/14.4	45.0/16.0	47.5/24.8	45.0/26.4	45.0/19.2	30.0/8.8
Insurance, Banking[b]	10.0/8.8	12.5/6.4	12.5/8.8	12.5/8.0	15.0/11.2	10.0/12.0	7.5/16.0	7.5/17.6
Business[c]	12.5/16.0	17.5/23.2	15.0/20.0	12.5/16.8	15.0/16.0	10.0/17.6	12.5/18.4	15.0/20.8
Journalism[d]	0/5.6	0/4.0	0/4.0	0/3.2	0/3.2	2.5/2.4	5.0/2.4	5.0/1.6
Education	0/2.4	0/4.0	0/4.0	0/3.2	0/3.2	2.5/2.4	2.5/3.2	2.5/4.0
Healing Arts[e]	0/1.6	2.5/0	2.5/0	0/0.8	0/2.4	0/2.4	0/4.8	2.5/3.2
Miscellaneous								
White Collar[f]	5.0/4.0	2.5/4.8	2.5/6.4	0/6.4	0/5.6	5.0/8.0	5.0/8.0	15.0/7.2
Blue Collar[g]	0/1.6	0/0.8	2.5/0.8	2.5/1.6	2.5/4.0	2.5/1.6	2.5/1.6	2.5/5.6
Not available	5.0/4.8	5.0/0.8	5.0/0.8	5.0/4.0	0/4.0	7.5/4.0	5.0/2.4	5.0/8.0

TABLE C-4 (continued)

New Jersey (Senate/Assembly)

Legislative Session Beginning	1960	1962	1964	1966	1968	1970	1972	1974
Average Age (Years)[a]	49.2/47.1	51.6/45.7	51.3/46.3	51.2/45.5	50.5/43.3	52.6/46.3	48.7/44.4	50.1/44.5
Age 35 or Under (%)[a]	0/8.3	0/16.7	0/11.7	3.5/11.7	0/17.5	0/15.0	7.5/12.5	2.5/18.8
Women (%)	0/10.0	0/5.0	0/5.0	3.5/1.7	0/1.3	0/2.5	2.5/3.8	5.0/7.5
Black (%)	NA	NA	NA	0/5.0	0/6.3	0/5.0	2.5/7.5	2.5/7.5
Occupations (%)								
Agriculture	0/0	0/0	4.8/0	3.4/0	2.5/1.3	2.5/1.3	0/1.3	0/0
Attorney	66.7/48.3	71.4/55.0	61.9/53.3	62.1/53.3	65.0/41.3	65.0/37.5	50.0/30.0	35.0/25.0
Insurance, Banking[b]	14.3/10.0	14.3/16.7	14.3/11.7	3.4/5.0	10.0/15.0	10.0/15.0	7.5/15.0	10.0/11.3
Business[c]	4.8/15.0	4.8/6.6	4.8/13.3	10.3/10.0	17.5/17.5	17.5/18.8	25.0/20.0	25.0/21.3
Journalism[d]	4.8/0	0/0	0/0	0/0	2.5/0	2.5/1.3	2.5/1.3	2.5/1.3
Education	0/8.3	0/3.3	0/3.3	6.9/3.3	0/5.0	0/7.5	2.5/3.8	10.0/8.8
Healing Arts[e]	0/0	0/0	0/0	3.4/0	0/1.3	0/0	2.5/1.3	2.5/0
Miscellaneous								
White Collar[f]	9.5/5.0	9.5/3.3	0/8.3	6.9/16.7	2.5/13.8	2.5/12.5	7.5/20.0	5.0/26.3
Blue Collar[g]	0/10.0	0/10.0	14.3/6.7	3.4/8.3	0/5.0	0/5.0	0/5.0	10.0/2.5
Not available	0/3.3	0/5.0	0/3.3	0/3.3	0/0	0/1.3	2.5/2.5	0/3.8

Oregon (Senate/House)

Legislative Session Beginning	1959	1961	1963	1965	1967	1969	1971	1973
Average Age (Years)[a]	50.8/49.7	50.6/48.2	53.9/46.4	56.3/45.5	55.3/45.2	54.2/45.8	52.0/45.8	48.9/42.4
Age 35 or Under (%)[a]	3.3/16.7	3.3/13.3	3.3/13.3	0/13.3	3.3/15.0	3.3/18.3	6.7/8.3	13.3/31.7
Women (%)	6.7/13.3	3.3/10.0	3.3/13.3	3.3/11.7	0/8.3	3.3/6.7	6.7/8.3	6.7/15.0
Black (%)	0/0	0/0	0/0	0/0	0/0	0/0	0/0	0/1.7
Occupations (%)								
Agriculture	13.3/18.3	16.7/21.7	13.3/18.3	20.0/15.0	16.7/18.3	23.3/11.7	20.0/10.0	16.7/11.7
Attorney	33.3/11.7	33.3/10.0	33.3/15.0	26.7/23.3	33.3/16.7	33.3/21.7	40.0/15.0	30.0/11.7
Insurance, Banking[b]	13.3/13.3	16.7/18.3	13.3/20.0	20.0/20.0	20.0/23.3	13.3/21.7	10.0/20.0	10.0/18.3
Business[c]	16.7/30.0	23.3/20.0	20.0/18.3	20.0/18.3	16.7/13.3	20.0/16.7	20.0/16.7	23.3/13.3
Journalism[d]	3.3/1.7	3.3/3.3	3.3/1.7	3.3/1.7	3.3/1.7	3.3/3.3	0/5.0	0/5.0
Education	3.3/3.3	0/3.3	3.3/3.3	3.3/1.7	0/8.3	3.3/3.3	0/18.3	6.7/15.0
Healing Arts[e]	3.3/3.3	0/1.7	0/6.7	0/6.7	0/5.0	0/10.0	3.3/5.0	3.3/1.7
Miscellaneous								
White Collar[f]	10.0/6.7	3.3/11.7	3.3/10.0	0/5.0	3.3/3.3	3.3/1.7	3.3/5.0	6.7/11.7
Blue Collar[g]	3.3/5.0	0/3.3	0/3.3	0/5.0	3.3/6.7	0/5.0	3.3/1.7	3.3/5.0
Not available	0/6.7	3.3/6.7	10.0/3.3	6.7/3.3	3.3/3.3	3.3/3.3	0/3.3	0/6.7

TABLE C-4 (continued)

South Dakota (Senate/House)

Legislative Session Beginning	1959	1961	1963	1965	1967	1969	1971	1973
Average Age (Years)[a]	53.1/51.1	55.1/53.1	54.6/52.7	52.6/52.3	52.0/53.8	57.1/53.2	53.1/52.0	50.9/46.6
Age 35 or Under (%)[a]	2.9/9.3	2.9/8.0	0/6.7	5.7/5.3	2.9/4.0	2.9/6.7	5.7/6.7	2.9/24.3
Women (%)	0/2.7	0/4.0	0/2.7	0/4.0	0/2.7	0/2.7	0/4.0	2.9/7.1
Black (%)	0/0	0/0	0/0	0/0	0/0	0/0	0/0	0/0
Occupation (%)								
Agriculture	48.6/62.6	42.8/54.7	37.1/57.3	42.8/45.3	31.4/40.0	34.3/46.7	40.0/46.7	48.6/45.7
Attorney	8.6/6.7	11.4/2.7	20.0/8.0	20.0/9.3	14.3/12.0	8.6/14.7	11.4/10.7	5.7/8.6
Insurance, Banking[b]	20.0/5.3	14.3/8.0	20.0/12.0	8.6/9.3	11.4/16.0	11.4/12.0	11.4/10.7	5.7/10.0
Business[c]	17.1/17.3	22.9/21.3	20.0/14.7	17.1/18.7	25.7/16.0	28.6/12.0	17.1/20.0	14.3/14.3
Journalism[d]	0/1.3	0/1.3	0/1.3	0/0	0/2.7	0/2.7	2.9/0	2.9/1.4
Education	0/4.0	0/4.0	0/4.0	2.9/8.0	2.9/4.0	2.9/2.7	2.9/5.3	11.4/10.0
Healing Arts[e]	2.9/0	0/2.7	0/2.7	2.9/1.3	8.6/2.7	5.7/4.0	5.7/1.3	5.7/1.4
Miscellaneous								
White Collar[f]	0/2.7	2.9/4.0	0/0	0/0	0/1.3	2.9/2.7	2.9/4.0	5.7/7.1
Blue Collar[g]	2.9/0	5.7/0	2.9/0	2.9/2.7	5.7/1.3	5.7/1.3	5.7/1.3	0/1.4
Not available	0/0	0/1.3	0/0	2.9/5.3	0/4.0	0/1.3	0/0	0/0

Tennessee (Senate/House)

Legislative Session Beginning	1959	1961	1963	1965	1967	1969	1971	1973
Average Age (Years)[a]	45.7/48.1	48.8/46.6	44.4/44.0	47.5/44.9	45.5/44.2	49.9/44.4	47.7/44.4	49.2/42.5
Age 35 or Under (%)[a]	15.2/23.2	18.2/25.3	24.2/35.4	12.1/27.3	15.2/31.3	15.2/27.3	3.0/20.2	3.0/25.3
Women (%)	0/1.0	0/3.0	0/4.0	0/2.0	3.0/1.0	0/2.0	0/2.0	0/5.1
Black (%)	0/0	0/0	0/0	0/1.0	0/5.7	3.0/6.1	3.0/6.1	3.0/7.1
Occupation (%)								
Agriculture	15.2/19.2	18.2/18.2	9.1/11.1	6.1/8.1	3.0/6.1	9.1/9.1	3.0/8.1	3.0/7.1
Attorney	36.4/30.3	33.3/28.3	54.5/45.5	42.4/36.4	45.5/38.4	39.4/27.3	42.4/20.2	39.4/17.2
Insurance, Banking[b]	6.1/16.2	6.1/15.2	9.1/10.1	12.1/9.1	15.2/10.1	6.1/18.2	9.1/16.2	9.1/17.2
Business[c]	24.2/16.2	21.2/21.2	15.2/14.1	24.2/28.3	21.2/26.3	30.3/20.2	27.3/25.2	30.3/22.2
Journalism[d]	3.0/1.0	6.1/0	3.0/1.0	3.0/0	3.0/0	3.0/0	3.0/0	3.0/2.0
Education	0/4.0	0/3.0	0/5.1	3.0/5.1	6.1/2.0	3.0/4.0	3.0/2.0	3.0/6.1
Healing Arts[e]	0/7.1	9.1/4.0	3.0/0	3.0/0	6.1/5.1	6.1/6.1	6.1/6.1	6.1/4.0
Miscellaneous								
White Collar[f]	12.1/5.1	6.1/5.1	0/10.0	3.0/10.1	0/9.1	3.0/8.1	6.1/11.1	6.1/12.1
Blue Collar[g]	0/0	0/0	3.0/0	0/0	0/2.0	0/2.0	0/3.0	0/3.0
Not available	3.0/1.0	0/5.0	3.0/3.0	0/3.0	0/1.0	0/5.1	0/7.1	0/9.1

TABLE C-4 (continued)

Sources: Data on black representation in Delaware, Kansas, and New Jersey are taken from Congressional Quarterly, Revolution in Civil Rights, 4th ed. (Washington, D.C.: Congressional Quarterly, 1968), p. 115; National Roster of Black Elected Officials, mimeo. (Washington, D.C.: Metropolitan Applied Research Center, 1966), pp. 21, 35, 60-62; National Roster of Black Elected Officials, vol. 1 (Washington, D.C.: Joint Center for Political Studies, 1971), front matter; National Roster of Black Elected Officials, vol. 3 (Washington, D.C.: Joint Center for Political Studies, 1973), front matter; National Roster of Black Elected Officials, vol. 4 (Washington, D.C.: Joint Center for Political Studies, 1974), p. xix. Sources for other data are described in Appendix B. (Sources for biographical data on Tennessee, listed in Appendix B, have been augmented by additional material covering missing data.)

[a]The average age is based on the number of legislators for whom ages were available. The percentage of legislators aged 35 or under is based on the total membership in the chamber.

[b]Category also includes public accountants.

[c]Category includes owners of businesses and top level executives.

[d]Category includes broadcasters, publishers, and writers.

[e]Category includes medical doctors, dentists, pharmacists, and veterinarians.

[f]Category includes clergymen, clerks, typists, and lower level executives.

[g]Category also includes labor union officials.

TABLE C-5

Percentage Distribution of Central City, Suburban, and Nonmetropolitan Seats within Republican and Democratic Parties in the Six Sample States by Chamber, 1959-74 [a][b]

				Delaware				
	1959	1961	1963	1965	1967	1969	1971	1973
Senate Reps (N)	(6)	(6)	(7)	(5)	(9)	(13)	(13)	(11)
Central City	16.7	16.7	14.3	0.0	11.1	7.7	7.7	9.1
Suburban	50.0	33.3	42.9	80.0	55.6	61.5	61.5	81.8
Nonmetro	33.3	50.0	42.9	20.0	33.3	30.8	30.8	9.1
Senate Dems (N)	(11)	(11)	(10)	(13)	(9)	(6)	(6)	(10)
Central City	9.1	9.1	10.0	30.8	33.3	33.3	33.3	20.0
Suburban	18.2	27.3	20.0	30.8	33.3	33.3	33.3	30.0
Nonmetro	72.7	63.6	70.0	38.5	33.3	33.3	33.3	50.0
House Reps (N)	(10)	(15)	(10)	(5)	(23)	(25)	(23)	(21)
Central City	10.0	6.7	10.0	0.0	17.4	4.0	8.7	9.5
Suburban	40.0	33.3	50.0	100.0	52.2	68.0	69.6	81.0
Nonmetro	50.0	60.0	40.0	0.0	30.4	28.0	21.7	9.5
House Dems (N)	(25)	(20)	(25)	(30)	(12)	(14)	(16)	(20)
Central City	16.0	20.0	16.0	26.7	33.3	35.7	25.0	20.0
Suburban	24.0	25.0	20.0	36.7	33.3	28.6	31.3	30.0
Nonmetro	60.0	55.0	64.0	36.7	33.3	35.7	43.8	50.0

				Kansas				
	1959	1961	1963	1965	1967	1969	1971	1973
Senate Reps (N)	(32)	(32)	(32)	(27)	(27)	(32)	(32)	(27)
Central City	6.3	6.3	6.3	22.2	22.2	28.1	28.1	25.9
Suburban	3.1	3.1	3.1	7.4	7.4	15.6	15.6	14.8
Nonmetro	90.6	90.6	90.6	70.4	70.4	56.3	56.3	59.3
Senate Dems (N)	(8)	(8)	(8)	(13)	(13)	(8)	(8)	(13)
Central City	12.5	12.5	12.5	23.1	23.1	37.5	37.5	46.2
Suburban	12.5	12.5	12.5	15.4	15.4	0.0	0.0	7.7
Nonmetro	75.0	75.0	75.0	61.5	61.5	62.5	62.5	46.2
House Reps (N)	(69)	(81)	(89)	(81)	(77)	(87)	(84)	(80)
Central City	2.9	4.9	4.5	9.9	20.8	18.4	21.4	18.8
Suburban	1.4	3.7	3.4	6.2	13.0	12.5	11.9	16.3
Nonmetro	95.7	91.4	92.1	84.0	66.2	69.0	66.7	65.0
House Dems (N)	(56)	(44)	(36)	(44)	(48)	(38)	(41)	(45)
Central City	12.5	18.2	22.2	22.7	43.8	55.3	46.3	48.9
Suburban	5.4	4.5	5.6	2.3	4.2	2.6	4.9	4.4
Nonmetro	82.1	77.3	72.2	75.0	52.1	42.1	48.8	46.7

TABLE C-5 (continued)

New Jersey

	1960	1962	1964	1966	1968	1970	1972	1974
Senate Reps (N)	(11)	(11)	(15)	(10)	(31)	(31)	(24)	(10)
Established								
Central City	9.1	9.1	13.3	20.0	32.3	32.3	16.7	30.0
New Central City[C]	[9.1]	[9.1]	[13.3]	[20.0]	[9.7]	[9.7]	16.7	10,0
Suburban	36.4	36.4	46.7	50.0	54.8	54.8	58.3	50.0
Nonmetro	54.5	54.5	40.0	30.0	12.9	12.9	8.3	10.0
Senate Dems (N)	(10)	(10)	(6)	(19)	(9)	(9)	(16)	(29)
Established								
Central City	40.0	40.0	50.0	52.6	66.7	66.7	62.5	34.5
New Central City[C]	[20.0]	[20.0]	[33.3]	[15.8]	[33.3]	[33.3]	18.8	20.7
Suburban	40.0	40.0	16.7	36.8	0.0	0.0	18.8	41.4
Nonmetro	20.0	20.0	33.3	10.5	33.3	33.3	0.0	3.4
Assembly Reps (N)	(26)	(22)	(33)	(19)	(58)	(59)	(39)	(14)
Established								
Central City	34.6	13.6	21.2	10.5	24.1	27.1	17.9	21.4
New Central City[C]	[11.5]	[13.6]	[9.1]	[15.8]	[17.2]	[16.9]	17.9	14.3
Suburban	38.5	50.0	54.5	52.6	55.2	52.5	53.8	50.0
Nonmetro	26.9	36.4	24.2	36.8	20.7	20.3	10.3	14.3
Assembly Dems (N)	(34)	(38)	(27)	(41)	(22)	(21)	(40)	(66)
Established								
Central City	61.7	55.3	63.0	53.7	77.3	71.4	45.0	37.9
New Central City[C]	[11.8]	[13.2]	[18.5]	[12.2]	[9.1]	[9.5]	22.5	18.2
Suburban	26.5	31.6	18.5	31.7	13.6	19.0	32.5	40.9
Nonmetro	11.8	13.2	18.5	14.6	9.1	9.5	0.0	3.0

Oregon

	1959	1961	1963	1965	1967	1969	1971	1973
Senate Reps (N)	(11)	(10)	(9)	(11)	(11)	(14)	(14)	(12)
Central City	27.3	30.0	33.3	27.3	18.2	14.3	14.3	16.7
Suburban	18.2	20.0	44.4	36.4	45.5	35.7	28.6	50.0
Nonmetro	54.5	50.0	22.2	36.4	36.4	50.0	57.1	33.3
Senate Dems (N)	(19)	(20)	(21)	(19)	(19)	(16)	(16)	(18)
Central City	42.1	40.0	47.6	52.6	57.9	68.8	68.8	61.1
Suburban	10.5	10.0	4.8	5.3	0.0	0.0	6.3	5.6
Nonmetro	47.4	50.0	47.6	42.1	42.1	31.3	25.0	33.3
House Reps (N)	(27)	(29)	(29)	(32)	(38)	(38)	(34)	(27)
Central City	51.9	44.8	41.4	37.5	36.8	31.6	26.5	33.3
Suburban	14.8	13.8	17.2	12.5	15.8	18.4	17.6	14.8
Nonmetro	33.3	41.4	41.4	50.0	47.4	50.0	55.9	51.9
House Dems (N)	(33)	(31)	(31)	(28)	(22)	(22)	(26)	(33)
Central City	33.3	38.7	48.4	53.6	59.1	68.2	69.2	51.5
Suburban	9.1	9.7	9.7	14.3	9.1	4.5	7.7	30.3
Nonmetro	57.6	51.6	41.9	32.1	31.8	27.3	23.1	18.2

TABLE C-5 (continued)

South Dakota

	1959	1961	1963	1965	1967	1969	1971	1973
Senate Reps (N)	(15)	(24)	(26)	(18)	(29)	(27)	(24)	(17)
Central City	13.3	8.3	7.7	11.1	13.8	14.8	16.7	17.6
Nonmetro	86.7	91.7	92.3	88.9	86.2	85.2	83.3	82.4
Senate Dems (N)	(20)	(11)	(9)	(16)	(6)	(8)	(11)	(18)
Central City	0.0	0.0	0.0	0.0	0.0	0.0	0.0	11.1
Nonmetro	100.0	100.0	100.0	100.0	100.0	100.0	100.0	88.9
House Reps (N)	(43)	(57)	(58)	(45)	(64)	(59)	(49)	(35)
Central City	16.3	14.0	15.5	20.0	14.1	15.3	12.2	5.7
Nonmetro	83.7	86.0	84.5	80.0	85.9	84.7	87.8	94.3
House Dems (N)	(32)	(18)	(17)	(30)	(11)	(16)	(26)	(35)
Central City	3.1	0.0	0.0	0.0	0.0	0.0	11.5	22.9
Nonmetro	96.9	100.0	100.0	100.0	100.0	100.0	88.5	77.1

Tennessee

	1959	1961	1963	1965	1967	1969	1971	1973
Senate Reps (N)	(5)	(6)	(6)	(8)	(8)	(12)	(13)	(13)
Central City	0.0	16.7	16.7	25.0	25.0	41.7	46.2	46.2
Suburban	20.0	16.7	16.7	12.5	12.5	8.3	7.7	7.7
Nonmetro	80.0	66.7	66.7	62.5	62.5	50.0	46.2	46.2
Senate Dems (N)	(28)	(27)	(27)	(25)	(25)	(21)	(19)	(19)
Central City	28.6	25.9	37.0	40.0	48.0	42.9	42.1	42.1
Suburban	7.1	7.4	7.4	8.0	8.0	9.5	10.5	10.5
Nonmetro	64.3	66.7	55.6	52.0	44.0	47.6	47.4	47.4
House Reps (N)	(17)	(19)	(21)	(24)	(41)	(49)	(43)	(48)
Central City	17.6	15.8	19.0	20.8	41.5	42.9	46.5	45.8
Suburban	5.9	5.3	9.5	4.2	4.9	8.2	7.0	8.3
Nonmetro	76.5	78.9	71.4	75.0	53.7	49.0	46.5	45.8
House Dems (N)	(82)	(80)	(78)	(75)	(58)	(49)	(56)	(51)
Central City	23.2	23.8	35.9	36.0	43.1	42.9	39.3	43.1
Suburban	4.9	5.0	5.1	6.7	6.9	4.1	5.4	3.9
Nonmetro	72.0	71.3	59.0	57.3	50.0	53.1	55.4	52.9

Sources: See Appendix B.

[a]The classification of districts is described in Chapter One.

[b]Years indicate first legislative sessions following elections.

[c]New central city counties are those central counties recognized after 1970. Percentages for those areas prior to 1970 are given in brackets and not counted in overall tabulations; prior to 1970 these counties are included in the nonmetropolitan category.

TABLE C-6

Percentage Distribution of Committee Chairmanships according to Party and Constituency in the Six Sample Legislatures by Chamber, 1959-74 [a]

Legislative Session Beginning[b]	1959 (1960)		1961 (1962)		1963 (1964)	
	Senate	House	Senate	House	Senate	House
Delaware						
Republican	0	0	0	0	0	0
Central City	9.1	19.2	9.1	15.4	9.1	15.4
Suburban	22.7	19.2	27.3	23.1	18.2	15.4
Nonmetropolitan	68.2	61.5	63.6	61.5	72.7	69.2
Kansas						
Republican	100.0	100.0	100.0	100.0	100.0	100.0
Central City	6.5	2.3	6.3	0	6.3	2.2
Suburban	3.2	2.3	3.1ᵛ	0	6.3	0
Nonmetropolitan	90.3	95.4	90.6	100.0	87.5	97.8
New Jersey						
Republican	100.0	0	100.0	0	100.0	100.0
Established Central City	8.3	66.7	0	58.3	16.7	16.7
New Central City[c]	(8.3)	(8.3)	(16.7)	(16.7)	(8.3)	(8.3)
Suburban	41.7	25.0	33.3	25.0	41.7	33.3
Nonmetropolitan	50.0	8.3	66.7	16.7	41.7	50.0
Oregon						
Republican	14.3	10.0	25.0	5.3	30.0	10.0
Central City	38.1	35.0	35.0	36.8	40.0	50.0
Suburban	9.5	5.0	20.0	15.8	10.0	10.0
Nonmetropolitan	52.4	60.0	45.0	47.4	50.0	40.0
South Dakota						
Republican	11.5	96.2	100.0	100.0	100.0	100.0
Central City	7.7	19.2	17.6	13.0	12.5	26.1
Nonmetropolitan	92.3	80.8	82.4	87.0	87.5	73.9
Tennessee						
Republican	12.5	18.8	5.3	15.0	18.8	18.2
Central City	12.5	18.8	21.1	20.0	31.3	18.2
Suburban	6.3	6.3	5.3	5.0	6.3	4.5
Nonmetropolitan	81.3	75.0	73.7	75.0	62.5	77.3

Sources: See Appendix B.

TABLE C-6 (continued)

1965 (1966)		1967 (1968)		1969 (1970)		1971 (1972)		1973 (1974)	
Senate	House	Senate	House	Senate	House	Senate	House	Senate	House
0	0	0	100.0	100.0	100.0	100.0	100.0	100.0	100.0
31.8	29.6	36.4	11.8	11.7	7.1	8.3	12.5	8.3	13.3
36.4	37.0	40.9	58.8	64.7	71.4	66.7	81.3	83.3	73.3
31.8	33.0	22.7	29.4	23.5	21.4	25.0	6.3	8.3	13.3
100.0	100.0	100.0	100.0	100.0	100.0	100.0	100.0	100.0	100.0
21.9	2.2	21.9	22.2	16.7	20.0	16.7	26.1	38.9	28.6
3.1	0	6.3	6.7	11.1	8.0	16.7	13.0	16.7	19.0
75.0	97.8	71.9	71.1	72.2	72.0	66.7	60.9	44.4	52.4
0	0	100.0	100.0	100.0	100.0	100.0	61.1	0	0
61.5	61.5	25.0	25.0	29.4	29.4	20.0	33.3	50.0	38.5
(7.7)	(23.1)	(12.5)	(18.8)	(11.8)	(17.6)	20.0	5.6	10.0	15.4
30.8	15.4	62.5	50.0	58.8	52.9	60.0	55.6	40.0	46.2
7.7	23.1	12.5	25.0	11.8	17.6	0	5.6	0	0
30.0	81.3	42.9	87.5	47.6	88.2	47.1	100.0	0	7.7
45.0	37.5	33.3	43.8	47.6	23.5	35.3	27.3	73.3	53.8
10.0	6.3	14.3	6.3	19.1	23.5	17.6	9.1	6.7	23.1
45.0	56.3	52.4	50.0	33.3	52.9	47.1	63.6	20.0	23.1
100.0	100.0	100.0	100.0	100.0	100.0	100.0	100.0	0	0
25.0	24.0	25.0	24.0	18.8	12.0	7.1	0	7.1	7.1
75.0	76.0	75.0	76.0	81.2	88.0	92.9	100.0·	92.9	92.9
27.8	25.0	20.0	30.8	33.0	57.1	33.0	0	28.6	0
33.3	30.0	35.0	23.1	16.7	12.5	16.7	30.0	28.6	36.4
11.1	10.0	10.0	3.8	16.7	0	16.7	10.0	14.3	9.1
55.6	60.0	55.0	73.1	66.7	85.7	66.7	60.0	57.1	54.5

[a]Figures are percentages of all standing committee chairmanships held by legislators in the category designated. The classification of constituencies is described in Chapter One.

[b]Even-numbered years are for New Jersey only.

[c]New central city counties are those central city counties recognized after 1970. Percentages for these counties prior to 1972 are given in parentheses and should be considered components of the nonmetropolitan figures.

TABLE C-7

Distribution of Legislators' Responses to Question of Whether Reapportionment Had Induced Changes in Chamber Organization and Procedure in the Six Sample Legislatures

State	Chamber	Yes	No	Don't Know or Not Answered	(N)
Delaware	Senate	44.4%	33.3%	22.2%	(9)
	House	43.8	43.8	12.5	(16)
	Combined	44.0	40.0	16.0	(25)
Kansas	Senate	65.2	30.4	4.3	(23)
	House	66.7	17.5	15.9	(63)
	Combined	66.3	20.9	12.8	(86)
New Jersey	Senate	33.3	66.7	0	(15)
	Assembly	24.1	48.3	27.6	(29)
	Combined	27.3	54.5	18.2	(44)
Oregon	Senate	53.3	40.0	6.7	(15)
	House	54.2	29.2	16.7	(24)
	Combined	53.8	33.3	12.8	(39)
South Dakota	Senate	30.0	60.0	10.0	(20)
	House	25.0	50.0	25.0	(32)
	Combined	26.9	53.8	19.2	(52)
Tennessee	Senate	40.0	40.0	20.0	(10)
	House	43.8	37.5	18.8	(32)
	Combined	42.9	38.1	19.0	(42)

Source: Responses to the 1973 survey of state legislators in the six sample states.   See question #6 in the questionnaire reprinted in Appendix A.

TABLE C-8

Percentage Distribution of Legislators' Responses to Question of Whether Reapportionment Had Induced Changes within Their Respective Parties in the Six Sample Legislatures

State	Chamber	Party	Yes	No	Don't Know or Not Answered	(N)
Delaware	Senate	Dem.	66.7%	33.3%	0%	(3)
	House	Dem.	50.0	33.3	16.7	(6)
	Senate & House	Dem.	55.6	33.3	11.1	(9)
	Senate	Rep.	66.7	16.7	16.7	(6)
	House	Rep.	80.0	20.0	0	(10)
	Senate & House	Rep.	75.0	18.8	6.3	(16)
Kansas	Senate	Dem.	66.7	33.3	0	(6)
	House	Dem.	57.9	26.3	15.8	(19)
	Senate & House	Dem.	60.0	28.0	12.0	(25)
	Senate	Rep.	76.5	11.8	11.8	(17)
	House	Rep.	56.8	20.5	22.7	(44)
	Senate & House	Rep.	62.3	18.0	19.7	(61)
New Jersey	Senate	Dem.	20.0	60.0	20.0	(5)
	Assembly	Dem.	46.7	26.7	26.7	(15)
	Senate & Assembly	Dem.	40.0	35.0	25.0	(20)
	Senate	Rep.	80.0	0	20.0	(10)
	Assembly	Rep.	50.0	50.0	0	(14)
	Senate & Assembly	Rep.	62.5	29.2	8.3	(24)
Oregon	Senate	Dem.	66.7	33.3	0	(9)
	House	Dem.	76.9	7.7	15.4	(13)
	Senate & House	Dem.	72.7	18.2	9.1	(22)
	Senate	Rep.	33.3	66.7	0	(6)
	House	Rep.	18.2	63.6	18.2	(11)
	Senate & House	Rep.	23.5	64.7	11.8	(17)
South Dakota	Senate	Dem.	42.9	28.6	28.6	(7)
	House	Dem.	71.4	21.4	7.1	(14)
	Senate & House	Dem.	61.9	23.8	14.3	(21)
	Senate	Rep.	30.8	61.5	7.7	(13)
	House	Rep.	50.0	33.3	16.7	(18)
	Senate & House	Rep.	41.9	45.2	12.9	(31)
Tennessee	Senate	Dem.	66.7	33.3	0	(6)
	House	Dem.	63.6	18.2	18.2	(11)
	Senate & House	Dem.	64.7	23.5	11.8	(17)
	Senate	Rep.	100.0	0	0	(4)
	House	Rep.	57.1	28.6	14.3	(21)
	Senate & House	Rep.	64.0	24.0	12.0	(25)

Source: Responses to 1973 survey of state legislators in the six sample states. See question #7 in the questionnaire reprinted in Appendix A.

TABLE C-9

Legislators' Perceptions of Reapportionment's Impact on the Most Important Sources of Legislative Conflict in the Six Sample States by Chamber, 1973

			Reapportionment's Impact			
State	Chamber	Conflict Rank	Increased Conflict	No Effect	Decreased Conflict	(N)[a]
Delaware	Senate	1.Partisan	37.5%	62.5%	0.0%	(8)
		2.Lib-cons.	87.5	12.5	0.0	(8)
		3.Urban-rural	71.4	14.3	14.3	(7)
	House	1.Partisan	46.7	40.0	13.3	(15)
		2.Lib-cons.	80.0	13.3	6.7	(15)
		3.Urban-rural	81.3	12.5	6.3	(16)
Kansas	Senate	1.Urban-rural	100.0	0.0	0.0	(22)
		2.Partisan	52.2	43.4	4.4	(23)
		3.Pro-anti Gov.	35.0	65.0	0.0	(20)
	House	1.Urban-rural	93.4	6.6	0.0	(61)
		2.Partisan	51.8	26.8	21.4	(56)
		3.Pro-anti Gov.	42.1	54.4	3.5	(57)
New Jersey	Senate	1.Partisan	25.0	58.3	16.7	(12)
		2.Urban-suburban[b]	8.3	--	--	(12)
		3.Lib-cons.	53.8	38.5	7.7	(13)
	Assembly	1.Partisan	52.6	42.1	5.3	(19)
		2.Lib-cons.	61.1	38.9	0.0	(18)
		3.Urban-suburban[b]	10.5	--	--	(19)
Oregon	Senate	1.Partisan	42.9	57.1	0.0	(14)
		2.Lib-cons.	73.3	20.0	6.7	(15)
		3.Urban-rural	80.0	13.3	6.7	(15)
	House	1.Lib-cons.	73.7	26.3	0.0	(19)
		2.Urban-rural	73.7	15.8	10.5	(19)
		3.Partisan	63.2	36.8	0.0	(19)
South Dakota	Senate	1.Partisan	58.8	35.3	5.9	(17)
		2.Lib-cons.	58.8	23.5	17.6	(17)
		3.Urban-rural	77.8	16.7	5.6	(18)
	House	1.Urban-rural	93.1	0.0	6.9	(29)
		2.Partisan	35.7	42.9	21.4	(28)
		3.Lib-cons.	58.6	41.4	0.0	(29)
Tennessee	Senate	1.Partisan	60.0	10.0	30.0	(10)
		tie Urban-rural	60.0	20.0	20.0	(10)
		3.Lib-cons.	90.0	10.0	0.0	(10)
	House	1.Partisan	76.7	20.0	3.3	(30)
		2.Urban-rural	80.0	10.0	10.0	(30)
		3.Lib-cons.	64.0	36.0	0.0	(25)

Source: Responses to the 1973 survey of state legislators in the six sample states. See question #4 in the questionnaire reprinted in Appendix A.

[a]N is the number of legislators who answered the particular question, not the total number responding to the questionnaire. Percentages are based on N.

[b]The figure given is the percentage of legislators who voluntarily named this type of conflict in relation to the average number of respondents, for the different components of question #4. See the text for further explanation.

TABLE C-10

Legislators' Responses to Question of Whether Reapportionment Had Affected Legislation Introduced in the Six Sample Legislatures

	Yes	No	Don't Know	Not Mentioned	(N)
Delaware					
Senate	44.4%	55.5%	0%	0%	(9)
House	43.8	25.0	31.3	0	(16)
Combined	44.0	36.0	20.0	0	(25)
Kansas					
Senate	65.2	30.4	4.3	0	(23)
House	60.3	22.2	15.9	1.6	(63)
Combined	61.6	24.4	12.8	1.2	(86)
New Jersey					
Senate	53.3	33.3	13.3	0	(15)
Assembly	31.0	48.3	20.7	0	(29)
Combined	38.6	43.2	18.2	0	(44)
Oregon					
Senate	53.3	40.0	6.7	0	(15)
House	66.7	16.7	16.7	0	(24)
Combined	61.5	25.6	12.8	0	(39)
South Dakota					
Senate	55.0	35.0	5.0	5.0	(20)
House	50.0	28.1	18.8	3.1	(32)
Combined	51.9	30.8	13.5	3.8	(52)
Tennessee					
Senate	50.0	40.0	10.0	0	(10)
House	34.4	28.1	31.3	6.3	(32)
Combined	38.1	31.0	26.2	4.8	(42)

Source: Responses to 1973 survey of state legislators in the six sample states. See question #10 in the questionnaire reprinted in Appendix A.

TABLE C-11

Legislators' Responses to Question of Whether Reapportionment Had Affected Legislation Adopted in the Six Sample Legislatures

	Yes	No	Don't Know	Not Mentioned	(N)
Delaware					
Senate	55.5%	33.3%	11.1%	0%	(9)
House	75.0	12.5	12.5	0	(16)
Combined	68.0	20.0	12.0	0	(25)
Kansas					
Senate	69.6	17.4	13.0	0	(23)
House	68.3	23.8	6.3	1.6	(63)
Combined	68.6	22.1	8.1	1.2	(86)
New Jersey					
Senate	66.7	26.7	6.7	0	(15)
Assembly	37.9	44.8	17.2	0	(29)
Combined	47.7	38.6	13.6	0	(49)
Oregon					
Senate	60.0	26.7	13.3	0	(15)
House	58.3	20.8	20.8	0	(24)
Combined	58.9	23.1	17.9	0	(39)
South Dakota					
Senate	50.0	40.0	5.0	5.0	(20)
House	62.5	28.1	9.4	0	(32)
Combined	57.7	32.7	7.7	1.9	(52)
Tennessee					
Senate	70.0	20.0	10.0	0	(10)
House	46.9	28.1	21.9	3.1	(32)
Combined	52.4	26.2	19.0	2.4	(42)

Source: Responses to 1973 survey of state legislators in the six sample
           states. See question #9 in the questionnaire reprinted in
           Appendix A.

TABLE C-12

Proportion of State Highway Expenditures on State-Administered Roads Expended in Metropolitan Counties in the Six Sample States, 1965 and 1972 [a]

State	County Type[b]	1965 Capital	1965 Maintenance	1972 Capital	1972 Maintenance
Delaware	Central City (and Suburban)	40.8%	25.9%	30.3%	15.0%
Kansas	Central City	17.0	3.5	23.2	5.0
	Suburban	9.0	2.7	5.6	3.3
New Jersey	Established Central City	23.9	7.7	22.9	7.2
	Suburban	28.8	17.8	31.1	16.8
Oregon	Central City[c]	18.4	8.8	30.4	10.5
	Suburban	6.2	4.5	15.5	7.6
South Dakota	Central City	6.0	3.3	3.9	3.4
Tennessee	Central City	35.4	8.2	29.3	11.2
	Suburban	7.0	3.3	4.9	3.9

Sources: Figures are computed from data in the following sources: U.S., Department of Transportation, Federal Highway Administration, Highway Statistics 1965, table SF-4, p. 76, and table SF-15, pp. 84-90; U.S., Department of Transportation, Federal Highway Administration, Highway Statistics 1972, table SF-4, p. 54, and table SF-15, pp. 102-108.

[a] Figures given are expenditures of state highway departments (on state-administered roads) in the counties designated as a percentage of total state disbursements for state-administered roads. The sources used for the data do not make clear whether total state disbursements for state-administered roads and total state highway department expenditures for such roads are identical figures. Therefore, the percentages reported in this table, though not the patterns of change between 1965 and 1972, should be viewed with some caution.

[b] Except as noted, the specific counties in each category are the same as those designated in Table 6-1.

[c] The category includes only Lane and Multnomah Counties.

A Selected Bibliography

The following list is limited primarily to works dealing directly with state legislative apportionment. The list is divided into three parts: (1) books, articles in books, and monographs; (2) journal articles; and (3) unpublished works. Most of the references cited in the text of the paper are listed in the bibliography, although some background citations not directly related to the central theme have been omitted. References to various volumes of *The Book of the States,* recurrent throughout the text, and legal citations have also been excluded. A number of works not cited in the text have been added to the bibliography in order to provide the interested reader with a more complete listing of relevant research. (Also see Appendix B.)

Books, Articles in Books, and Monographs

Auerbach, Carl A. "Commentary." In *Reapportionment in the 1970s,* edited by Nelson W. Polsby, pp. 74-90. Berkeley: University of California Press, 1971.

Baker, Gordon E. "Gerrymandering: Privileged Sanctuary or Next Judicial Target?" In *Reapportionment in the 1970s,* edited by

Nelson W. Polsby, pp. 121-42. Berkeley: University of California Press, 1971.

————. *The Reapportionment Revolution: Representation, Political Power, and the Supreme Court.* New York: Random House, 1966.

Balmer, Donald G. "Oregon." In *Impact of Reapportionment on the Thirteen Western States,* edited by Eleanore Bushnell, pp. 241-62. Salt Lake City: University of Utah Press, 1970.

Berger, Raoul. *Government By Judiciary: The Transformation of the Fourteenth Amendment.* Cambridge, Mass.: Harvard University Press, 1977.

Best, James J. "The Impact of Reapportionment on the Washington House of Representatives." In *State Legislative Innovation,* edited by James A. Robinson, pp. 136-82. New York: Praeger Publishers, 1973.

Bickel, Alexander M. "The Supreme Court and Reapportionment." In *Reapportionment in the 1970s,* edited by Nelson W. Polsby, pp. 57-74. Berkeley: University of California Press, 1971.

Bicker, William H. "The Effects of Malapportionment in the States—A Mistrial." In *Reapportionment in the 1970s,* edited by Nelson W. Polsby, pp. 151-201. Berkeley: University of California Press, 1971.

Burns, John, and the Citizens Conference on State Legislatures. *The Sometime Governments: A Critical Study of the Fifty American Legislatures.* New York: Bantam Books, 1971.

Congressional Quarterly, *Representation and Apportionment.* Washington, D.C.: Congressional Quarterly, 1966.

Cornelis, William G., ed. *Southeastern State Legislatures.* Atlanta, Ga.: Emory University, 1968.

Cortner, Richard C. *The Apportionment Cases.* Knoxville: University of Tennessee Press, 1970.

Council of State Governments. *Reapportionment in the Seventies.* Lexington, Ky.: Council of State Governments, 1973.

David, Paul T., and Eisenberg, Ralph. *Devaluation of the Urban and Suburban Vote: A Statistical Investigation of Long-Term Trends in State Legislative Representation.* 2 vols. Charlottesville: Bureau of Public Administration, University of Virginia, 1961-62.

————. *State Legislative Districting.* Chicago: Public Administration Service, 1962.

Davis, I. Ridgeway. *The Effects of Reapportionment on the Con-*

necticut Legislature—Decade of the Sixties. New York: National Municipal League, 1972.

De Grazia, Alfred. Essay on Apportionment and Representative Government. Washington, D.C.: American Enterprise Institute for Public Policy Research, 1963.

Dixon, Robert G., Jr. "The Court, the People, and 'One Man, One Vote.'" In Reapportionment in the 1970s, edited by Nelson W. Polsby, pp. 7-46. Berkeley: University of California Press, 1971.

————. Democratic Representation: Reapportionment in Law and Politics. New York: Oxford University Press, 1968.

————. "Representation Values and Reapportionment Practice: The Eschatology of 'One Man, One Vote.'" In Representation, Nomos X, edited by J. Roland Pennock and John W. Chapman, pp. 167-95. New York: Atherton Press, 1968.

Dye, Thomas R. Politics, Economics, and the Public: Policy Outcomes in the American States. Chicago: Rand McNally. 1968.

Elliott, Ward E. Y. The Rise of Guardian Democracy: The Supreme Court's Role in Voting Rights Disputes, 1845-1969. Cambridge, Mass.: Harvard University Press, 1974.

Francis, Wayne A. Legislative Issues in the Fifty States: A Comparative Analysis. Chicago: Rand McNally, 1967.

Friedman, Robert S. "State Politics and Highways." In Politics in the American States: A Comparative Analysis, 2d ed., edited by Herbert Jacob and Kenneth N. Vines, pp. 477-519. Boston: Little, Brown & Co., 1971.

Gatlin, Douglas S. "The Development of a Responsible Party System in the Florida Legislature." In State Legislative Innovation, edited by James A. Robinson, pp. 1-45. New York: Praeger Publishers, 1973.

Goldwin, Robert A., ed. Representation and Misrepresentation: Legislative Reapportionment in Theory and Practice. Chicago: Rand McNally, 1968.

Gove, Samuel K. "Policy Implications of Legislative Reorganization in Illinois." In State Legislative Innovation, edited by James A. Robinson, pp. 101-35. New York: Praeger Publishers, 1973.

Graham, Gene. One Man, One Vote: Baker v. Carr and the American Levellers. Boston: Little, Brown & Co., 1972.

Grumm, John G. "The Effects of Legislative Structure on Legislative Performance." In State and Urban Politics: Readings in Comparative Public Policy, edited by Richard I. Hofferbert and Ira Sharkansky, pp. 298-322. Boston: Little, Brown & Co., 1971.

————. "The Kansas Legislature: Republican Coalition." In *Midwest Legislative Politics*, edited by Samuel C. Patterson, pp. 37-66. Iowa City: Institute of Public Affairs, University of Iowa, 1967.

Hacker, Andrew. *Congressional Districting*. Washington, D.C.: Brookings Institution, 1963.

Hamilton, Howard. "Some Observations in Ohio: Single-Member Districts, Multi-Member Districts, and the Floating Fraction." In *Reapportioning Legislatures: A Consideration of Criteria and Computers*, edited by Howard Hamilton, pp. 73-95. Columbus: Charles E. Merrill, 1966.

Hanson, Roger, and Crew, Robert. "The Effects of Reapportionment on State Policy Out-Puts." In *The Impact of Supreme Court Decisions: Empirical Studies*, 2d ed., edited by Theodore L. Becker and Malcom M. Freeley, pp. 155-74. New York: Oxford University Press, 1973.

Hanson, Royce. *The Political Thicket: Reapportionment and Constitutional Democracy*. Englewood Cliffs: Prentice-Hall, 1966.

Harder, Marvin L., and Rampey, Carolyn. *The Kansas Legislature: Procedures, Personalities, and Problems*. State Legislative Service Project of the American Political Science Association. Lawrence: The University Press of Kansas, 1972.

Havard, William C., and Beth, Loren P. *The Politics of Misrepresentation: Rural-Urban Conflict in the Florida Legislature*. Baton Rouge: Louisiana State University Press, 1962.

Hawkins, Brett W. "Consequences of Reapportionment in Georgia." In *State and Urban Politics: Readings in Comparative Public Policy*, edited by Richard I. Hofferbert and Ira Sharkansky, pp. 273-298. Boston: Little, Brown & Co., 1971.

Heath, Robert, and Melrose, Joseph H., Jr. *Pennsylvania Reapportionment: A Study in Legislative Behavior*. New York: National Municipal League, 1972.

Jewell, Malcolm E. *Legislative Representation in the Contemporary South*. Durham, N.C.: Duke University Press, 1967.

————. *Metropolitan Representation: State Legislative Districting in Urban Counties*. New York: National Municipal League, 1969.

————. *The State Legislature: Politics and Practice*. New York: Random House, 1962.

————. ed. *The Politics of Reapportionment* (New York: Atherton Press, 1962.

Jewell, Malcolm E., and Greene, Lee S. *The Kentucky and Tennessee Legislatures.* Lexington: Department of Political Science, University of Kentucky, 1967.

Keefe, William J., and Ogul, Morris S. *The American Legislative Process: Congress and the States,* 4th ed. Englewood Cliffs, N.J.: Prentice-Hall, 1977.

Key, V. O., Jr. *American State Politics: An Introduction.* New York: Alfred A. Knopf, 1956.

Lehne, Richard. *Legislating Reapportionment in New York.* New York: National Municipal League, 1971.

————. *Reapportionment of the New York Legislature: Impact and Issues.* New York: National Municipal League, 1972.

McKay, Robert B. *Reapportionment: The Law and Politics of Equal Representation.* New York: Twentieth Century Fund, 1965.

National Legislative Conference and the Council of State Governments. *Reapportionment in the States.* Lexington, Ky.: National Legislative Conference and the Council of State Governments, 1972.

National Municipal League. *Apportionment in the Nineteen Sixties,* rev. ed. New York: National Municipal League, 1970.

————. *Compendium on Legislative Apportionment.* New York: National Municipal League, 1962.

O'Rourke, Terry B. *Reapportionment: Law, Politics, Computers.* Washington, D.C.: American Enterprise Institute for Public Policy Research, 1972.

Rae, Douglas W. "Reapportionment and Political Democracy." In *Reapportionment in the 1970s,* edited by Nelson W. Polsby, pp. 91-112. Berkeley: University of California Press, 1971.

Rosenthal, Alan. *Legislative Performance in the States: Explorations of Committee Behavior.* New York: Free Press, 1974.

Schubert, Glendon A., ed. *Reapportionment.* New York: Charles Scribner's Sons, 1965.

Segal, Morley, and Fritschler, A. Lee. "Emerging Patterns of Intergovernmental Relations." In *The Municipal Yearbook: 1970,* pp. 13-38. Washington, D.C.: International City Management Association, 1970.

Shank, Alan. *New Jersey Reapportionment Politics: Strategies and Tactics in the Legislative Process.* Rutherford, N.J.: Fairleigh Dickenson University Press, 1969.

Sharkansky, Ira, and Hofferbert, Richard I. "Dimensions of State

Policy." In *Politics in the American States: A Comparative Analysis,* 2d ed., edited by Herbert Jacob and Kenneth N. Vines, pp. 315-53. Boston: Little, Brown & Co., 1971.

Stoiber, Susanne A., ed. *Legislative Politics in the Rocky Mountain West: Colorado, New Mexico, Utah, and Wyoming.* Boulder: Bureau of Government Research and Service, University of Colorado, 1967.

U.S. Advisory Commission on Intergovernmental Relations. *Apportionment of State Legislatures.* Washington, D.C.: U.S. Government Printing Office, 1962.

Wahlke, John C.; Eulau, Heinz; Buchanan, William; and Ferguson, LeRoy C. *The Legislative System: Explorations in Legislative Behavior.* New York: John Wiley & Sons, 1962.

Walker, Jack L. "The Diffusion of Innovations Among the American States." In *State and Urban Politics: Readings in Comparative Public Policy,* edited by Richard I. Hofferbert and Ira Sharkansky, pp. 377-412. Boston: Little, Brown & Co., 1971.

Wells, Donald T., ed. *Power in American State Legislatures: Case Studies of the Arkansas, Louisiana, Mississippi, and Oklahoma Legislatures.* New Orleans: Department of Political Science, Tulane University, 1967.

Journal Articles

Baker, Gordon E. "One Man, One Vote, and 'Political Fairness'—or How the Burger Court Found Political Happiness by Rediscovering *Reynolds v. Sims.*" *Emory Law Journal* 23 (Summer 1974): 701-23.

Banzhaf, John F., III. "Multi-Member Electoral Districts—Do They Violate the 'One Man, One Vote' Principle." *Yale Law Journal* 75 (July 1966): 1309-38.

Beiser, Edward N. "A Comparative Analysis of State and Federal Judicial Behavior: The Reapportionment Cases." *American Political Science Review* 62 (September 1968): 788-95.

Boyd, William J. D. "Apportionment and Districting: Problems of Compliance." *National Civic Review* 60 (April 1971): 199-203.

Brady, David, and Edmonds, Douglas. "One Man, One Vote—So What?" *Transaction* 4 (March 1967): 941-46.

Broach, Glen T. "A Comparative Dimensional Analysis of Partisan and Urban-Rural Voting in State Legislatures." *Journal of Politics* 34 (August 1972): 905-21.

Bryan, Frank M. "The Metamorphosis of a Rural Legislature." *Polity* 1 (Winter 1968): 191-212.

————. "Who Is Legislating?" *National Civic Review* 56 (December 1967): 627-32, 644.

Cantrall, William R., and Nagel, Stuart S. "The Effects of Legislative Reapportionment on Nonexpenditure Legislation," *Annals of the New York Academy of Sciences* 219 (9 November 1973): 269-79.

Carmines, Edward G. "The Mediating Influence of State Legislatures on the Linkage Between Interparty Competition and Welfare Policies." *American Political Science Review* 68 (September 1974): 1118-24.

Casper, Gerhard. "Apportionment and the Right to Vote," *The Supreme Court Review* (1973): pp. 1-32.

Cho, Yong Hyo, and Frederickson, H. George. "Apportionment and Legislative Responsiveness to Policy Preferences in the American States." *Annals of the New York Academy of Sciences* 219 (9 November 1973): 248-68.

Clem, Alan L. "Party and Bloc Voting in the 1969 South Dakota Legislature." *Public Affairs,* no. 38, 15 August 1969, pp. 1-6.

————. "Roll Call Voting Behavior in the South Dakota Legislature." *Public Affairs,* no. 25, 15 May 1966, pp. 1-8.

Cobb, Edwin L. "Representation and the Rotation Agreement: The Case of Tennessee." *Western Political Quarterly* 23 (September 1970): 516-29.

————. "Representation Theory and the Floterial District: The Case of Texas." *Western Political Quarterly* 22 (December 1969): 790-805.

Dauer, Manning J. "Multi-member Districts in Dade County: Study of a Problem and a Delegation." *Journal of Politics* 29 (August 1966): 617-38.

Dauer, Manning J., and Kelsay, Robert G. "Unrepresentative States." *National Municipal Review* 44 (December 1955): 571-75, 587.

David, Paul T. "One Member vs. 2, 3, 4, or 5." *National Civic Review* 60 (February 1966): 75-81.

De Rubertis, William, "How Apportionment with Selected Demographic Variables Relates to Policy Orientation." *Western Political Quarterly* 22 (December 1969): 904-20.

Dines, Allan. "A Reapportioned State." *National Civic Review* 55 (February 1966): 70-74, 99.

Dixon, Karl H. "Reapportionment and Reform: The Florida Example," *National Civic Review* 62 (November 1973): 548-53.

Dixon, Robert G., Jr. "One Man, One Vote—What Happens Next?" *National Civic Review* 60 (May 1971): 259-66.

Dye, Thomas R. "Malapportionment and Public Policy in the States." *Journal of Politics* 27 (August 1965): 586-601.

Edsall, Preston W. "State Legislatures and Legislative Representation." *Journal of Politics* 30 (May 1968): 277-90.

Eimers, Robert F. "Legislative Apportionment: The Contents of Pandora's Box and Beyond," *Hastings Constitutional Law Quarterly* 1 (Spring 1974): 289-309.

Elliot, Ward E. Y. "Prometheus, Proteus, Pandora and Procrustes Unbound: The Political Consequences of Reapportionment." *University of Chicago Law Review* 37 (Spring 1970): 474-93.

Engstrom, Richard L. "The Supreme Court and Equipopulous Gerrymandering: A Remaining Obstacle in the Quest for Fair and Effective Representation," *Arizona State Law Journal* 1976, no. 2 (1976): 277-319.

Erikson, Robert S. "Malapportionment, Gerrymandering, and Party Fortunes in Congressional Elections." *American Political Science Review* 66 (December 1972): 1234-45.

———. "The Partisan Impact of State Legislative Reapportionment." *Midwest Journal of Political Science* 15 (February 1971): 57-71.

———. "Reapportionment and Policy: A Further Look at Some Intervening Variables," *Annals of the New York Academy of Sciences* 219 (9 November 1973): 280-90.

Ferejohn, John A. "On the Decline of Competition in Recent Congressional Elections." *American Political Science Review* 71 (March 1977): 166-75.

Firestine, Robert E. "The Impact of Reapportionment upon Local Government Aid Receipts within Large Metropolitan Areas." *Social Science Quarterly* 54 (September 1973): 394-402.

Frederickson, H. George, and Cho, Yong Hyo. "The Effects of Reapportionment: Subtle, Selective, Limited." *National Civic Review* 63 (July 1974): 357-62.

———. "Legislative Apportionment and Fiscal Policy in the American States." *Western Political Quarterly* 27 (March 1974): 5-37.

———. "Sixties' Reapportionment: Is it Victory or Delusion?" *National Civic Review* 60 (February 1971): 73-78, 85.

Furness, Susan W. "The Response of the Colorado General Assembly to Proposals for Metropolitan Reform." *Western Political Quarterly* 26 (December 1973): 747-65.

Hamilton, Howard. "Legislative Constituencies: Single-Member Districts, Multi-Member Districts, and Floterial Districts." *Western Political Quarterly* 20 (June 1967): 321-40.

Hardin, Charles M. "Issues in Legislative Reapportionment." *Review of Politics* 27 (April 1965): 147-72.

Hardy, Leroy C. "Considering the Gerrymander," *Pepperdine Law Review* 4 (Spring 1977): 243-84.

Hardy, Leroy C., and Sohner, Charles P. "Constitutional Challenge and Political Response: California Reapportionment, 1965." *Western Political Quarterly* 28 (December 1970): 733-51.

Heath, Robert, and Melrose, Joseph H., Jr. "New Lawmakers?" *National Civic Review* 58 (October 1969): 410-14.

Hill, A. Spencer. "The Reapportionment Decisions: A Return to Dogma?" *Journal of Politics* 31 (February 1969): 186-213.

Hofferbert, Richard I. "The Relationship Between Public Policy and Some Structural and Environmental Variables in the American States." *American Political Science Review* 60 (March 1966): 73-82.

Hofstetter, C. Richard. "Malapportionment and Roll Call Voting in Indiana, 1923-1968: A Computer Simulation." *Journal of Politics* 33 (February 1971): 92-111.

Irwin, William P. "Representation and Election: The Reapportionment Cases in Retrospect." *Michigan Law Review* 67 (February 1969): 729-55.

Jacob, Herbert. "The Consequences of Malapportionment: A Note of Caution." *Social Forces* 43 (December 1964): 256-71.

Jewell, Malcolm E. "How Many Members?" *National Civic Review* 57 (February 1968): 75-80, 100.

Kaiser, Henry F. "A Measure of the Population Quality of Legislative Apportionment." *American Political Science Review* 62 (March 1968): 208-15.

Kenton, Carolyn L., and Want, Susan W. "Reapportionment: The Issues." *State Government* 45 (August 1972): 214-22.

LeBlanc, Hugh. "Voting in State Senates: Party and Constituency Influences." *Midwest Journal of Political Science* 13 (February 1969): 33-57.

LeMay, Michael C. "The States and Urban Areas: A Comparative Assessment," *National Civic Review* 61 (December 1972): 542-48.

McKay, Robert B. "Reapportionment: Success Story of the Warren Court." *Michigan Law Review* 67 (December 1968): 223-36.

"More Clues to the Impact of Reapportionment." *National Civic Review* 66 (April 1967): 217.

Nehring, Earl A. "Metropolitan Integration in the Kansas House of Representatives." *Your Government* 23 (15 November 1967): unpaged.

Noragon, Jack L. "Redistricting, Political Outcomes, and Gerrymandering in the 1960s." *Annals of the New York Academy of Sciences* 219 (9 November 1973): 314-33.

Pulsipher, Allan G. "Empirical and Normative Theories of Apportionment." *Annals of the New York Academy of Sciences* 219 (9 November 1973): 334-41.

Pulsipher, Allan G., and Weatherby, James R., Jr. "Malapportionment, Party Competition, and the Functional Distribution of Governmental Expenditures." *American Political Science Review* 62 (December 1968): 1207-19.

"Reapportionment—Nine Years into the Revolution and Still Struggling." *Michigan Law Review* 70 (January 1972): 586-616.

Robeck, Bruce W. "Legislative Partisanship, Constituency, and Malapportionment: The Case of California." *American Political Science Review* 66 (December 1972): 1246-55.

————. "Urban-Rural and Regional Voting Patterns in the California Senate Before and After Reapportionment." *Western Political Quarterly* 23 (December 1970): 785-94.

Rosenthal, Alan. "Turnover in State Legislatures." *American Journal of Political Science* 18 (August 1974): 609-16.

Schubert, Glendon A., and Press, Charles. "Measuring Malapportionment." *American Political Science Review* 58 (June 1964): 302-27.

————. "Malapportionment Remeasured." *American Political Science Review* 58 (December 1964): 966-70.

Sharkansky, Ira. "Reapportionment and Roll Call Voting: The Case of the Georgia Legislature." *Social Science Quarterly* 51 (June 1970): 120-37.

Sickels, Robert J. "Dragons, Bacon Strips, and Dumbbells—Who's Afraid of Reapportionment?" *Yale Law Journal* 75 (July 1966): 1300-08.

Silva, Ruth C. "Compared Values of the Single- and Multi-Member Legislative District." *Western Political Quarterly* 17 (September 1964): 504-16.

————. "Relation of Representation and the Party System to the Number of Seats Apportioned to a Legislative District." *Western Political Quarterly* 17 (December 1964): 742-69.

Slingsby, Stephen D. "Community the Key." *National Civic Review* 58 (February 1969): 61-66.

Smith, George Bundy. "The Failure of Reapportionment: The Effect of Reapportionment on the Election of Blacks to Legislative Bodies," *Howard Law Journal* 18, no. 3 (1975): 639-84.

Sokolow, Alvin D. "Legislative Pluralism, Committee Assignments, and Internal Norms: The Delayed Impact of Reapportionment in California." *Annals of the New York Academy of Sciences* 219 (9 November 1973): 291-313.

Sokolow, Alvin D., and Brandsma, Richard W. "Partisanship and Seniority in Legislative Committee Assignments: California After Reapportionment." *Western Political Quarterly* 24 (December 1971): 740-60.

"States Make Size, Electoral Changes." *National Civic Review* 57 (February 1968): 94-97.

Taylor, Peter J. "A New Shape Measure for Evaluating Electoral District Patterns." *American Political Science Review* 67 (September 1973): 947-50.

Tufte, Edward R. "The Relationship between Seats and Votes in Two-Party Systems." *American Political Science Review* 67 (June 1973): 540-54.

"*United Jewish Organizations* v. *Carey* and the Need to Recognize Aggregate Voting Rights," *Yale Law Journal* 87 (January 1978): 571-602.

White, John P., and Thomas, Norman C. "Urban and Rural Representation and State Legislative Apportionment." *Western Political Quarterly* 17 (December 1964): 724-41.

Unpublished Materials

Brady, David W., and Murray, Richard. "Reformers and Skeptics: Testing for the Effects of Apportionment Patterns on Policy Outputs." Paper presented at the 1972 Annual Meeting of the Southern Political Science Association, 2-4 November 1972 at Atlanta, Ga.

Broach, Glen T. "Party, Apportionment and Conflict in State Legislatures: A Comparative Roll Call Analysis." Ph.D. dissertation, University of Alabama, 1971.

Firestine, Robert E. "Some Effects of Reapportionment on State Government Fiscal Activity." Ph.D. dissertation, Syracuse University, 1971.

Furness, Susan. "The Response of the Colorado General Assembly to Metropolitan Reform in the Denver Metropolitan Area: 1961-1970." Ph.D. dissertation, University of Colorado, 1971.

Isaacs, John S., II. "An Analysis of Voting Behavior in the Delaware House of Representatives, 1965-1970." Master's thesis, University of Delaware, 1971.

Matthews, Paul A. "The Impact of Reapportionment in Tennessee." Senior History Honors Seminar, Duke University, 1974.

O'Rourke, Timothy G. "The Impact of Reapportionment on State Legislatures: An Interpretative Analysis." Master's thesis, Duke University, 1973.

Patterson, Samuel C. "Political Representation and Public Policy." Paper presented at the Social Science Research Conference on the Impacts of Public Policies, 3-5 December 1971, at St. Thomas, U.S. Virgin Islands.

Todd, John Richard. "Reapportionment and Legislative Outputs: A Florida Case Study." Ph.D. dissertation, University of Florida, 1971.

Uslaner, Eric M., and Weber, Ronald E. "The Electoral Impact of Reapportionment." Paper presented at the 1973 Annual Meeting of the Southern Political Science Association, 1-3 November 1973, at Atlanta, Ga.

Van Meter, Donald Stuart. "The Policy Implications of State Legislative Reapportionment: A Longitudinal Analysis." Ph.D. dissertation, University of Wisconsin, 1972.

Index

Alabama, 9

Baker v. Carr. See
  Reapportionment, legal
  aspects
Balmer, Donald G., 35
Best, James J., study of
  Washington by, 9, 164
Bickel, Alexander M., 159
Brady, David W., 9, 140
Braybrooke, David, 34
Broach, Glen T., 9, 109-10
Burns, John, 86-87

California, 9
Cantrall, William R., 144 n.-45 n.
Central city and suburban
  representation, impact of
  reapportionment on, 3-9, 12-
  13, 16-21, 41-42, 48-53, 58-65,
  74-83, 88-92, 97-114, 120-39,

149-56. See also listing under
  specific states
Characteristics of legislators,
  impact of reapportionment on
  age, experience, occupation,
  race, and sex, 5, 8-9, 36-43,
  148-49, 153, 155
Cho, Yong Hyo, 140, 145 n.
Clem, Alan L., 111-12
Colorado, 9, 65-66
Connecticut, 8-9

David, Paul T., 6
Davis, I. Ridgeway, 9
Dauer, Manning J., 6, 8-12, 55
Delaware, impact of
  reapportionment on: central
  city and suburban
  representation, 12-13, 16-21,
  41-42, 48, 53, 64-65, 78-83, 88-
  90, 103, 113-14, 120-30, 131,

135; characteristics of legislators, 37-42; gerrymandering, 56; interest group activity, 137-38; legislative chamber leadership, 81-83; legislative conflict, 100-03, 107-08, 113-15; legislative districts, modification of number and size, 15, 29, 32-33, 58; legislative procedure, 84, 88-90; legislative standing committees, 74-80, 84, 88, 92; legislative turnover, 28-29; legislator-constituency relations, 32, 35; party competition, 48-56, 67-68, 78-79, 102-03, 107-08, 113-14, 156-57; party organization, 64-65, 78-83, 90-92; policy, 122-39; single-member and multimember districts, 33, 58; summary of findings, 148-51, 153-54, 156-57

Democratic party. See Party competition, Party organization
Dolan, Paul, observations of, 177 n.
Dye, Thomas R., 140-41

Edmonds, Douglas, 140
Eisenberg, Ralph, 6
Elliott, Ward E. Y., 158
Erikson, Robert S., 53-57

Firestine, Robert E., study by, 141 n.-42 n.
Florida, 8-9
Francis, Wayne L., 7, 96-97, 101-06
Frederickson, H. George, 140, 145 n.
Fritschler, A. Lee, 142 n.
Furness, Susan W., study of Colorado by, 9

Gatlin, Douglas S., study of Florida by, 8-9
Georgia, 8, 41
Gerrymandering, impact of reapportionment on, 2, 23 n.,

32-34, 56-57, 68, 69 n.-70 n.
Glazer, Nathan, 158-59
Gove, Samuel K., study of Illinois by, 9
Greene, Lee S., observations of, 59-60, 93 n.-94 n., 116 n.
Grumm, John G., 7, 102-03, 110-11

Harder, Marvin L., 86, 102, 111, 136
Hawkins, Brett W., study of Georgia, 8; methodology of, 75
Heath, Robert, study of Pennsylvania by, 9, 36
Hofferbert, Richard I., 140

Illinois, 9
Indiana, 109
Interest group activity, impact of reapportionment on, 136-38, 151
Isaacs, John S., II, 113-14

Jacob, Herbert, 140
Jewell, Malcolm E., 35, 41, 63, 65-67, 110

Kansas, impact of reapportionment on: central city and suburban representation, 12-13, 16-21, 41-42, 48, 53, 75-78, 81-83, 88, 90, 92, 102, 110-11, 120-38; characteristics of legislators, 37-43; gerrymandering, 32-33, 56-57; interest group activity, 137-38; legislative chamber leadership, 81-83; legislative conflict, 99-102, 107, 110-11, 115, 138-39; legislative districts, modification of number and size, 29, 32-34, 58; legislative procedure, 84-88; legislative standing committees, 74-80, 84-86, 88, 92; legislative turnover, 28-29; legislator-constituency relations, 32-34; party competition, 48, 53-57, 68, 101-02, 107, 110-11; party organization, 64-65, 81, 90-92; policy, 122-39; single-member and multimember districts, 33, 58; summary of findings, 148-53

Kelsay, Robert G., 6, 8-12, 55

LeBlanc, Hugh, 111-13
Lehne, Richard, study of New York by, 9, 36
Legislative conflict, impact of reapportionment on, 4-6, 8-9, 95-115, 150-56
Legislative leadership and procedure, impact of reapportionment on: chamber leadership, 80-83, 150-51, 153-56; procedure, 84-90, 92-93, 150-51, 153-56; standing committee chairmen, 5, 74-80, 92, 150-51, 153-56; standing committee operations, 84-90, 93, 150, 155
Legislative standing committees. See legislative leadership and procedure
Legislative turnover, impact of reapportionment on, 3, 5, 9, 27-29, 36-37, 84, 148, 152-53, 155-56
Legislators, characteristics of. See Characteristics of legislators
Legislator-constituency relations, impact of reapportionment on, 32-36, 148-49

McKay, Robert B., 158-59
Melrose, Joseph H., Jr., study of Pennsylvania by, 9, 36
Multimember districts. See Single-member districts
Murray, Richard, 9

Nagel, Stuart S., 144 n.-45 n.
Nevada, 6
New Jersey, impact of reapportionment on: central city and suburban representation, 12-13, 16-21, 41-42, 48-53, 60-65, 68, 78-80, 83, 92, 103-04, 122-35;

characteristics of legislators, 37-44; gerrymandering, 57; interest group activity, 137-38; legislative chamber leadership, 81-83; legislative chamber leadership, 81-83; legislative conflict, 103-05, 107-08, 112-13, 115; legislative districts, modification of number and size, 15, 29, 32-34, 38-39, 41-44, 58, 60-63, 84, 87, 113; legislative procedure, 84-90, 92-93; legislative standing committees, 74-80, 84-87, 90-93; legislative turnover, 28-29; legislator-constituency relations, 32-34; party competition, 48-55, 60-63, 68, 102-05, 112-13; party organization, 64-68, 78-80, 83, 90-92; policy, 122-39; single-member and multimember districts, 33, 41-44, 58, 60-63; summary of findings, 148-56

New York, 9, 36

Ohio, 41
Oregon, impact of reapportionment on: central city and suburban representation, 6, 12-13, 16-21, 53, 59, 64-65, 79-80, 83, 92, 105-06, 122-39; characteristics of legislators, 37-44; gerrymandering, 57; interest group activity, 137-38; legislative chamber leadership, 81-83, 88-90; legislative conflict, 105-08, 114-15, 138-39; legislative districts, modification of number and size, 15, 29, 32-36, 39-40, 43-44, 58-59; legislative procedure, 84, 88-90; legislative standing committees, 74-80, 84, 92; legislative turnover, 28-29; legislator-constituency relations, 29, 32-36; party competition, 53, 58-59, 62-63, 68, 88-90, 105-06, 108; party

organization, 64-65, 67-68, 90-
92; policy, 122-39; single-
member and multimember
districts, 33-36, 39-40, 43-44,
58-59, 62-63, 68; summary of
findings, 148-51, 155-56

Party competition, impact of
reapportionment on:
Democratic and Republican
success, 3-9, 47-68, 149-50,
153-55, 157-58, 159 n.;
legislative conflict, 4-9, 95-115,
150-56
Party organization, impact of
reapportionment on: county
chairmen's power, 65-68, 150,
155; legislative parties, 5-6, 63-
65, 68, 90-92, 149-50, 152-56
Pennsylvania, 9, 36
Policy, impact of reapportionment
on, 8-9, 119-41, 141 n.-44 n.,
151, 158-59
Pulsipher, Allan G., 140

Questionnaire, 1973 survey of
state legislators: description
of, 13, 163-68; results of, 29,
32-36, 66-67, 88-92, 96-108, 130-
39

Rampey, Carolyn, 86, 102, 111, 136
Reapportionment, impact of:
possible effects considered, 3-
8, 27-28, 36-37, 47-48, 73-74,
95-96, 119-20; previous
research, summary of findings
for other states, 8-9, 28, 35, 41,
53-57, 63, 65-67, 109, 139-41;
summary of findings in six
state study, 148-56. See also
individual states, specific
areas (e.g., Policy, Party
competition), various authors
Reapportionment, legal aspects, 1-
2, 15, 22 n.-23 n., 56, 58, 69 n.-
70 n., 158-60
Reynolds v. Sims. See
Reapportionment, legal
aspects

Robeck, Bruce W., 9
Rosenthal, Alan, 28, 87, 112

Segal, Morley, 142 n.
Single-member districts, versus
multimember districts: legal
aspects, 2, 22 n.-23 n., 58, 69
n.-70 n.; political
consequences, 33-35, 39-44,
57-63, 65-68
South Dakota, impact of
reapportionment on: central
city and suburban
representation, 12-13, 16-21,
53, 64-65, 79-80, 81-83, 92, 105-
06, 112, 122-35; characteristics
of legislators, 37-42;
gerrymandering, 33, 56;
interest group activity, 137-38;
legislative chamber
leadership, 81-83, 88-90;
legislative conflict, 105-06,
108, 111-12, 115, 138-39;
legislative districts,
modification of number and
size, 15, 29, 32-33, 35, 58;
legislative procedure, 84, 88-
90; legislative standing
committees, 74-80, 84, 92;
legislative turnover, 28-29;
legislator-constituency
relations, 33-35; party
competition, 53-54, 56, 62-63,
68, 79, 90, 105-06, 111-12; party
organization, 64-65, 90-92;
policy, 122-39; single-member
and multimember districts,
33, 41-42, 58, 62-63; summary
of findings, 148-51, 155-56
Suburban representation. See
Central city and suburban
representation

Tennessee, impact of
reapportionment on: central
city and suburban
representation, 12-12, 16-21,
41-42, 48, 53, 59-60, 64-65, 67-
68, 78, 80-83, 88, 90-92, 97, 101-
02, 109-10, 120-35;
characteristics of legislators,

37-43; gerrymandering, 57, 69 n.-70 n.; interest group activity, 137-38; legislative chamber leadership, 81-83; legislative conflict, 9, 97-102, 107-10, 115, 138-39; legislative districts, modification of number and size, 15, 29, 32-34, 41, 58; legislative procedure, 84, 88-90; legislative standing committees, 74-80, 84, 88, 92; legislative turnover, 28-29; legislator-constituency relations, 32-34; party competition, 48-53, 57-60, 62-63, 67-68, 97-101, 109-10, 115; party organization, 63-65, 67-68, 90-92; policy, 122-39; single-member and multimember districts, 33, 41, 58-60, 62-63; summary of findings, 148-53

Thomas, Norman C., 6-8, 20, 156
Tufte, Edward R., 55

Urban-rural representation and conflict. *See* Central city and suburban representation, Legislative conflict
Uslaner, Eric M., 55-56

Walker, Jack L., 140
Wahlke, John C., et al., 96-101, 103-04
Warren, Earl, 158
Washington (state), 9, 164
Weatherby, James R., Jr., 140
Weber, Ronald E., 55-56
White, John P., 6-8, 20, 156

Zeller, Belle, 101